Undomesticated Ground

Undomesticated Ground

Recasting

Nature

as

Feminist

Space

Stacy Alaimo

Cornell University Press
Ithaca & London

First published 2000 by Cornell University Press

First printing, Cornell Paperbacks, 2000

Printed in the United States of America

Library of Congress Cataloging-in-Publication Data

Alaimo, Stacy
    Undomesticated ground : recasting nature as feminist space / Stacy Alaimo.
        p.   cm.
    Includes bibliographical references and index.
    ISBN 0-8014-3735-0 (cloth) — ISBN 0-8014-8643-2 (pbk.)
    1. Feminist theory.   2. Philosophy of nature.   3. Ecofeminism.   4. Nature in literature.   I. Title.
HQ1190.A4 2000
305.42'01—dc21

                                                                    00-022676

Cloth printing   10 9 8 7 6 5 4 3 2 1
Paperback printing   10 9 8 7 6 5 4 3 2 1

FSC   FSC Trademark © 1996 Forest Stewardship Council A.C.
      SW-COC-098

For Emma

Contents

Illustrations

Acknowledgments

This project, which began nearly ten years ago, has benefited at every stage from Cary Nelson's encouragement and incisive critique. Cary's political engagement, generosity, and commitment to his students have been an inspiration. Amanda Anderson, Michael Bérubé, and Robert Dale Parker were extraordinary readers. They saw potential in ideas that had yet to come to fruition and challenged my work in productive ways. Their comments resonate still. Rick Canning, Barry Faulk, Brady Harrison, Mary Hocks, and Lauren Onkey carefully read through very early drafts—with a patience that could only emanate from friendship—giving me a wealth of insightful suggestions and helping me to work through many conflicting ideas. Bob McRuer and Sagri Dhairyam offered productive criticism of individual chapters. The members of University of Illinois' Feminist Theory Reading Group, especially Amanda Anderson, Janet Lyon, and Carol Neely, created an intellectual environment that helped shape my theoretical positions.

I am grateful to the Americanists here at the University of Texas at Arlington, especially Phil Cohen, Tim Morris, and Ken Roemer, for their interest in my work. I also thank Ken for reading one of my chapters and for a multitude of doorway discussions. Rajani Sudan sustains me with daily discussions of cultural studies and critical theory. Bruce Levy, of Southern Methodist University, generously shared his materials and ideas on Mary Austin. I also thank Ben Agger for his comments on this project and the College of Liberal Arts for a Faculty Development Leave that enabled me to complete my research. Thanks also to UTA's interlibrary loan office, especially Beatrice Cantu and Diana Hines, for providing me with a steady stream of materials.

Feminist Studies published an earlier version of the final chapter, entitled "Cyborg and Ecofeminist Interventions: Challenges for Environmental Feminism." Donna Haraway, a reader for that piece, gave me extensive and invaluable comments. *Studies in American Fiction* published a condensed version of the third chapter, "The Undomesticated Ground of Feminism: Mary Austin and the Progressive Women Conservationists." I am grateful to Melody Graulich for her rigorous reading of that essay. Many thanks to Barbara Kruger and the Estate of Ana Mendieta for allowing me to include their artwork and to Mary Boone Gallery and Galerie Lelong. I am quite grateful to the anonymous readers for Cornell University Press, especially the one who provoked me to add an entirely new chapter. Many thanks to my editors, Alison Shonkwiler and Catherine Rice, for transforming my manuscript into a book.

Finally, I'd like to thank my entire family for their support. The greatest thanks, however, go to Evan Engwall, who read and reread numerous drafts, helped me track down sources and illustrations, and gave generously of his wide-ranging knowledge and insight. Thank you, Evan, for enriching my life in every way. I dedicate this book to my daughter Emma, who helps me imagine feminist futures.

STACY ALAIMO

Dallas, Texas

Undomesticated Ground

Introduction

Feminist Theory's Flight from Nature

[I]t must be recalled that during her earliest years on this conti-
nent, the Euro-American woman seems to have been the unwill-
ing inhabitant of a metaphorical landscape she had no part in
creating—captive, as it were, in the garden of someone else's
imagination.

(Annette Kolodny, *The Land Before Her*)

Disney's recent blockbuster *Pocahontas,* advertised with previews
featuring the "Indian maiden" gracefully cascading hundreds of feet down
a waterfall into an Edenic pool, feeds that ravenous American hunger for
"unspoiled" nature, preferably inhabited by accommodating, feminine,
dark-skinned beings. *Pocahontas,* emblematic of the enduring imaginative potency that "nature" carries in this culture, also betrays the way nature has been entangled with ideologies of race and gender: even more
than the Euro-American women Kolodny describes, Pocahontas is captive
in "the garden of someone else's imagination." This study traces the genealogy of such captivating gardens in order to explore how North American women writers—ensnared within inhospitable landscapes—have
written neither captivity narratives nor escape tales, but have instead, in a
myriad of ways, negotiated, contested, and transformed the discourses of
nature that surround them. A remarkably diverse range of women's writings insist that it is crucial for feminism to contend with the nature that
has been waged against women. The struggle for birth control in the
1920s, Marxist-feminism of the 1930s, and contemporary battles against
racism and heterosexism all grapple with the shifting but nonetheless po-

litically potent meanings of nature. Even more surprisingly, many texts demonstrate that nature has been and continues to be a place of feminist possibility. Catherine Sedgwick, Emma Goldman, Mary Austin, Toni Morrison, Leslie Marmon Silko, Donna Haraway, and others transform nature into a hospitable space for feminism. The fact that most feminist theory distances woman from nature only underscores the importance of understanding how and why feminists inhabit nature as an undomesticated ground.

The Nature of Feminist Theory

Feminism has long struggled with the historically tenacious entanglements of "woman" and "nature." Mother earth, earth mothers, natural women, wild women, fertile fields, barren grounds, virgin lands, raped earths, "a woman in the shape of a monster/a monster in the shape of a woman,"[1] the repulsively breeding aliens of horror films—these creatures portray nature as female and women as not exactly human. As Carolyn Merchant documents in *The Death of Nature: Women, Ecology, and the Scientific Revolution,* European cultures have long imagined nature as feminine. By the sixteenth century, pastorals depicted nature as mother and bride who would "soothe the anxieties of men distraught by the demands of the urban world," comforting them with nurturing, "subordinate," and "essentially passive" female natures.[2] The scientific revolution replaced an organicist worldview with a mechanistic one and envisioned nature as an even less appealing figure, "a female to be controlled and dissected through experiment." This image endorsed the exploitation of natural "resources" by promoting an ideology of power over nature and a "methodology of 'penetration' into her innermost secrets."[3] Such cadaverous images have not only provoked the prodding and piercing of the natural world, but have also embalmed "woman" as corporeal, passive matter. As Denise Riley argues, philosophers and theologians from the sixteenth through the eighteenth centuries expanded nature's domain to engulf "woman" herself. Casting woman as synonymous with nature actually constituted woman as "woman," that is, as a completely sexed being.[4] Defining woman as that which is mired in nature thrusts woman outside the domain of human subjectivity, rationality, and agency.

In a dauntingly impermeable formulation, woman is not only constituted as nature, but nature is invoked to uphold the propriety of this very constitution, as when Rousseau baldly asserts that the "laws of nature" created woman "to please and be subjected to man." A multitude of feminist demands have been met with the cocksure contention that woman's inferior role is—of course—"natural." The dual meanings of nature converge at the site of woman, fixing her in a vortex of circular arguments: woman is closer to nature and is thus inferior; woman is inferior because nature has made her so. Perhaps it is the misogynist logic of this formulation that obscures the contradictory meanings of the term "nature," which is subordinate to Man, and yet contains Man's Truths.

Since nature has been at the heart of a plethora of misogynist arguments and ideologies, grappling with the concept of nature has been an extraordinarily important component of feminist thought. On the one hand, feminists have countered the claim that women's inferiority is "natural" by insisting that women are socially constructed (as I will discuss below). On the other hand, feminists have identified the pervasive association of woman with nature as itself a root cause of misogyny and have advocated a feminist flight from this troublesome terrain. Simone de Beauvoir, for example, suggests that one of the reasons women are "the second sex" is that they are nearly indistinguishable from the natural world: "woman is related to nature; she incarnates it: vale of blood, open rose, siren, the curve of a hill, she represents to man the fertile soil, the sap, the material beauty and soul of the world."[5] Whereas men mark their own transcendent subjectivity by separating themselves from the natural world, women, seen as the embodiment of nature, are doomed to immanence and otherness. Dorothy Dinnerstein, in *The Mermaid and the Minotaur,* attributes the "universal exploitation of women" to the fact that women have been responsible for infants and have thus been experienced as indistinguishable from nature.[6] Similarly, Sherry Ortner claims that women's "pan-cultural" inferior status results from women being viewed as "*closer* to nature than men."[7] Ortner explains that woman's body makes her more involved with "natural" biological activities such as giving birth, while man is free to engage in cultural pursuits. These bodily activities then "place her in *social roles* that in turn are considered to be at a lower order of the cultural process than man's," thus giving women a different "psychic structure" which is seen as closer to nature.[8] Ortner believes that "woman is not 'in reality' any closer to (or further from) nature than man" and that this "scheme is a construct of culture rather than a fact of nature."[9] Ironically however, by presenting a seamless, cross-cultural narrative of woman's oppression that originates in her body, Ortner naturalizes woman's oppression.

If woman's perceived proximity to nature is responsible for her oppression, then her liberation, it would seem, is contingent on her distance from nature. Ortner, for example, urges us to change both the institutions and representations that position or paint woman as "closer" to nature.[10] She does not argue that we need to reevaluate why cultures debase nature, but instead accepts the nature/culture hierarchy in order to transfer women into the elevated category. Similarly, Beauvoir endorses the process of subjectivity that has elevated man over nature even while she deplores the consequent objectification of woman.

> The support of life became for man an activity and a project through the invention of the tool: but in maternity woman remained closely bound to her body, like an animal. It is because humanity calls itself into question in the matter of living—that is to say, values the reasons for living above mere life—that, confronting woman, man assumes mastery. Man's design is not to repeat himself in time: it is to take control of the instant and mold the future. It is male activity that in creating values has made of existence itself a value; this activity has prevailed over the confused forces of life; it has subdued Nature and Woman.[11]

Freed from his body, the existentialist man masters woman, prevails over the "confused forces of life," and subdues nature. Beauvoir sanctions these descriptions of dominance by endowing them with the values that define "humanity" itself. Instead of critiquing this model of subjectivity, she suggests that woman, too, needs to rise up from her degraded bestial position and embark on the same route to transcendence.

Given that "woman" has been defined in much of Western thought as that which is mired in "nature," it is no wonder that feminist theory has struggled to extricate her from this quicksand. By attempting to disentangle "woman" from the web of associations that bind her to "nature," however, nature is kept at bay—repelled—rather than redefined. It is not only ironic but deeply problematic that the "aggressive, intellectual 'flight from the feminine' " that motivated Cartesian rationalism[12] has been followed by feminist flights from all that Descartes attempted to transcend—"impure" matter, bodies, and nature. The recent rage to purge feminism of all vestiges of "essentialism," for example, is one of the most striking instances of feminist theory's flight from nature. Working within rather than against predominant dualisms, many important feminist arguments and concepts necessitate a rigid opposition between nature and culture.

In response to the oft-repeated contention that woman is inferior by nature, for example, feminists have asserted that women are products of culture—not nature. Nascent and contemporary theories of social construction assume nature is static and culture is dynamic, making feminist change contingent on the systematic removal of woman from the category of nature. Long before Simone de Beauvoir insisted that one is not born but *becomes* a woman, feminist theorists including Mary Astell and Mary Wollstonecraft argued that nurture, not nature, created woman as she is; thus the proper education of women can effect social change.[13] More recently, Juliet Mitchell's important essay, "Women: The Longest Revolution," concludes: "The liberation of women under socialism will not be 'rational' but a human achievement, in the long passage from Nature to Culture that is the definition of history and society."[14] Placing Nature and Culture at opposite ends of a teleological spectrum, this passage asserts that the further we progress from nature, the closer women will be to liberation. Moreover, feminist theory's most revolutionary concept, the concept of "gender"—as distinct from biological sex—is predicated on a sharp opposition between nature and culture. Gayle Rubin's influential theory of the "sex/gender" system explains, for example, how the social apparatus "takes up females as raw materials and fashions domesticated women as products."[15] While the language here suggests a parallel between the exploitation of woman and that of nature ("raw materials" become "products"), to redefine nature as something other than a mere resource for culture would muddy, if not collapse, the notion of the sex/gender system. Nature, in short, must be all that culture is not for the sex/gender system to explain the process of social construction. The slash not only distinguishes sex from gender but severs nature from culture.

Monique Wittig extends the idea of social construction, arguing that even the category of sex is not natural, but "political and economic."[16] In Wittig's view, both women's bodies and their minds are manufactured products of (hetero)sexist ideology: "We have been compelled in our bodies and in our minds to correspond, feature by feature, with the *idea* of nature that has been established for us."[17] Insisting that there is "no nature within society" allows Wittig to make the wonderfully provocative claim that lesbians are not women, "since what makes a woman is a specific social relation to a man"—not anything biological.[18] Wittig offers a cogent critique of the way heterosexist regimes create "biology" in order to enforce destiny, and her radical denaturalization of the category of sex encourages bold lesbian-feminist utopias. Ironically, however, though the lesbian in Wittig's terms is neither man nor woman, her path to liberation—cut from the absolute denial of nature—is disturbingly similar to the male subject who triumphs by transcending a gendered ground. Though it is crucial for any feminist who invokes "nature" to be wary of its foundational role in heterosexism, to banish nature from culture, as Wittig does, risks the return of the repressed and forecloses the possibilities for subversive feminist rearticulations of the term. Moreover, expanding the domain of the social and barring nature from entrance denies any space for the workings of bodies and natures (whether hetero-sexed or not, whether retrogressively or progressively articulated). While it would be difficult to overestimate the explanatory and polemical force of feminist theories of social construction, such theories are haunted by the pernicious notions of nature that propel them. The more brilliant and compelling the arguments for social construction, the more they seem to concede, or even implicitly rely on, the "nature" of misogyny. Thrust aside, completely removed from culture, this nature—the repository of essentialism and stasis—nonetheless remains dangerously intact.

Although Luce Irigaray understands the connections between woman and nature in Western thought to be profoundly deleterious, unlike many feminist theorists she refuses to distance women from nature. Departing from the predominant strain of feminist thought in this manner, her work has long been critiqued for its essentialism. Though Irigaray, like Beauvoir, argues that male subjectivity is produced against the ground of women and nature, she does not advocate that women transcend this ground. Instead, playing with the word "mimesis" to suggest representation is both the foundation of culture and a mere imitation of nature, she shows that women, by their very "closeness" to nature, are necessary for the culture that erects itself upon them. "Is not the 'first' stake in mimesis that of re-producing (from) nature? Of giving it form in order to appropriate it for oneself? As guardians of 'nature,' are not women the ones who maintain, thus who make possible, the resource of mimesis for men? For the logos?"[19] Exposing how the male logos does not merely reproduce nature but reproduces "(*from*) nature," Irigaray's parentheses playfully mirror the mechanisms of concealment. Such mechanisms serve to deny that the language, knowledge, culture, and subjectivity of men are produced from the very (female) matter that they disavow. Rather than encouraging women to abandon their role as "guardians of 'nature' " and to step into the "culture" side of this equation (if such a thing were even possible), Irigaray suggests an alternate route. She urges women to inhabit the feminine space in discourse in order to transform it: "One must assume the feminine role deliberately. Which means already to convert a form of subordination into an affirmation, and thus to begin to thwart it."[20]

This feminist mimesis, or miming, playfully affirms the feminine role as a strategy to open up an enclosed system that endlessly replicates male subjectivity. Miming, as imitation, highlights the feminine role *as* a mere role—making it a rather unstable and unappealing site for the erection of male subjectivity. Mimicry, however, must reiterate the very relations it critiques. The following passage, for example, represents the positions of woman and the earth as indistinguishable.

> If there is no more "earth" to press down/repress, to work, to represent, but also and always to desire (for one's own), no opaque matter which in theory does not know herself, then what pedestal remains for the ex-sistence of the "subject"? If the earth turned and more especially turned upon herself, the erection of the subject might thereby be disconcerted and risk losing its elevation and penetration. For what would there be to rise up from and exercise his power over? And in?[21]

Significantly, "the earth" "herself" becomes a subject here, as she refuses to serve as the bedrock for male subjectivity. The earth displays her agency by turning upon herself, displacing the vertical delineation of dominance with the nonhierarchical motion of rotation. "Woman" and the "earth" are conflated in this passage in order to parody the process by which the male subject erects himself and to suggest a space in which another subjectivity—one not predicated on transcending the earth, matter, and woman—could emerge. Unlike Beauvoir, Irigaray does not seek to evade women's association with nature—to do so would only reproduce the already prolific posture of elevated mastery. Instead, she strategically occupies "woman's" position within discourse, which confuses the very categories of male and female, culture and nature, subject and object—since the silent ground is not supposed to speak.

In some of Irigaray's later work, however, it seems that "woman" and the "earth" have shifted ontologically, from discursive constructions to "the real." Instead of disrupting the conventional oppositions between male and female, she reaffirms them. In a speech given at the festival of women of the Italian Communist Party on the theme "Life after Chernobyl," Irigaray argues that Chernobyl shows we can no longer assume that nature will "fulfill its role as regulator of our energies and our lives," so "the race of men needs the help of persons whose function would be to promote self-understanding among men and to set limits."[22] Women should play this role, she argues, because as societal outsiders they can offer a more "objective" critique.[23] Women, moreover, should act as ecological naysayers:

> We need some regulation that matches the rhythms of nature: we need to cultivate this affiliation with nature and not to destroy it in order to impose a double nature that has been split off from our bodies and their elementary environment. Women suffer more grievously from the rupture with cosmic checks and balances. Therefore it is up to women to say *no*. Without a *yes* from women the world of men cannot continue and develop.[24]

Refusing to applaud the male march of progress is hardly the most dynamic form of political intervention. Furthermore, just saying "no" calcifies conservative gender roles (women are always supposed to say no) and deepens the nature/culture divide. Endowed with a special knowledge of the "rhythms of nature," women are positioned in a pure and innocent realm outside of culture, that is, the "world of men." Though it aims to prevent environmental catastrophe, this ecological Lysistrata strengthens the very conceptions of woman and nature that undermine feminism and environmentalism. Such mimicry strikes a bit too close to the original.

Despite the serious shortcomings of this passage, Irigaray serves as an apt contrast to Beauvoir, highlighting two opposite directions for feminism's relation to the category of nature.[25] Most feminist theory has followed Beauvoir and distanced itself from nature. Some radical feminists, however, such as Adrienne Rich or Mary Daly, imagine and promote feminist possibilities by looking toward nature as a realm untouched by the stalwart reach of patriarchal culture. Ecofeminism makes even more explicit links between nature and feminism. Susan Griffin's *Woman and Nature,* for example, speaks for both of her subjects in order to protest their mutual oppressions and to create alliances between them. Although I cannot discuss the many forms of contemporary ecofeminism here—liberal, Marxist, radical, postmodern—I would like to touch briefly on the way in which ecofeminism has often been summarily dismissed by feminist theorists. This dismissal no doubt emerges from feminist theory's long flight from nature, but it also betrays a rather chilling chasm between some feminist academics and feminist social activism. Though I do not wish to minimize the problems with some ecofeminist arguments,[26] I would like to warn against hasty dismissal. The ease with which many ecofeminist texts are labeled essentialist betrays a narrow rigidity on the part of the predominant feminist positions. Noël Sturgeon, in her study of ecofeminist movements, provocatively argues not only that essentialist moments in ecofeminism have distinct and significant political purposes but that the "radically democratic movement structures . . . destabilize essentialist ecofeminist formulations," making careful contextual understanding necessary.[27] Furthermore, feminist theory can approach ecofeminism from a different angle, examining how some ecofeminist conceptions of nature actually undermine the very ground of essentialism. Instead of dismissing ecofeminism from serious consideration, it would be more productive to bring its perspectives to bear on the continuing debates about strategic essentialism, performative identities, postmodern feminism, and difference.

For example, since ecofeminists desire not only a transformation of gender relations but also a radically *different* way for humanity to interact with nature, it is not surprising that they would promote "difference" feminisms. The contrast between Sherry Ortner and Nancy Hartsock is telling. Ortner argues that because culture devalues nature, women, in order to achieve equality, must distance themselves from the representations, institutions, and practices that position them as "closer" to nature. Hartsock, by contrast, develops an environmentalist-feminist epistemology out of the same "natural" tasks of subsistence and child rearing that Ortner claims denigrate woman. Hartsock argues that women's experience of "continuity and relation—with others, with the natural world, of mind with body" provides the basis for developing a society that "need not operate through the denial of the body, the attack on nature, or the death struggle between self and other."[28] Hartsock offers a compelling connection between feminism and environmentalism, but one fraught with problems. For one, the fact that fewer women (exclusively) perform or identify themselves with traditionally female work may undermine the foundation of this alternative epistemology. Another problem with this theory is that its account of traditionally female work downplays race and class differences while glorifying a female realm that has been produced by the system of gender oppression itself.

Yet, if we are all constituted by discourses implicated in oppressive systems, there is never any untainted path to liberation, only, as Judith Butler would have it, the possibility of "reworking that very matrix of power by which we are constituted."[29] The fact that women's bodies, experiences, and labor have long been denigrated for their supposed proximity to a degraded natural world creates the potential for feminist epistemological positioning and discursive reworkings that challenge the constitution of both "woman" and "nature." Though "women" are constituted differently along several axes of power—race, class, and sexuality, for example—

many of these axes are also inflected by pernicious notions of nature, which lays the groundwork for a diversity of women to rework "the very matrix of power by which we are constituted." Thus, as the works of Agnes Smedley, Nella Larsen, Toni Morrison, Jane Rule, and many others demonstrate, feminists need not follow a transcendent path to liberation, but can instead engage in a kind of "situated theorizing"[30] that dwells precisely at the places where the discourses of nature are implicated in classism, sexism, racism, and heterosexism. Such situated theorizing, operating through a kind of grounded immersion rather than bodiless flight, is not only appropriate for environmental feminisms but for all feminisms that refuse Cartesian models of knowledge, agency, and subjectivity.

We can also shift the ground of feminist theory's debates about difference by redefining nature itself. If nature is no longer a repository of stasis and essentialism, no longer the mirror image of culture, then the female body need not be misogyny's best resource. Disrupting the opposition between nature and culture opens up spaces for feminisms that neither totally affirm nor totally deny difference. Feminism can instead cobble together a myriad of adulterated alternatives that neither seek an untainted, utterly female space outside of culture nor cast off bodies, matter, and nature as that which is forever debased.

Since the opposition between nature and culture is so fundamental to Western thought, however, reformulating these categories is no small matter. Attempts to reconceptualize "nature" often end up back within the very terms that they seek to transform. Rosi Braidotti, for example, argues quite persuasively that feminists who reject "all that is polarized around 'nature' as an ideological trap . . . end up freezing the conflict between the sexes in a sealed world where there is no gap." She critiques how the "categories of masculine and feminine, culture and nature, are used in that instance as fixed categories, given points of reference, as if the frontier between them, and the limits of the domain of reflection they determine were clearly established, once and for all."[31] As Braidotti explains, the feminist flight from all that has been tainted by essentialism may end up solidifying the very nature/culture dichotomy that grounds essentialism in the first place. Braidotti's solution, however, is to realize that "nature is a cultural construction," since "the notions of nature and culture can only be formulated inside an *already established* cultural order."[32] Stepping back may allow us to see nature and essentialism as cultural constructs, but this glimpse in and of itself does not provide a way of transforming the categories of nature and culture. Braidotti's lifting of the curtain is actually implicated in the very categories she critiques, since it assumes that understanding nature and culture as (mere) cultural constructs signals a kind of progress—presumably because the categories are then less recalcitrant, more open to change. The relief with which something is declared cultural betrays an assumption that culture is dynamic and nature static.

The rigidity of the nature/culture dichotomy has reverberated throughout much of feminist theory. Indeed, Diana Fuss claims that "the current impasse in feminism" is "predicated on the difficulty of theorizing the social in relation to the natural."[33] Feminism's difficulty in charting the relation between the social and the natural is connected to the problematic position of nature in poststructuralist theory and criticism. Poststructuralism offers indispensable insights for the textual and political analysis of the relations between nature and feminism. Yet within poststructuralist theory, nature occupies an untenable space. Fuss charges, for example, that "essentialism is *essential* to social constructionism" as its grounding, contrasting, and defining term. She warns against the assumption that the category of essence is " 'always already' knowable" and the parallel tendency to " 'naturalize' the category of the natural."[34] Poststructuralism has portrayed culture as a fluid field of signification by implicitly or explicitly contrasting it to the silent, static, and, hence, rather dull horizon of nature.[35] Within this cosmology, nature need not be examined, since it serves as the self-evident—indeed, the natural. As the toxic repository of essentialism, nature has been pushed further outside the poststructuralist field of vision. Mark Seltzer describes the "rule of thumb that has guided much recent criticism":

> When confronted by the nature/culture opposition, choose the culture side. This criticism has proceeded as if the deconstruction of the traditional dichotomy of the natural and the cultural indicated merely the elimination of the first term and the inflation of the second.[36]

The inflation of the cultural at the expense of the natural situates nature as a discursive vanishing frontier, a space of enabling alterity for the cultural or textual, a space that disappears with the approach of logos.[37]

Seltzer suggests that instead of endlessly proving that everything is cultural, we investigate "how the relays between what counts as natural and what counts as cultural are differently articulated, invested, and regulated."[38] Seltzer's approach allows us to examine historically varied discursive formations and their effects, as his remarkable book *Bodies and Machines* aptly demonstrates. Ironically, however, by mapping "what counts," the investigation is, of course, solidly within the realm of "culture." The nature/culture opposition is nearly impossible to escape. Nature's very alterity invites its exploration, but as soon as it is approached it vanishes with its own status as a frontier. As long as nature is imagined as the outside of culture, the advance of language pushes the frontier of "nature" further away. Culture and textuality then become self-enclosed systems for which nature is always outside. This denies any significance to a nature that is other than, or more than, a discursive formation and denies the possibility that nature could intervene or affect cultural systems.

Jody Berland and Jennifer Daryl Slack sum up the difficulties here when they ask, "[H]ow can we understand something as discursive and non-discursive at the same time?"[39] While nature cannot be understood apart from its discursive construction, it may *act* in ways that jostle or jolt that very construction. This partially accounts for both the discursive construction of nature and its simultaneous existence outside of discourse. Carolyn Merchant's "ecological approach to history," for example, "reasserts the idea of nature as historical actor";[40] its actions may challenge the very cultural constructions through which it is understood. Viewing nature as an actor radically challenges the idea that nature is passive matter, there for cultural consumption.

Other postmodern conceptions of nature emphasize nature's agency, activity, and ability to signify. Deleuze and Guattari's *A Thousand Plateaus,* for example, eludes centuries of dualistic, anthropocentric Western thought by forwarding concepts such as rhizomes, strata, and assemblages that not only transgress boundaries between the psychological, philosophical, and economic but also intrepidly ignore divisions between human life and nonhuman nature.[41] *A Thousand Plateaus* disorients its readers, denying them the familiarity and stability of a landscape where nature and culture are clearly demarcated. Their extraordinary cartography redefines "nature" to such an extent that feminism can forge alliances with it—even while escaping the cumbersome cultural baggage that such alliances threaten to deliver. Donna Haraway's cyborgs, "material-semiotic actors," trickster coyotes, and "artifactual" natures that are *made* by humans and nonhumans also blur the boundaries between nature and culture as they insist on nature's agency and semiotic force.[42] Such postmodern cartographies effectively disentangle "woman" from "nature"— but they do so without condemning nature to a vacuous wilderness. As Val Plumwood argues, a "nonreductive resolution requires both that we reconceive ourselves as more animal and embodied, more 'natural,' and that we reconceive nature as more mindlike."[43] Along with Plumwood, Braidotti, Haraway, and others, I believe that neither a feminist retreat into nature where we pose as "angel[s] in the ecosystem,"[44] nor a feminist flight from nature is the answer. Instead, we must transform the gendered concepts—nature, culture, body, mind, object, subject, resource, agent, and others—that have been cultivated to denigrate and silence certain groups of humans as well as nonhuman life.

Despite the transhistorical tenacity of these potent concepts, it is important to examine how they function within specific historical and political contexts. For, as I demonstrate in the next section, the discursive landscape that women writers inhabit is no virgin land—at any given historical moment "nature" is not only a profoundly gendered realm but a site of many other struggles for power and meaning. Perhaps it is this rich though dizzying landscape that allows for the complex, protean, and forceful "situated theorizing" of women writers and activists. For whereas feminist theory's flight from nature leaves nature dangerously abject, a remarkable range of women's texts inhabit nature in order to transform it, not only contending with the natures that have been waged against women but writing nature as feminist space.

Nature, Cultural Studies, and American Literature

European colonists set foot on the "New" World of "virgin" land only to inscribe that land with the same old stories of violation. Frederick Turner's *Beyond Geography*, for example, depicts the "coming of European civilization to the wilderness" as a "spiritual story," but the chapter titles expose an unabashed narrative of carnal conquest. They proceed from "Mythic Zones" to "Defloration," to "Penetration," to "Things of Darkness," and finally "Possession."[45] Sexualizing conquest and colonialism naturalizes those processes while depicting women, the land, and indigenous peoples as mysterious zones that invite their own violation. Indeed, the very glorification of "nature" as a quintessentially American ideal is complicit with a conquest mentality. For example, Frederick Jackson Turner's 1893 "frontier hypothesis" argues that "the existence of an area of free land, its continuous recession, and the advance of American settlement westward explain American development."[46] As Henry Nash Smith explains, "nature" becomes the democratic "norm of value" when Turner depicts "the influence of free land as a rebirth, a regeneration, a rejuvenation of man and society constantly recurring where civilization came into contact with the wilderness."[47] As many have noted, the convenient characterization of the continent as "free land"—that is, as "nature"—begs the question of colonialism by mentally obliterating the multitude of cultures already here. Although American mythology endows nature with value, nature is seen as "empty," not full; in other words, nature is *"terra nullius"* in Plumwood's terms, "available for annexation . . . empty, passive and without a value or direction of its own" that spurs on the delirious pioneer visions of unlimited freedom.[48] While the American landscape as *terra nullius* may not seem flagrantly female (no breastlike rolling hills protrude from this particular portrait), it is nonetheless a gendered representation, since, as Plumwood argues, women have long been positioned as a blank background for masculine exploits.

Just as the conquest of the continent was staged on a feminine ground, so too was the later conflict between an American pastoral ideal and the industrial revolution. In *The Machine in the Garden* Leo Marx notices that the ubiquitous "crude, aggressive" machines and the "tender," "submissive" gardens they violate are gendered male and female.[49] Not until Annette Kolodny's *The Lay of the Land*, however, did anyone fully explore the persistently feminized landscape of American literature. Examining texts from 1500 until the present, Kolodny argues that "the land-as-woman" is the "central metaphor of American pastoral experience."[50] Male texts present the land as the feminine principle of gratification, as a mother, a lover, or both; but when the land fails to live up to a pastoral ideal, she becomes a "victim [of] masculine activity": "For all her promise, her bounty, her seductive beauty, nature must be *made* to provide for man; he dare not wait for all to be given."[51]

In this book I examine how North American women have written about nature, given their immersion within such narratives and discourses. Both Kolodny and Vera Norwood have posed similar questions; however, my findings, especially on the issue of the domestic, differ greatly from theirs.[52] In *The Land before Her: Fantasy and Experience of the American Frontiers, 1630–1860,* Kolodny traces Euro-American women's response to the frontier. She argues that Euro-American women cultivated the symbol of the garden, confining themselves to the " 'innocent . . . amusement' of a garden's narrow space" not only in order to evade gendered metaphors of nature, but also to avoid "male anguish at lost Edens and male guilt in the face of the raping of the continent."[53] According to Kolodny, it was women's exclusion from masculine wilderness narratives that encouraged them to create an alternative, less grandiose mythology of the frontier.

> Having for so long been barred from the fantasy garden, American women were also, at first, wary of paradisal projections onto the vast new landscape around them. Their imaginative play, instead, focused on the spaces that were truly and unequivocally theirs: the home and the small cultivated gardens.[54]

The frontier women Kolodny describes imagine their gardens as an extension of domestic space, a ground within the sphere of their influence, a space of their own.

Euro-American women's desire to transform the wilderness into domestic space continues through the nineteenth and into the twentieth century, according to Vera Norwood. Norwood's *Made from This Earth: American Women and Nature*, a wonderfully rich study of American women writers, illustrators, gardeners, taxidermists, and others, argues that nineteenth- and twentieth-century American women participated in naturalist activities "because they believed that the particular environmental agendas supported values deriving from domestic culture" and, conversely, that women gained a "public voice" in the nineteenth and early twentieth centuries because "the values of middle-class family life were conflated with the domestication of the landscape to justify expansionist goals."[55] While it is important to consider the role that domestic ideologies played in granting women of racial and class privilege a public voice, Norwood's history tends to flatten out women's responses to nature by equating women with the domestic. For example, referring to Delia Akeley and other female animal behaviorists, Norwood states that "[w]omen who take up residence alongside wild animals extend the boundaries of home to include wolves' dens and elephants' gathering places."[56] Yet to argue that female naturalists extended the domestic realm into nature and built a women's space in the wilderness from "their domestic roles as wives and mothers"[57] forecloses the possibility that women entered the wilderness, literally, or imaginatively, precisely in order to throw off—or complement, subvert, or bracket—their domestic roles. Many women have, in fact, invoked nature in order to critique cultural roles, norms, and assumptions and to escape from the confines of the domestic.

Unlike the frontier women Kolodny describes, who cultivated real and imaginary gardens, various women writers, beginning with Catherine Sedgwick in 1824 and continuing through the mid-twentieth century, searched for an undomesticated space in nature. I argue that these women looked outward toward a natural realm precisely because this space was *not* already designated as "truly and unequivocally theirs" and thus was not replete with the domestic values that many women wished to escape. Nature, then, is undomesticated both in the sense that it figures as a space apart from the domestic and in the sense that it is untamed and thus serves as a model for female insurgency. In addition, several of the texts examined here that are environmentalist as well as feminist insist that nature is undomesticated in order to stress its wildness, sovereignty, or agency. Gripping, provocative, and remarkably inventive, such cartographies of undomesticated ground demonstrate how nature has served as an important space for the cultural work of feminism. For example, the female individualism advocated by Sedgwick's *Hope Leslie,* which is rooted in nature as an alternative ground of values, significantly departs from the domestic feminism that reigned during the nineteenth century. The hybrid landscapes of Sarah Orne Jewett and Mary Wilkins Freeman, which confound and confuse the boundaries between nature and the domestic, serve to gently uproot rigid notions of gender. Most dramatically, perhaps, Mary Austin paints the land beyond the borders as a feminist refuge where women can dodge domestic confinement and cast off gender as if it were an ill-fitting shoe.

Traveling to nature as an undomesticated space for feminism, many American women writers implicitly—or in the case of Marxist-feminist theorists of the 1930s, explicitly—interrogated the grounds of female social construction. Imagining a place in which women could be untamed, unruly, and unregenerate critiques the "unnatural" social forces that have constructed women as obedient subjects. In a strange twist on the history of feminist claims that women are created by culture, not nature, writers such as Mary Inman and Rebecca Pitts turn toward nature to condemn the *social* "manufacturing" of females, arguing that it is oppressive because it is "unnatural." A "natural woman" in these theories does not call up a flower-adorned earth goddess or a barefoot and pregnant drudge but instead a free, self-determined, and not particularly "feminine" individual. Feminists have long drawn on nature not only as an ally for "difference" or "gender maximizing" feminisms but also for nascent poststructuralist, or "gender minimizing," feminisms. In such formulations, it is culture that enforces rigid notions of gender, while nature is imagined as a space utterly free from such confining concepts, values, and roles. Nature, posed as a space apart, serves as an indispensable site for feminist cultural critique. If, as Hortense Spillers argues, the domestic is the very root of gender, then nature as a nondomestic—sometimes even antido-mestic space—can provide a site for unraveling gender.[58]

Characterizing nature as a liberatory wilderness, however, poses sev-eral potential problems: it may widen the nature/culture divide, and it may be complicit in the American glorification of "free land," which has underwritten colonialist exploits by depicting nature as an empty space. Despite these difficulties, feminist writers such as Mary Austin resist the colonization of nature by representing it as an active, forceful, and sover-eign entity, even while depicting it as a space apart from culture. It may be paradoxical, but Austin maps nature as a liberatory place apart from cul-ture even as she erases the conventional borders that divide nature from culture. Several other feminists blur the boundaries between nature and culture even as they grant nature its own domain. Along with Austin, such a diverse group of writers as Octavia Butler, Marian Engel, and Leslie Marmon Silko demonstrate that nature cannot be entirely known, con-trolled, or predicted. Their writings not only offer a less domineering de-piction of the natural world but also challenge the conception of nature as a ground of fixed essences, rigid sexual difference, and already apparent norms, values, and prohibitions. Such reconceptualizations of nature are of considerable importance for feminism, especially in light of the history of racist and sexist attempts to mark and denigrate difference by rooting it within the static realm of nature.

At the same time that feminists have traveled to nature as an open, un-determined space, they have also enlisted the cultural potency of nature as an ally for their struggles, as I discuss in the next few paragraphs. While the fact that nature has been represented as both an empty space and a field replete with cultural values may make it a peculiarly paradoxical place, this paradox may actually make it an auspicious terrain for femi-nism.[59] Both the ideological saturation of nature and the concomitant po-sitioning of nature as outside of culture make it the perfect site for the "movement" that engenders "the subject of feminism," as de Lauretis ex-plains: "It is a movement between the (represented) discursive space of the positions made available by hegemonic discourses and the space-off, the elsewhere, of those discourses."[60] Rather than fleeing from or retreat-ing to an already defined realm of nature, many women writers instead undertake this very movement between the hegemonic constructions of nature and the elsewhere beyond them. This movement characterizes women's attempts to write nature as a feminist space.

The cultural authority of the pastoral, for example, has motivated American women to inscribe nature as a feminist domain. Lawrence Buell argues that "American pastoral representation cannot be pinned down to a single ideological position. Even at its seemingly most culpable—the moment of willful retreat from social and political responsibility—it may be more strategized than mystified."[61] Indeed, pastoral representations have underwritten colonialist, racist, and misogynist enterprises, but they have also been taken up in order to battle those same forces. Though the pastoral is certainly not ideologically one-dimensional, it has been a potent ideological site. Women have endorsed their social visions by drawing on the pastoral tradition in American literature that has saturated "nature" with democratic values and held it up as the conscience of culture. Women have enlisted this ideal in support of specific political struggles and as an imaginative space for equality and freedom. Whereas early twentieth-century conservation discourse, macho wilderness cults, and the popular exploits of "Nature Man" veiled their brawny attempts to reestablish dominance by planting them within the supposedly apolitical realm of nature, leftist writers such as Agnes Smedley, Emma Goldman, Fielding Burke, and Tillie Olsen validated their anarchist, socialist, and communist ideals by invoking pastoral values. Various groups sought to align their interests with the endorsement of a disinterested nature. A "contest of mapping" ensued (see Chapter 4).

Despite the wide range of ideological positions that have taken root in the pastoral, it has never been ideologically innocent or neutral—especially when it claims to be. As the early twentieth-century wilderness mania demonstrates, the very idealization of nature as a pure field apart from social struggles constitutes it as the ideal site for playing out—while repressing—anxieties about threats to white male middle- to upper-class social power.[62] Karl Kroeber's *Ecological Literary Criticism: Romantic Imagining and the Biology of Mind* performs a similar retreat into the "apolitical" sphere of nature by contrasting "ecological thinking" with "Cold War oppositionalist mentality" that would "substitute for one dogmatic system its mirror opposite—for instance, substituting for imperialism anti-imperialism, or replacing a canon excluding female artists of color with a canon excluding white males."[63] Presumably to rescue white males from canonical extinction, Kroeber invokes "nature's" values of "interdependency," "interactivity," and "diversity" to neutralize politically engaged literary criticism by staking out a position that is supposedly beyond "self-defensively exclusivist terms, nationalistic, ethnic, or ideological."[64] To take one example, Kroeber exhorts ecological criticism to restore the true (i.e., biological/ecological) meaning of "diversity" that "has been threatened by recent postmodern separatist critics."[65] This valorization of diversity as a normative principle, however, does not promote an ecological criticism that transcends political struggles—as if such a thing were possible or even desirable—but instead, uses nature as a site from which to launch a conservative backlash.

Kroeber has set up camp in a rather crowded site—a multitude of literary, popular, and philosophical depictions of nature have cordoned it off from the clamoring, messy battlefields of the political, even when, or especially when, they have used nature as a site from which to launch political battles. "Nature" becomes a most pernicious and potent weapon when it is paradoxically both devoid of and overflowing with meaning. Functioning as a "point de capiton," or quilting point, nature seems "a point of supreme density of meaning," yet "its role is purely structural, purely performative . . . it is a 'signifier without the signified.' "[66] Always oversaturated with meanings yet never pointing directly toward any particular meaning, nature serves to hold in place a multitude of other, always shifting meanings. Idealized as beyond politics, nature simultaneously bolsters gender, race, class, colonialist, and sexual ideologies that are defended with specious tautological arguments. Nature has served as a repository for culture's moralism[67] and prejudice: the claim that something is "natural" justifies it, while at various times higher education for women, "miscegenation," single motherhood, and homosexuality have been condemned as "unnatural." (Somehow, a country of strip malls, nuclear weapons, and Twinkies has no problem proclaiming something "bad" because it is supposedly "unnatural.") On the other hand, the erection of culture above a denigrated nature has fortified racist ideologies by charting a chain of being in which African, Mexican, and Native Americans dwell "closest" to a debased nature. Ronald Takaki's *Iron Cages* offers numerous examples of how a "rational," "free," disciplined white American identity was formed by projecting bodily, bestial, and other "natural" attributes onto people of color.[68]

Nature holds in place a multitude of conflicting, ever shifting meanings that are nonetheless potent ideological pivots. This overdetermined symbolic landscape is often a treacherous terrain. Writing a feminist nature, in fact, is often akin to lifting the lid on Pandora's box—many evils rush out and cannot be recontained. For example, when Margaret Atwood's *Surfacing* allies feminism with nature, it also catalyzes a heterosexist ideology that demands not only "a man" but procreation for wholeness. Furthermore, some of the white writers in this study forge their own "feminist" position out of racist materials. For example, the women conservationists of the Progressive Era performed valuable conservation work—but it was probably the xenophobic pedestal these "ladies" mounted that allowed them to be heard. And the protagonist of Fielding Burke's *Call Home the Heart* succeeds in controlling her own reproductive capacities by symbolically projecting the denigrated corporeal aspects of nature onto a black woman's body as she herself flees to more ethereal pastures.

The perplexing ways in which "nature" becomes enmeshed in such an astonishing array of social struggles can be understood with the help of Ernesto Laclau and Chantal Mouffe's post-Marxist theory, put forth in *Hegemony and Socialist Strategy: Towards a Radical Democratic Politics.* For Laclau and Mouffe, "elements" have no necessary or preordained meaning; their significance arises from how they are "articulated" or connected into discursive systems, systems which are themselves never entirely stable.[69] This theory not only helps us to understand how the meaning and significance of nature can shift and transform, but suggests a mode of analysis that examines how feminists intervene in already established, though never quite fixed, discursive terrains. For example, whether the "nature" feminist writers engage is that of Enlightenment, Romantic, Darwinist, Social Darwinist, utilitarian, or postmodern thought (or more often a heterogeneous mixture of these) shapes but does not foreclose feminist transformations. Women, of course, do not stand outside the conceptions of nature that they seek to transform. Nor do women enjoy some sort of special relationship to nature that their writings will reflect. Instead, because women are positioned differently within gendered discourses of nature that usually work to their disadvantage, feminists often attempt to reconfigure these discourses by severing, connecting, or transmuting various elements in such a way as to profoundly alter their meaning and political force.

Such complicated, intermeshed, even overwrought symbolic landscapes seem a far cry from the vision of nature as a prelapsarian Eden, a pastoral utopia, or a wilderness fantasy. Yet such discursive landscapes provide apt models for the ways in which women's texts carve their feminisms out of the very materials that hem them in. De Lauretis explains that a feminist perspective, "a view from 'elsewhere,'" cannot succeed in representing something utterly different: "For that 'elsewhere' is not some mythic distant past or some utopian future history: it is the elsewhere of discourse here and now, the blind spots, or the space-off, of its representations."[70] Feminists inhabit the margins and blind spots of the very representations that have operated against them, including the association of woman with nature. Emma Goldman and several radical women writers of the 1930s, for example, recruit the bountiful "Mother Earth"—usually a benign, maternally selfless icon—as their comrade in arms. Similarly, Mary Austin takes the same sexualized image of nature that Kolodny describes in *The Lay of the Land,* but instead of representing her as the victim of the rape narratives, she transforms her into a powerful mistress who delights in disrupting domesticity. Although Darwin and many of his followers have used evolution to assert male supremacy, several late nineteenth-century women, including Mary Wilkins Freeman and Sarah Orne Jewett, transformed Darwin's theory into an argument for the untrammeled "evolution" of woman, as they seized upon the way in which Darwin's narrative of human origins—unwittingly perhaps—diminishes the significance of sexual difference itself. Carving their own spaces in the "space-offs" of representation, North American women writers and theorists have transformed nature into a crucial place for the cultural work of feminism.

The gendering of the American landscape as feminine and the constellation of classist, racist, and heterosexist ideologies of "nature" complicate—even thwart—the search for an undomesticated space of feminist possibility. Just as the American landscape was hardly "virginal" terrain (someone indeed *had* already been here), so the discursive realm of "nature" is always populated by someone else's intentions, someone else's desires. Feminist conceptions of nature do not stand outside of dominant cultural views; they stage dialogues, protests, and contests for the meaning of "nature" and the "natural." Thus, this book does not trace a consistent tradition of American women's conceptions of nature; no central metaphor, concept, or narrative could rein in the diverse, contradictory, but often overlapping ways in which North American women have written themselves into, out of, and through nature. In fact, the wide array of literary texts were chosen to demonstrate how the relationship between feminism and nature cannot be understood by extracting the two terms from their social and historical context, but only by analyzing what these terms have meant within specific historical moments. Thus, each chapter concentrates on a different nexus of social issues and political movements—the "Indian Wars" of the early nineteenth century; the influence of Darwin in the late nineteenth century; the aims of the progressive women conservationists; the fight for reproductive freedom in the 1920s; the communist, socialist, and anarchist movements of the early twentieth century; and contemporary environmentalism.

Although I analyze several convention speeches, magazine articles, visual arts, and films, works of fiction often take center stage. Narrative fiction, as a genre, is invaluable for writing nature as a feminist space. Even Emma Goldman—not exactly known as a fiction writer—pens fables when she writes of "Mother Earth." Fiction allows Goldman, like other writers, to transform what is into what could be. Certainly much of the political force of fiction emanates from its utopian moments—its ability to conjure up in concrete, gripping, and memorable ways a more desirable social order that implicitly critiques the status quo. Moreover, the symbolic and discursive richness of fiction—the way it wraps its arms around a cacophonous array of competing social codes, assumptions, and ideals—makes it a productive site for the transformation of meaning and, in this case, for the articulation of feminist "natures." Fiction also offers a space for women to imagine themselves beyond the strictures of their roles, values, and subject positions. The form of narrative itself gives a sense of unfolding, traversing, and traveling that is consonant with writing nature as a feminist space. This sense of movement—exemplified by Austin's "Walking Woman"—is not primarily about occupying a specific subject position[71] but about disidentifying from sedimented notions of womanhood. Since most notions of womanhood have been squarely rooted within the domestic realm, these fictions venture outward, imagining nature as an undomesticated space. I should also note that with the exception of Austin's work, the fictions studied here would not be classed as conventional "nature writing." The critical category of "nature writing" should certainly be enlarged, as Patrick D. Murphy has persuasively argued, but my primary aim in discussing an extraordinarily diverse group of literary texts that are often seemingly not "about" nature at all is to demonstrate how indispensable nature has been for a range of feminist social interventions.

The book is organized chronologically and divided into three thematic sections. In Part I, "Feminist Landscapes," I explore three extraordinarily different spatial-symbolic landscapes and the extent to which these landscapes serve as an undomesticated ground for feminism. In Part II, "Nature as Political Space," I trace how early twentieth-century writers engaged in a "contest of mapping," protesting against the normative "nature" used to condemn birth control while aligning a utopian nature with working-class feminism. In Part III, "Feminism, Postmodernism, Environmentalism," I examine the natures currently circulating through postmodern theory, contemporary feminist novels, and popular culture texts in order to determine their feminist and environmentalist valences. The remarkable range of feminist rearticulations of nature and the fact that nature appears in the most unlikely places underscores how crucial nature has been for the cultural work of feminism. Despite its role as the bedrock of oppressive ideologies, nature has also been a space of feminist possibility, an always saturated but somehow undomesticated ground.

Part I
Feminist Landscapes

Chapter One: Feminism at the Border

Nature, Indians, and Colonial Space

We may trust your wild-wood bird; her flights are somewhat de-
vious, but her instincts are safer than I once thought them.
                                        Catherine Sedgwick, *Hope Leslie*

Catherine Maria Sedgwick's early nineteenth-century novel *Hope Leslie* enacts a paradoxical cartography: nature is at once an undomesticated ground for (white) female freedom and an abject realm of racial subjection. Even though Sedgwick clearly intended to pen a "pro-Indian" novel, the novel advances territorially, mining nature as a ground of alternative values while erecting race as a barrier against the howling void of the wilderness. Does the novel's feminism become unwittingly entangled in racist discourses, or is it actually dependent on a racially stratified landscape? And if nature is, like fantasy, "a fundamental impossibility, a screen masking a void," then how should feminist texts approach this impossible space?[1]

Sedgwick's novel travels to nature in order to depart from the prevalent domestic ideals that "woman's fiction" promoted, yet Sedgwick is an odd candidate for such a departure.[2] Nina Baym classifies four of Sedgwick's other novels as "woman's fiction," including her 1822 *New England Tale*, which was the first novel of this genre. Baym explains that in woman's fiction, domesticity "is set forth as a value scheme for ordering all of life" so that woman's influence would be expanded.[3] Despite the fact that Sedgwick never married, the ideal "that she was hostage to . . . was to become a compleat [*sic*] wife and mother in her own dream home."[4] Though a prolific author, she "regarded her literary endeavors as a pale substitute for what she believed should be the calling of a true woman."[5] *Hope Leslie*, shaped by neither the ideology nor the form of woman's fiction, may betray a dissent from domesticity, however. As Carol J. Singley succinctly states, "[I]n *Hope Leslie* no home is glorified."[6] The novel in fact skirts domestic settings, presenting instead expansive natural space. If, as Gillian Brown argues, in the nineteenth century the domestic came to signify individualism—but "an individualism most available to (white) men,"[7] then *Hope Leslie* deserts the domestic in the hope that nature would extend a space for female individualism.

Nineteenth-century representations of nature can hardly be considered apart from images of "Indians," since Indians were rarely considered distinct from the natural world. Take Columbus, for example, who "in his naturalist's enthusiasm" (and in the delirium of a colonialist shopping spree), wanted "to take specimens of all kinds back to Spain: trees, birds, animals, and Indians."[8] Later European colonists conceived of Indians less as objects for acquisition and more as creatures that were disturbingly indistinguishable from the threatening wilderness: "Sweeping out of the forest to strike, and then melting back into it, savages were almost always associated with the wilderness."[9] The Indian and the wild animal merge into one figure in Harriet Prescott Spofford's 1860 story "Circumstance," which depicts a Euro-American woman held captive in the woods all night long by a panther. The heroine wards off death and metaphorical rape with her civilizing influence: she sings to the animal to stop the "savage caresses that hurt like wounds."[10] In case the reader neglects to notice the similarities between this tale and Indian captivity narratives, Spofford helpfully names the panther "The Indian Devil." Helen Hunt Jackson's *Ramona* (1884), which attempted to arouse public sentiment on the behalf of Indians, as *Uncle Tom's Cabin* had done for slaves, also depicts Indians as synonymous with nature. If, as Carl Gutiérrez-Jones argues, the novel's "most fundamental object of denial is the central character's mestiza identity,"[11] nature—as the authenticator of Ramona's Indian identity—effects this denial. Although Ramona has been raised by a prosperous Mexican family and for most of her life has not even known that she is half Indian, when she escapes with her Indian lover, nature itself transforms her into her "true" identity. Thrilled with her new life outdoors, she says to her lover, "This seems to me the first home I have ever had. Is it because I am Indian, Alessandro, that it gives me such joy?"[12] Later, when Ramona happily tells Alessandro he "speak[s] as the trees speak, and like the rock yonder, and the flowers, without saying anything!" he replies, "[W]hen you say that, you speak in the language of our people; you are as we are."[13]

In other words, to be an Indian means to speak and to comprehend the language of nature. Lydia Maria Child romanticizes Indians even more in her 1846 story "She Waits in the Spirit Land," which protests Victorian sexual codes by celebrating the utopian life of the Indians in the wilderness, who, like the animals to which they are compared, enjoy sexuality without the constraints of artificial culture.[14] In some ways this story is the romanticized flip side of "Circumstance." While Child portrays the natural world as a utopia, Spofford depicts nature as "red in tooth and claw." For both, however, Indians are devoid of culture and inseparable from the natural world.

Sedgwick's historical romance *Hope Leslie,* written in 1827 but set in seventeenth-century New England, tells of the spirited white heroine's triumphs over puritanical patriarchal authority. The overarching romance narrative, in which three women love the same man, is nearly eclipsed by adventurous subplots in which Hope and the Pequod Indian Magawisca rescue various Indian and white characters from captivity and death. Writing during a decade of "Indian Removal," when whites were forcing Cherokees and Choctaws off their land, Sedgwick attempts to intervene in contemporary debates by rewriting the past.[15] She prefaces her novel with a strong critique of historical accounts that misrepresent Indians as "surly dogs" and insists that history and literature would be very different if written from an Indian perspective: "Their own historians or poets, if they had such, would as naturally, and with more justice, have extolled their high-souled courage and patriotism."[16] The novel also breaks miscegenation taboos and illustrates its theory that the difference between races "arises mainly from difference in condition" (6) when Hope's sister Faith "becomes" an Indian by living with the Pequods and chooses to stay with her Indian husband instead of her family. Sedgwick reveals the import of such didactic narratives by writing "metafictional" scenes which illustrate that narrative and sentiment can transform political positions. For example, when Magawisca describes the slaughter of her people to Everell, who has never before considered the Indian Wars from an Indian perspective, he responds as Sedgwick's ideal white reader, his consciousness transformed by "sympathy and admiration for her heroic and suffering people" (54).

Although the plots of the novel are far too complex to summarize here, a brief outline will illuminate that most of them contest patriarchal authority. From the offstage beginning of the novel, which describes a dogmatic father who cruelly severs two lovers, to the climax of the tale, in which Hope frees Magawisca from her Puritan prison, the novel denounces patriarchal control and applauds its subversion. Setting the novel in a seventeenth-century Puritan community renders the power that the male elders wield symbolic of American patriarchy itself, as the elders, the court, and the Bible stand as one rigid wall of authority. In one instance Magawisca defies her Indian father's authority by leaping under his hatchet to save Everell from decapitation—she sacrifices her arm to save his head. In most of the novel, however, it is white patriarchy that Hope and various Indian characters defy. Hope, for instance, rescues Nelema, an Indian woman, from her unjust imprisonment and, along with Everell's backstage help, Hope cleverly sneaks Magawisca out of jail. Unlike Lydia Maria Child's 1824 *Hobomok,* in which the forest only momentarily serves as a space for daughterly rebellion, *Hope Leslie* puts forth a coherent vision of nature as a ground of transcendental values. Throughout, Sedgwick justifies Hope's rebellious, impetuous, and even illegal actions by appealing to something beyond the law, rooted in the heart and in nature—a "natural" ethic that the Indians share.

Like other fiction of its time, *Hope Leslie* represents Native Americans as coextensive with nature. Indian characters speak and are spoken about in similes and metaphors of the natural world. When Mrs. Fletcher explains to Magawisca how fortunate she is to be her servant, soaking up white culture, because Indian ways are "little superior to those of wolves and foxes," Magawisca retorts by affirming her connection to nature. She explains that she is not tired from her journey: "The deer tires not of his way on the mountain, nor the bird of its flight in the air" (24). Less happily, Magawisca's father describes how his people "were swept away like withered leaves before the wind" (75). Examples abound. Although it may ring a bit precious to modern ears, the Indians' poetic language upstages the Puritans' stiff pronouncements and biblical injunctions. This rhetorical struggle, in which a romantic sensibility edges out authoritative discourse, helps enlist readers' support for the anti-authoritarian plots.

If the plots that pit Hope Leslie and Indian characters against the white patriarchs ally feminists with Native Americans, their propinquity to nature allies them even more. Hope Leslie's free spirit, courage, and defiance of authority—in short, her feminism (if I may be permitted the anachronistic use of the term)—emanates from nature. Worried that Hope's liberal attitudes about women and Indians may seem anachronistic, Sedgwick explains that "like the bird that spreads his wings and soars above the limits by which each man fences in his own narrow domain, she enjoyed the capacities of her nature, and permitted her mind to expand beyond the contracted boundaries of sectarian faith" (123). The simile idealizes

Hope's capacity to escape from the narrow confines of religion by elevating her natural freedom high above her tethering culture.[17] Natural tropes consistently figure freedom throughout the novel. Hope, for instance, springs up as the model for nineteenth-century women because of her riparian nature:

> Nothing could be more unlike the authentic "thoroughly educated," and thoroughly disciplined young ladies of the present day, than Hope Leslie; as unlike as a mountain rill to a canal—the one leaping over rocks and precipices, sportive, free, and beautiful, or stealing softly on, in unseen, unpraised loveliness; the other, formed by art, restrained within prescribed and formal limits, and devoted to utility. (121)

Sedgwick's analogy celebrates Hope's "natural" freedom, energy, and activity, contrasting the mountain stream to the young ladies who have been rigidly channeled by a dourly utilitarian culture. Sedgwick draws upon nature as a domain free from the reach of cultural construction in order to envision the possibility of a free-spirited feminist heroine. Unlike much feminist theory, which assumes nature is adamantine and culture is malleable, Hope's feminism condemns the rigidity of culture while envisioning nature as a ground of freedom.

At moments, Hope seems to share the Pequod's reverence for nature. When Magawisca and Hope accidentally meet at their mothers' graves, Magawisca reveals to her that the Great Spirit is not only present in temples, but "beneath the green boughs of the forest." Hope muses, "There was certainly something thrilling in Magawisca's faith" (189). Earlier, in a letter to Everell, Hope herself narrates—at great length and with an ecstasy that is rivaled by nothing else in the novel—her experience of climbing a mountain: "My senses were enchanted on that high place. I listened to the mighty sound that rose from the forest depths of the abyss, like the roar of the distant ocean, and to the gentler voice of nature, borne on the invisible waves of air" (101). Sedgwick strips the innocence from Hope's ecstasy, however, by noting the colonialist purpose for climbing the mountain—they were scoping out sites for Puritan villages. The prime site was conveniently "marked out for them by clusters of Indian huts" (100). Whites cannot enjoy an untroubled "bond with nature" when they gain their access to (free) land by way of massacres.

Despite this darkly ironic moment, the novel creates a space for Hope's feminism by drawing on "Indian" ideals of nature. For the Indians literally and for Hope symbolically, nature offers freedom, expansiveness, and liberation. *Hope Leslie* embodies Paula Gunn Allen's contention that white feminism has long been indebted to the ideals it adopted from Native American cultures. Allen argues that American feminism was influenced by early contact between white women and Native American cultures that valued femaleness, promoted freedom and egalitarianism, and derided "authoritarian structures."[18] Later feminists would self-consciously exploit Native histories for their own gain. Gail H. Landsman outlines how the woman suffragists from the mid-nineteenth through the early twentieth century argued for white women's equality by portraying the Iroquois matriarchy as an "alternative to American patriarchy" and as "proof that in some cultures the natural rights of woman as equal of man were recognized."[19] Though *Hope Leslie* does not exhibit Indian culture as a matriarchy where female equality flourishes, it does enact a struggle of values in which nature encompasses an anti-authoritarian alternative that both Indian culture and white feminism embrace.

Not content to let these alternative values languish in the margins of culture, Sedgwick's historical revision asserts their centrality to American patriotism. Sedgwick was not the first to link American democratic values with the American landscape. As discussed in the preceding chapter, the notion of "free land" has long saturated nature with "American" values. In 1782 J. Hector St. John de Crévecoeur asserted in *Letters from an American Farmer* that equal access to the land grants Americans their democratic rights: "[I]t has established all our rights; on it is founded our rank, our freedom, our power as citizens, our importance as inhabitants of such a district."[20] Sedgwick takes up the potent association between an expansive nature and democratic values, but eschewing the image of the male pioneer or farmer, she articulates a democratic nature with feminist challenges to patriarchal authority. When Hope asks Digby, a lower class white character, whether he thinks she has been "too headstrong" in wanting her "own way," he responds:

> Oh, no! my sweet mistress—no—why this having our own way, is what every body likes; it's the privilege we came to this wilderness world for; and though the gentles up in town there, with the Governor at their head, hold a pretty tight rein, yet I can tell them, that there are many who think what blunt Master Blackstone said, "that he came not away from the Lords-bishops, to put himself under the Lord's brethren." (225)

Digby insists that the "gentles" pervert the very ideals of egalitarianism and liberty that brought them to the wilderness.

The antidemocratic sovereignty of the town patriarchs reigns during

Magawisca's trial when everyone—except for the judges—decides that Magawisca should be free: "every voice, save her judges, shouted 'liberty!—liberty! grant the prisoner liberty!' " (293). In the speech that provokes this outcry, Magawisca proudly asserts that she is an enemy of white civilization ("Take my own word, I am your enemy"); yet she also positions herself as a "patriot." Her speech contrasts the freedom of the natural world with her dungeon and demands that they grant her either liberty or death:

> . . . if ye send me back to that dungeon—the grave of the living, feeling, thinking soul, where the sun never shineth, where the stars never rise nor set, where the free breath of heaven never enters, where all is darkness without and within . . . ye will even now condemn me to death, but death more slow and terrible than your most suffering captive ever endured from Indian fire and knives . . . I demand of thee death or liberty. (293)

By alluding to Patrick Henry, a revolutionary hero, Sedgwick (ironically) has Magawisca articulate nature, freedom, and American patriotism into one anti-authoritarian trumpet blast. The links between nature and resistance to authority become more overt when Everell tries to convince the ever-obedient and submissive Esther that she should help Magawisca escape from jail: "I should think the sternest conscience would permit you to obey the generous impulses of nature, rather than to render this slavish obedience to the letter of the law" (278). Nature, in other words, incites justified civil disobedience.

Esther's obedience makes her less appealing to her fiancé Everell, as he longs for Hope and her "unfettered soul" (280), which brings us to the romance plot in which the three heroines—Magawisca, Esther, and Hope, all of whom vie for Everell's affection—are contrasted. Despite Sedgwick's depiction of Faith's interracial marriage, by the last third of the novel, the long-felt attraction between Magawisca and Everell is bracketed as Magawisca fades from the contest. Although a husband is a dubious trophy for a feminist heroine, by rewarding Hope with Everell, instead of Esther, the plot suggests that Hope's feminist spirit triumphs over Esther's submission. More importantly, despite Carol Singley's provocative argument that the novel rejects dichotomous views of women and nature since "Magawisca and Hope are as capable as their male counterparts of participating in nature and society,"[21] Magawisca, Hope, and Esther do indeed embody a symbolic structure: Esther, ever-obedient to cultural dictates, becomes synonymous with culture; Magawisca, predictably, merges with nature;

and Hope occupies a mediating position, taking the "best" from each. The space of possibility for Hope's white feminism occurs near the border because it is there that she can claim the freedom of nature in order to move beyond her own culture's rigidity, and at the same time remain safely sheltered within white culture by posing Magawisca as a boundary against the wilderness.

Julia Kristeva's conception of "the abject" aptly characterizes Magawisca's precarious position as a border between nature and culture, a position that is itself disruptive of order, "in-between, ambiguous . . . composite."[22] Though Magawisca is relegated to this tenuous borderline zone in order to map out a space for Hope's securely white "feminism," the nagging residue from this very operation (which can never quite cover its tracks) constitutes Magawisca as a threat to the delusion of a "natural," self-contained, already constituted feminist subjectivity. Hope Leslie—the character, the novel, and the feminist position that the novel demarcates—may be disturbed by her dependence on her alter ego; Kristeva writes: "I experience abjection only if an Other has settled in place and stead of what will be 'me.' Not at all an other with whom I identify and incorporate, but an Other who precedes and possesses me, and through such possession causes me to be."[23] The intimate, even parasitic, relation between Hope's feminism and the representation of Magawisca results in Magawisca becoming an abject other who must be expelled far into the forest.

Magawisca's ultimate exile undermines the alliances forged between white feminism and Indians. Although the text sometimes undercuts Hope's speeches, the novel seems to endorse her last words on Magawisca. Hope implores Magawisca to stay with them because her "noble mind must not be wasted in those hideous solitudes" (332). When Magawisca replies that in nature there is no solitude because the "Great Spirit" is everywhere present, Hope's desire to convert her becomes all the more vehement:

> . . . the thought that a mind so disposed to religious impressions and affections, might enjoy the brighter light of Christian revelation—a revelation so much higher, nobler, and fuller, than that which proceeds from the voice of nature—made Hope feel a more intense desire than ever to retain Magawisca. (332)

This scene reasserts the superiority of Christianity (gleaming with Enlightenment metaphors of knowledge) over Indian paganism. *Hope Leslie* thus embodies the contradictory ways that white feminists would later draw on Indian culture to promote their own cause: first as a "symbol of women's past power and natural rights" and then as a "validation of [white] women's special 'civilizing' qualities."[24] Although Hope does not succeed in converting Magawisca, Hope's aspiration radiates the potential to civilize.

Magawisca's earlier words prove true: "Take my own word, I am your enemy; the sun-beam and the shadow cannot mingle. The white man cometh—the Indian vanisheth" (292). The Indians vanish symbolically when the text propels them back into nature, so that they may serve as the border to (white) culture. Several critics have noted that *Hope Leslie* advances a feminist position but fails to successfully articulate an anti-racist politics; I would argue that the novel actually constructs its feminism from a colonialist cartography.[25] The text progresses not unlike Trinh T. Minh-ha's "territorialized knowledge," which "secures for the speaker a position of mastery; I am in the midst of a knowing, acquiring, deploying world—I appropriate, own and demarcate my sovereign territory as I advance—while the 'other' remains in the sphere of acquisition."[26] Despite Hope's anti-racist actions and intentions, her "feminist" subjectivity operates from a position of mastery which denies its dependence on the others it subordinates. It is not surprising, then, that near the end of the novel one of the elders comments about Hope: "[W]e may trust your wildwood bird; her flights are somewhat devious, but her instincts are safer than I once thought them" (303). This evaluation reveals that Hope, for all her rebellions, has not disrupted the cultural order; the difference that she procured is safely bound.[27]

Within the colonialist cartography of *Hope Leslie,* nature and Indians serve as a space outside the bounds of the Puritan patriarchy, a place that white feminism mines in order to forge a position for itself; yet, Indians also serve as the boundary between nature and culture, a boundary that ensures that Euro-American feminism still inhabits the safe zone of colonialist culture. *Hope Leslie* moves in an all-too-familiar pattern: it advances into "Indian Territory" only to push that territory further away. Thus, although *Hope Leslie* begins by articulating an alternative constellation of democratic values that promote anti-authoritarian alliances between Indians and white feminists, it ultimately draws a self-serving, colonialist map that mirrors the policy of Indian Removal that it set out to critique.

Promoting Indians as repositories of alternative values, yet ultimately expelling them from the social order, *Hope Leslie* represents the Indian as "a social reality which is at once an 'other' and yet entirely knowable and visible."[28] Beyond the "entirely knowable and visible" border of the colonized representation of "the Indian," however, lies the nonvisible wilderness, which marks the limit of the knowable and the textual. Magawisca serves as a figure of fantasy, "filling out the empty space of a fundamental impossibility, a screen masking a void."[29] Magawisca, in fact, embodies the paradoxical "nature" of Manifest Destiny: nature serves both as a screen that cultural ideals are projected onto and an unsettling reminder that the screen is only a screen, and that "nature" in the form of the void lies beyond. Colonial desire for the land pushes the screen further and further into the "wilderness" but can never pierce through the screen itself.

In Žižek's reading of Lacan, the "fascinating presence" of the Other—for us the chimerical representations of nature—masks "not some other positivity but its own place, the void, the lack that it is filling in by its presence—the lack in the Other":

> To "unmask the illusion" does not mean that "there is nothing to see behind it": what we must be able to see is precisely this *nothing as such*—beyond the phenomena, there is nothing *but this nothing itself,* *"nothing" which is the subject.* To conceive the appearance as "mere appearance" the subject effectively has to go beyond it, to "pass over" it, but what he finds there is his own act of passage.[30]

This formulation renders coherent the paradoxical way nature serves both as a screen saturated with cultural fantasies and as a *terra nullius* or empty void. Yet while it is politically effective to traverse this illusion of a nature saturated with grounds for sexism, racism, and heterosexism, to recognize that these grounds are, precisely—nothing—or at least nothing "natural"—this schema, when applied to nature, lacks the recognition that the "nothing" of nature is also an illusion. This solipsistic formulation underscores how an environmental philosophy requires that when we attempt to traverse the chimerical screen of nature, we somehow find more on the other side than our own "act of passage."[31] While no one, of course, can ever venture "beyond ideology" and present an unmediated representation of nature, in part because language, even at the level of the word, is pierced by history and culture and every knowledge is a partial, situated one (in Donna Haraway's terms), there are significant differences between texts that represent nature as a saturated screen or a gaping void and those that attempt to represent something else, something "beyond" cultural constructions—even though the entire notion of nature as a place "beyond" is itself, of course, a cultural construction. As I explore in the following chapters, many women writers project their own feminist narratives onto the screen of nature, yet others, such as Mary Austin, Octavia Butler, Marian Engel, and Leslie Marmon Silko, wary of the screen itself, seek to represent the unrepresentable, to search for ways to write nature that do not merely pose it as a backdrop for anthro- (or gyno-) pocentric tales. Those who attempt to traverse the screen find, like the "Ones Who Walk Away from Omelas,"[32] that the place they go to exists beyond the bounds of the narrative—yet gesturing toward the very unrepresentableness of this place allows us to recognize that nature exceeds human desires to know it, to render it flatly visible, to rein it in.

Hope Leslie demonstrates, among other things, how nature is bound up with racist demarcations, borders that ironically undo the very valorization of Indians upon which the text's feminism is contingent. Mary Austin's work echoes Sedgwick's entangled portrayal of Indians, nature, and feminism in that Austin's reconception of nature depends on Native American philosophies. Like Sedgwick, Austin travels to nature as an undomesticated ground for feminism. Austin, however, does not pose Native Americans as a barrier between whites and nature, nor does she represent nature as a howling void or empty screen. Instead, Austin struggles to portray nature as both a place of feminist possibility and an independent force that exceeds and resists mastery. But before we move into the early part of the twentieth century with Austin, we first need to consider why nature does not in fact serve as an undomesticated ground for most nineteenth-century women's fiction, and why the late-nineteenth-century fiction of Sarah Orne Jewett and Mary Wilkins Freeman paints strange, hybrid places.

Chapter Two: Darwinian Landscapes

Hybrid Spaces and the Evolution of Woman in

Sarah Orne Jewett and Mary Wilkins Freeman

[T]he "woman's rights movement" is an attempt to rear, by a process of "unnatural selection," a race of monstrosities—hostile alike to men, to normal women, to human society, and to the future development of our race.

"The Woman's Rights Question Considered from a Biological Point of View"

I am a graft on the tree of womanhood. I am a hybrid. Sometimes I think I am a monster, and the worst of it is, I certainly take pleasure in it.

Mary Wilkins Freeman, quoted in Glasser

Catherine Sedgwick's 1827 *Hope Leslie,* which rejects the cult of domesticity and envisions nature as the ground of female individual liberty, stands as somewhat of an anomaly in the nineteenth century. The bulk of fiction written by women during this period promoted the values of the domestic life and envisioned those values radiating out into the "world." It would be difficult to imagine a body of literature more contrary to the idea of nature as an undomesticated ground for feminism, since in this schema not only do women embrace their identification with the domestic but the domestic seeks to envelop everything heretofore outside its grasp. The novels written between 1820 and 1870 that Nina Baym classifies as "woman's fiction," for example, espoused "a 'cult of do-

mesticity,' that is, fulfillment for women in marriage and motherhood,"
and promoted a "social reorganization wherein their special concept of
home was projected out into the world."[1] Mary Kelley terms twelve
women writers from this same period "literary domestics," arguing that
they not only saw themselves as "private beings primarily committed to
woman's role within the home," but envisioned the home as a "rarely
glimpsed, untouched, beloved paradise, a paradise that was a fantasy all
their own."[2] Jane Tompkins contends that "women writers of the nineteenth century" made "the home into an all-sufficient basis for satisfaction and fulfillment," writing "about domestic routines in such a way that
everything else seemed peripheral."[3]

While Tompkins, like many feminist critics, has lauded the philosophical heft and the political acumen of these women, reading their work primarily within the critical apparatus of the separate sphere, Amy Kaplan
exposes how their domestic ideals actually advance the projects of colonialist expansion. She contends that it is no coincidence that "the development of domestic discourse in America is contemporaneous with the
discourse of Manifest Destiny."[4] Catherine Beecher's 1841 *A Treatise on
Domestic Economy,* for example, "fuses the boundedness of the home with
the boundlessness of the nation," obliterating "the distinction between inside and outside" by the "expansion of the home/nation/temple to encompass the globe." Rather than understanding domesticity as a "static
condition," she conceives of it as "the process of domestication, which entails conquering and taming the wild, the natural, and the alien."[5] It is important to note the power and prevalence of this "process of domestication," both to account for the relative rarity of nineteenth-century
feminisms that rooted themselves in nature and to highlight how writers
such as Mary Austin radically depart from such a paradigm.

But before we travel westward with Austin into the early part of the
twentieth century, two northeastern late nineteenth-century writers,
Sarah Orne Jewett and Mary Wilkins Freeman, deserve our attention.
Jewett and Freeman are pivotal figures between nineteenth-century domestic feminism and Austin's "undomesticated" feminism. Their fiction
carefully documents the details of domestic space even while experiment-
ing with the potential to pose nature as an alternative (feminist) place.
Even more intriguing, however, is that both Freeman and Jewett narrate
hybrid spaces, places that do not conform to boundaries between nature
and culture, places where nature takes root in the domestic and the domestic opens out into nature. Perhaps with the waning of nineteenth-
century domestic feminism, Freeman and Jewett were reluctant to com-

pletely relinquish a female space, yet were attracted to the expansiveness figured by the natural world. Rather than representing the domestic as a colonizing force that tames and contains nature, nature often seems to have imploded into the domestic realm, leaving an odd, hybrid landscape for women to inhabit.

It is certainly no accident that such hybrid spaces would emerge in the late nineteenth century, since Charles Darwin's writings on evolution sought to dissolve the distinctions between humans and nature. Although the conclusion to Darwin's 1859 *The Origin of Species* only cautiously suggests that "[m]uch light will be thrown on the origin of man and his history," his 1871 *The Descent of Man* boldly declares that "man must be included with other organic beings in any general conclusion respecting his manner of appearance on this earth."[6] *The Descent of Man* demonstrates that human bodily structure, embryonic development, and rudimentary organs (such as the vestiges of a tail) mean that "man and all other vertebrate animals have been constructed on the same general model" and comprise one "community of descent."[7] Even more provocatively, Darwin argues that the human mind—not just the body—is no different in kind from that of the animal, as he asserts that "there is no fundamental difference between man and the higher mammals in their mental faculties."[8] He supports this assertion with a long series of charming, humorous, and sometimes poignant stories of animals who exhibit mental traits usually considered exclusively "human"—attention; reason; memory; language; tool use; aesthetic sense; sociability; emotions such as love, jealousy, and wonder; and a nascent moral sense. He tells of "puppies, kittens, lambs" and even insects "playing together, like our own children"; of a monkey "washing the faces of her young ones in a stream"; and a baboon whose maternal emotions were such that she "not only adopted young monkeys of other species, but stole young dogs and cats, which she continually carried about." He speculates that "an old dog with an excellent memory and some power of imagination" may dream about "his past pleasures or pains in the chase."[9] Even as they illustrate the rich emotional life of non-human animals, these stories evoke emotions in the human reader, conjuring up a kind of empathic bridge between human and animal. While humans may sometimes be generous about extending "human" characteristics to certain animals, we are for the most part less receptive to arguments that move in the opposite direction, "reducing" the transcendentally "human" to the level of the animal. Darwin's arguments moved in both directions; as Gertrude Himmelfarb wryly notes, Darwin "reduced language to the grunts and growls of a dog" and "reduce[d] religion to the lick of the dog's tongue and the wagging of his tail."[10] Not only are human achievements and institutions thus debased—in both senses of the word—so is the human (bodily) self. Reading Darwin, we imagine our own body, no longer an entity unto itself, as a site of metamorphosis, still bearing traces of its forebears, the "hairy, tailed quadruped," the "amphibian-like creature," the "fish-like animal," and finally, the "aquatic animal provided with branchiae, with the two sexes united in the same individual, and with the most important organs of the body (such as the brain and heart) imperfectly or not all developed."[11] As Gillian Beer explains, the "rapidity of Darwin's narrative made it difficult for him to render accurately the extreme slowness of the processes he was describing. Ontogeny and phylogeny might therefore be confused in the reader's mind—and even in the syntax of the text."[12] Even though evolution describes a process that occurs gradually through an almost unimaginable stretch of *time*, the catalogue of vivid examples presented in the *Descent*—which propel animal into human and human into animal— creates a dazzling *space* of collision, of admixture, of hybrids.

"Hybrid," in fact, is far too tame a term here, since it denotes the offspring of two discernible entities. None of evolution's creatures can be so clearly demarcated; none are unadulterated, solid, or stable. For many, to think of humans in such terms is nothing short of monstrous. Such monstrosity emerges, in fact, within Jewett and Freeman's portrayals of Mrs. Bonny and Jenny Christmas. These stories, however, also express the feminist possibilities for inhabiting spaces in which human and animal, nature and the domestic, merge and collide. Moreover, although Darwin and many of his followers have used evolution to assert the natural origin of what we now call gender, his story of human descent nonetheless allows feminists to diminish the significance of sexual difference in the distant past and in the perhaps not-so-distant future. Like Antoinette Brown Blackwell, Eliza Burt Gamble, and Lester Ward, Jewett and Freeman participated in the debate over the implications of Darwinism for feminism, narrating feminist visions of the evolution of woman and the origin of the species.

Sarah Orne Jewett's 1881 collection of stories and essays, *Country By-Ways*, muses on the relations of humans to nature and associates female freedom with the expansive natural world. The narrator in "An October Ride," presumably Jewett, reflects on her identity, exuberantly concluding that "I am only a part of one great existence which is called nature. The life in me is a bit of all life, and where I am happiest is where I find that which is next of kin to me, in friends, or trees, or hills, or seas, or beside a flower."[13] The opening essay, "River Driftwood," which deserves attention as environmentalist philosophy, meditates on the differences and commonalities between humans and nonhuman nature. Here Jewett reproaches humans for our rude, self-centered indifference to the "personality of our neighbors" who cannot "be made to understand a little of our own spoken language." She asks, "Who is going to be the linguist who learns the first word of an old crow's warning to his mate, or how a little dog expresses himself when he asks a big one to come and rout his troublesome enemy?" (4). Learning the languages of our nonhuman "neighbors" is but the first step in seeking a common ground with them.

> It is not necessary to tame [creatures] before they can be familiar and responsive; we can meet them on their own ground, and be surprised to find how much we may have in common. Taming is only forcing them to learn some of our customs; we should be wise if we let them tame us to make use of some of theirs. (5)

This passage echoes Darwin as it continues, arguing that humans and animals share many mental characteristics.[14] More interestingly, however, the encounter Jewett describes is not between two distinctly different realms of "nature" and "culture," but rather an intercultural meeting of "neighbors" in which both groups possess their own languages and customs. She sketches an ethic of reciprocity whereby humans should refrain from imposing our ways on other creatures, but should instead allow them to "tame us." Would this sort of "taming" be liberatory for humans? Would we become "wilder" or just fluent in the codes of another culture? Perhaps her perspective as a woman, and as a "lesbian,"[15] help her to value the languages that are not heard, the customs that have not been understood. Jewett in fact explicitly allies feminism and nature when she extends the emerging rights of woman to nonhuman creatures, envisioning "a more truly universal suffrage than we dream of now, when the meaning of every living thing is understood, and it is given its rights and accorded its true value" (6).

This spatial model of humans and nature meeting on a common ground serves both as an important ethical ideal and as an entry into some of the hybrid landscapes created by Jewett and Freeman. In these landscapes nature and culture merge, overlap, and collide. This model is consonant with the Darwinian erasure of the boundaries between nature and culture, human and animal, but it is also inflected by the question of what constitutes female space. Jewett calls attention to the question of female space when she reads the neglect of the household yard as an index of women's emancipation.

> The disappearance of many of the village front yards may come to be typical of the altered position of woman, and mark a stronghold on her way from the much talked-of slavery and subjection to a coveted equality. She used to be shut off from the wide acres of the farm, and had no voice in the world's politics; she must stay in the house, or only hold sway out of doors in this prim corner of land where she was queen. No wonder that women clung to their rights in their flower-gardens then, and no wonder that they have grown a little careless of them now, and that lawn mowers find so ready a sale. The whole world is their front yard nowadays! (120–21)

Reading spatial relations as social relations, Jewett rejoices that women are no longer bound within the domestic or cornered in a "prim" bit of land that is merely an extension of the home, but instead may venture out into "the whole world." During the 1870s and 1880s, as more privileged women began attending colleges in record numbers, they experienced life "outside the world of bourgeois domesticity": "To place a woman outside of a domestic setting, to train a woman to think and feel 'as a man,' to encourage her to succeed at a career, indeed to place a career before marriage, violated virtually every late-Victorian norm. It was literally to take her outside of conventional structures and social arrangements."[16] Whereas this enlargement of women's social opportunities—their opportunity to venture outside of the domestic—is often portrayed in Jewett's texts as venturing, quite literally, into the outdoors, other texts by Jewett and Freeman portray the implosion of nature into domestic space, and the strange, hybrid beings that result.

In Jewett's *Deephaven* (1877), for example, two young women from Boston, Kate Denis and Helen Lancaster, travel to a rural town spending "by far the greater part of the summer out of doors."[17] As Barbara A. Johns argues, "Kate and Helen are never held inside by either external or internal strictures; with no thought of being merely decorative, passive, or dependent on men for adventuresome lives, they presume their mobility and they presume that they are free to gather experience, to move in a rhythm of visits that will enlarge their knowledge."[18] Indeed, even though Deephaven is, as Judith Fetterley notes, "a gendered world," it allows Helen and Kate to "cross gender lines" and to participate in both male and female cultures.[19] Of course their ability to spend their days exploring is

contingent on class privilege, since servants perform the necessary domestic tasks. Such freedom allows them to ruminate on the lives of both
their human and nonhuman "neighbors"; Kate concludes that "the more
one lives out of doors the more personality there seems to be in what we
call inanimate things. The strength of the hills and the voice of the waves
are no longer only grand poetical sentences, but an expression of something real" (225). Ironically, even as Kate reaches toward nature as something "real" and critiques belletristic proclamations, her own musings become yet another "grand poetical sentence."

In the chapter that follows this epiphany, however, nature appears in a
less magnificent guise—feathered and squawking and perhaps a bit too
"real." Visiting "Mrs. Bonny," Kate and Helen encounter a "flock of hens
and one turkey" who greet them in the kitchen no less, signaling a household in disarray (234). As Ann Romines notes, there is "no clear boundary
between inside and out," and as Sarah Way Sherman explains, "Not only
does the barnyard penetrate her household, but Mrs. Bonny's household
extends into the barnyard, where her patient horse stands dressed in his
mistress's cast-off bonnet."[20] While philosophical musings on the possibility that nature could "tame" us are a noble pursuit, having chickens walk
through one's door and take up residence is another matter entirely. Nature, as "something real," appeals far less to Kate and Helen when it is "no
longer only grand poetical sentences." Though the parched Kate and
Helen ask Mrs. Bonny for a tumbler, they are suddenly "not so thirsty as
[they] had been" when they witness "some bunches of dried herbs, a tin
horn, a lump of tallow in a broken plate, a folded newspaper, and an old
boot, with a number of turkey-wings tied together," and other peculiar
things, fall out of the cupboard where the tumbler is supposed to reside
(241). While I agree with Sherman that Mrs. Bonny "seems to be on the
messy boundary between the tidy pastoral and the chaotic wilderness," especially as this opposition is inflected with class, I think it is quite revealing that this "chaotic wilderness" has broken into the domestic.[21] Given
that Kate and Helen perceive the inhabitants of Deephaven as figuring a
past time, Mrs. Bonny's domestic landscape seems particularly Darwinian, not only because of the obvious collapse of boundaries but because of
the way in which this collapse is figured as a grotesque concoction of
things. As Margot Norris writes, "Darwin's attention to monstrosity, excess, and incongruity makes his universe exceedingly strange and alienating."[22] The human being, for example, "contains little bits and traces of
other animals (the modified swim bladder of fish for its lungs, its hand
homologous to 'the foot of a dog, the wing of a bat, the flipper of a seal,'

aspects of male and female, and primitive instinctual glimmers suffused throughout its civilized behavior."[23] Not only does Mrs. Bonny's jumbled home correspond to this description, but so does her person, as she wears "a man's coat, cut off so that it made an odd short jacket, and a pair of men's boots much the worse for wear; also some short skirts, beside two or three aprons," as well as something that looked like a "nightcap" which "she had forgotten to take . . . off" (233–34). Mrs. Bonny's clothing and home are not unlike Darwin's writing, which according to Beer "emphasizes clutter and profusion" as it "relies on a nature which surges onward in hectic fecundity."[24]

While the chaotic implosion of nature into the domestic realm meets with disgust and Mrs. Bonny's doubly gendered attire meets with ridicule, Mrs. Bonny still holds a certain appeal for the young women, who "went to see her many times" after that initial visit (243). Living "deep in the woods," she "knew all the herbs and trees, and the harmless wild creatures who lived among them" (243). Her house, which opens out into a beautiful view, does not contain her, but is, rather, an extension of this "wild and unconventional" woman's outdoor life (243). Romines's finely nuanced reading concludes that Mrs. Bonny is an "unorthodox housekeeper" who "triumphs because [she] manage[s] to keep house *and* to keep [herself]."[25] Although this reading is compelling, I find Mrs. Bonny a deeply ambivalent figure. Mrs. Bonny simultaneously embodies the attraction and the revulsion that Kate and Helen feel toward the lower class. Moreover, she evokes anxiety about the loss of a domestic ideal even while proclaiming women's freedom from the domestic; she manifests the fear of Darwinian "monstrosity" even while lionizing a kinship between humans and nonhuman creatures.

Mary Wilkins Freeman's Christmas Jenny bears no small resemblance to Mrs. Bonny. Dragging behind her the evergreens for which she is named, Christmas Jenny looks, from a distance, "like a broad green moving bush."[26] Up close, the narrator's description becomes even more fantastical: "Her features were strong, but heavily cut. She made one think of those sylvan faces with features composed of bark-wrinkles and knotholes, that one can fancy looking out of the trunks of trees. She was not an aged woman, but her hair was iron-gray, and crinkled as closely as gray moss" (52). This proto-surrealistic portrait shuns anything feminine, depicting Christmas Jenny as solid and strong, an admixture of such natural elements as bark, moss, and iron. Although Leah Blatt Glasser claims that this "physical description . . . is a celebration of [Jenny's] unity with the natural environment,"[27] the rough and eerie images provoke and unsettle.

Just as Jenny's face blends into the trunk of a tree, her home merges with the natural world; "heaped with evergreens here and there" and "filled with bunches of brilliant dried flowers," it has a decidedly "sylvan air" (56, 57). But all is not cheery and bright. When the minister and Deacon Little come to investigate Christmas Jenny's house because the townspeople have rumored that she mistreats animals and a "deaf-and-dumb" boy, they are shocked by what they discover. Even though Freeman has demonstrated Christmas Jenny's remarkable kindness to animals (she sacrifices a much-needed new dress to purchase food for starving birds) and even though Freeman will later describe this visit as a "witch hunt" (59), she presents the following scene from the perspective of the two churchmen, which taints it with a kind of horror that even the "truth" of the matter cannot quite expunge.

> All around the room—hung on the walls, standing on rude shelves— were little rough cages and hutches, from which the twittering and chirping sounded. They contained forlorn little birds and rabbits and field-mice. The birds had rough feathers and small, dejected heads, one rabbit had an injured leg, one field-mouse seemed nearly dead. The men eyed them sharply . . . But they did not say what they thought, on account of the little deaf-and-dumb boy, whose pleasant blue eyes never left their faces. When they had made the circuit of the room, and stood again by the fireplace, he suddenly set up a cry. It was wild and inarticulate, still not wholly dissonant, and it seemed to have a meaning of its own. It united with the cries of the little caged wild creatures, and it was all like a soft clamor of eloquent appeal to the two visitors, but they could not understand it. (57)

Even though the plot turns on whether or not Jenny will be wrongfully blamed for the condition of these creatures, the spatial-symbolic impact of the scene resonates much further. The domestic becomes a kind of menagerie of decrepit forest creatures whose "rough cages and huts"— not unlike Jenny's "weather-beaten hut" (56)—mirror and mock the mechanisms of domestic enclosure. Even as they may need the "nurturing" of the domestic realm, their excessive and improper presence dissolves the domestic from within. When the churchmen make their official "circuit" about the room, it seems they are trying to reestablish a sense of domestic enclosure. But their efforts to distinguish nature from culture are overthrown by the "wild and inarticulate" cry of the boy, which unites with the "cries of the little caged wild creatures." Neither the humanity of the little boy, who "sat in the midst of evergreens," nor his gender can be firmly established, since he is "dressed like a girl, in a long, blue gingham pinafore" and has "pretty, soft, fair hair" which lay in a "smooth scallop" (56). Unable to decipher the scene before them or the cries that fuse man and beast, the guardians of propriety remain "perplexed."

Many feminists critics have lauded Christmas Jenny, reading her as a " 'love-cracked' subversive"; a "colossal . . . mythic, matriarchal power"; or even "the Virgin Mary, radically redefined";[28] I find the character of Christmas Jenny less fascinating, though, than her fantastic interior landscape, which confounds and confuses fundamental categories. In this case the "unreadable," "undecidable" elements of Freeman's fiction[29] result from the fact that Christmas Jenny inhabits a spatial-symbolic landscape in which the usual meanings have become unmoored. Janice Daniel argues that the images of enclosure in Freeman's fiction are not metaphors of confinement, because "her women protagonists make their own choices and thereby engage in acts of self-definition that redesign their spaces."[30] While this is certainly the case in many of Freeman's stories, one can read "Christmas Jenny" the other way around, understanding Jenny's environment not as something created solely through the will and actions of a character, but by the twin specters of Darwinian hybridity and feminist rejection of domestic enclosure. The resulting space, then—a collision of nature and culture, domesticity and the wild, the nurturing and the monstrous—allows the character to break with predictable patterns. Her "eccentricity, her possibly uncanny deviation from the ordinary ways of life" (59), is in fact inseparable from the spaces she inhabits—the nature that is her home, the home that fuses with nature. It is telling that the story begins with a stiff and stubborn old patriarch repeatedly falling on a patch of ice, for Jewett narrates a slippery sort of landscape. The "messiness" of "Christmas Jenny," as well as "Mrs. Bonny," is also apt, for they both undertake a "mobilization, subversive confusion, and proliferation" of the domestic, making "gender trouble"[31] by figuring wildly paradoxical, hybrid spaces that loosen the moorings of gender itself.

Sarah Orne Jewett's *The Country of the Pointed Firs* (1896)[32] contains several hybrid spaces, though none of them as messy as Mrs. Bonny's house. When the narrator of these stories returns to Dunnet Landing, a maritime village of Maine, she lodges with Mrs. Todd, a wise, self-possessed herbalist who will quickly become the center of these tales. As Elizabeth Ammons notes, in Mrs. Todd's home "domestic space outdoors and indoors intermingle, with the garden entering the house in the form of various scents and fragrances and Mrs. Todd moving between house and garden as between two rooms."[33] The garden itself is a kind of hybrid space, not as "feminine" as one would expect since the "few flowers [are] put at a disadvantage by so much greenery" (14). The narrator, in fact, calls it a "queer little garden and puzzling to a stranger" (14). Mrs. Todd's "domestic" space opens out not only into the garden, but into the wilder landscapes where she gathers herbs; conversely, the sea takes up residence in her home as "sea-breezes" blow into the house (14). Mrs. Todd's home is an extension of the landscape; likewise, as she tells the narrator in "A Queen's Twin," she has always thought of "the woods and all wild places" as "home" (137). Appropriately, Mrs. Todd's mother, Mrs. Blackett, dwells on "Green Island" in "one of those houses that seem firm-rooted in the ground, as if they were two-thirds below the surface, like icebergs" (40). Esther, the "Dunnet Shepherdess" who will become Mrs. Blackett's daughter-in-law, sleeps many a moonlit night in a little shed out amidst her sheep (124). These green, rooted interiors that blend with the wider natural world allow women to retain certain domestic values even while widening their prospects as they wander and partake of a broader realm. Significantly, female freedom is not linked to the consumerism of the public sphere but to greater access to natural forms of life. As Mrs. Blackwell says to her daughter Mrs. Todd, "You wanted more scope, didn't you, Almiry, an' to live in a large place where more things grew" (51). The narrator is electrified by exactly this sense of scope. As she climbs a hill on Green Island, she exclaims that the view "gave a sudden sense of space, for nothing stopped the eye or hedged one in,—that sense of liberty in space and time which great prospects always give" (46).

Even as the greening of the domestic allows for a specifically female sense of "liberty and space and time," it still cherishes domestic values. Green Island, for example, simultaneously offers that liberatory expansive view *and* a home, within which beats a room the narrator proclaims is "the real home, the heart of the old house on Green Island!" (52). When Mrs. Blackett and her son William treat their guests to a nearly tearful rendition of "Home, Sweet Home," we are awash in sentiment about the home, motherhood, and family. It may be no surprise then that Ann Romines holds up *The Country of the Pointed Firs* as the "American ur-text of household ritual."[34] Romines garners no small amount of evidence to support this claim, demonstrating that this "great domestic text" "excavates, teaches, validates, and preserves the language of domestic culture."[35] Romines makes a very strong case; nevertheless, I find this text much more ambivalent. The genre itself, as Vera Norwood explains, is a hybrid, a cross between "the literary domestic novel and the nature essay."[36] The women who inhabit such a hybrid literary space are likewise at cross purposes. They "are at the same time rooted *and* restless, enriched *and* impoverished, sustained by domestic routine *and* frustrated by it."[37]

"Poor Joanna" and her home are especially riven with contradictions. Poor Joanna, in a story by the same name, retreated to "shell-heap" island after being "crossed in love" (61). The heap of shells evokes the misogynist evaluation of spinsters as dead husks. Her exile is self-imposed, but it is nonetheless absolute; after moving to the island this "hermit" or "nun" "never stepped foot on the mainland again" (62). Though surrounded by the expansive sea, the island itself, as Mrs. Todd judges, "is a dreadful small place to make a world of" (62). The narrator, on the other hand, reflects "upon a state of society which admitted such personal freedom and a voluntary hermitage" (64). Does Joanna's exile demonstrate the ultimate act of individual freedom—the almost complete rejection of society—or a punitive domestic captivity? Or, as Romines puts it, "Is Joanna's life a rejection or an apotheosis of domesticity?"[38] The sparrows that light on Joanna's coffin seem to be testifying that Joanna lived in a state of "natural freedom," especially since they sing during the minister's eulogy and reduce him to silence. On the other hand, after living with Joanna these "wild sparrows" were now "as tame as could be" (72).

Joanna's interior landscape is equally perplexing, as its inclusion of nature may link it to the expansive hybrid space of Mrs. Todd or merely demonstrate a poor, perhaps failed, attempt at "good taste." Another character, Mrs. Begg, has decorated her house "with West Indian curiosities, specimens of conch shells and fine coral" (20); such decorations hardly bespeak the transformative entry of nature into the domestic sphere. Joanna's house, however, is a bit less proper, a bit more eccentric. She has furnished it with mats and cushions braided from rushes that grow in the swamp. She also "showed a good deal of invention" by picking up "pices o' wood and boards that drove ashore" (68). She has "flowers set about in shells fixed to the walls, so it did look sort of homelike, though lonely and poor" (68). Despite this seeming eccentricity, Joanna's decor may emulate the standards set forth in Catherine Beecher and Harriet Beecher Stowe's *The American Woman's Home* (1869), which "encouraged the use of a variety of 'natural' objects, including picture frames of pinecones, moss, and seashells; hanging baskets for plants," and other things because "the introduction of nature into the home offered its moral influence upon the character of those present."[39] Thus the natural objects in Joanna's home may not signal a hybrid space where domesticity itself comes into question, but merely a poor attempt to adhere to notions of propriety. Vera Norwood argues, in fact, that Esther and Joanna behave according to "women's role as conservator of the values of home, family, and civilization" and are hardly " 'natural' women in the contemporary meaning."[40]

Indeed, even though Mrs. Fosdick worries that Joanna may have been so lonely that she "soon came to makin' folks o' " the hens (65), she needn't trouble herself. *The Country of the Pointed Firs* is a long way from Mrs. Bonny's chaotic kitchen. When Mrs. Bonny's hens appear in this novel—as if uninvited—they are promptly exiled to their proper place. After the narrator notes that Mrs. Blackett's house is "broad and clean," for example, she spots the "brainless little heads of two half-grown chickens who were snuggled down among the mallows as if they had been chased away from the door more than once, and expected to be again" (41). Like Mrs. Blackett, Jewett chases the chickens away, infusing nature with a transcendentalist spirit in order to ward off the more disturbing "nature" of Darwin's works—a nature in which humans are kin to such lowly, "brainless" creatures. Even as the homes of Mrs. Todd, Mrs. Blackett, the "Dunnet Shepherdess," and "Poor Joanna" merge with the natural world, certain boundaries remain. Fear is certainly one of the forces that erects such boundaries; the narrator feels she and Mrs. Todd "were likely to be surrounded and overcome" by what Mrs. Todd describes as "wild Natur' ": "There was a vigor of growth, a persistence and savagery about the sturdy little trees that put weak human nature at complete defiance" (136). If the novel's emphasis on kinship, exemplified by the Bowden family reunion, is about "blood, clannishness, and inheritance," as Susan Gillman argues, and about "racial purity and white cultural dominance," as Ammons contends,[41] the colonialism and racism of this centripetal vision of kin are intimately bound up with the desire to "defy" the human relationship to the "savagery" of nature. Thus, *The Country of the Pointed Firs* is a haven not only for its narrator but for its author and its readers, since it retreats from the "disturbing" implications of Darwin's writings.

After the narrator expresses her fear that they would be overtaken by wild nature, Mrs. Todd asserts that unlike some, who are "afraid of the woods and all wild places," they have "always been like home" to her (137). The invocation of "home" here seems to clean up the threatening vision of nature as vigorous, persistent, and savage. More significantly, though, the narrator shifts her focus, seeing Mrs. Todd as embodying "some force of nature." Mrs. Todd, however, is not represented as kin to those threatening trees but as a "cousin" "to the ancient deities" (137). Many feminist critics have followed the narrator's lead, reading the novel in terms of a mythical and often maternal "feminism." For example, Elizabeth Ammons locates the "dramatic center" of *The Country of the Pointed Firs* at the point in which "the narrator and Mrs. Todd descend together into a silent, sacred, lush, female space in nature where past and present, self and other, myth and reality merge." They come together, in fact, "in the presence of the sacred earth, the healing Mother, herself."[42] Elsewhere Ammons argues that the "imagined world of mother-rule and female solidarity . . . represents an astutely political statement."[43] Josephine Donovan, in "Sarah Orne Jewett and the World of the Mothers," argues that the "narrator-visitor" represents the "historical anxieties of this generation of women, their distance from the matriarchal realm of their foremothers and their desire to reconnect with it."[44] Sarah Way Sherman reads the novel in terms of a Demeter-Persephone myth in which the protagonist is initiated "into the feminine world and its mysteries" by Mrs. Todd, who represents the earth goddess Demeter.[45]

Even as the novel reaches "back" toward a mythical, matriarchal place of earth goddesses and "mother rule," it registers its own ambivalence toward the "world of the mothers" it depicts. As Lynne Huffer argues in *Maternal Pasts, Feminist Futures,* nostalgic longings for maternal pasts are problematic because "in a nostalgic structure, an immutable lost past functions as a blueprint for the future, cutting off any possibility for uncertainty, difference, or fundamental change."[46] Rooting the maternal realm solidly within nature makes it even more difficult to imagine as yet unimagined futures. Jewett's pointed firs, are, in a sense, too firmly rooted, standing as testaments to a matriarchal tradition that is as limiting as it is enabling. Even as Jewett enshrines this particular landscape and all that it embodies, however, she also imports another strikingly different and provocatively distant "nature," a nature that unsettles the very ground of gender. The Arctic zone, residing at once within the narrative and far outside its spatial boundaries, gestures toward nature as a place "beyond"—beyond gender, beyond culture, beyond the solidly knowable. Captain Littlepage's story of an adventure at sea tells of a "strange sort of country 'way up north beyond the ice,' " "a town two degrees farther north than ships had ever been" (29–30). Michael David Bell reads this scene as a "community of fog-shaped *men,* an image of failed *male* power"—a contrast to Dunnet Landing, which is a community of women, and Margaret Roman reads these beings as a "symbolic representation of men and their traditional mode of interacting."[47] The text, however, refers to these creatures in gender-neutral terms as "strange folks," "inhabitants," and "shapes of folks." Though Littlepage does once call them "fog-shaped men," he later describes them as "folks, or whatever they were" (30). The narrator herself refers to them as "*human*-shaped creatures of fog and cobweb" (32, emphasis added). I concur with Judith Fetterley's reading of this place as one of "mediation, dissolution, blending," a place which, even though it "both obsesses and horrifies Captain Littlepage," it perhaps serves as a "desired goal" "for other characters and perhaps Jewett herself."[48] Fetterley notes, for example, Mrs. Blackett's satisfaction that William has been "son an' daughter both," and Roman asserts that "Dunnet Landing is unusually void of polarities between men and women resulting from rigid gender behavior."[49] Moreover, the icy place that haunts Littlepage exists beyond the proper "orientation" that gender demands: "Twa'n't a right-feeling part of the world, anyway; they had to battle with the compass to make it serve, an' everything seemed to go wrong" (31). When such seemingly stable categories as north, south, east, and west have no meaning and must be forced to "serve," other seemingly natural categories may also come into question. This Arctic zone is a perfect example of the "transitivity" in Jewett's fiction, which, as Marjorie Pryse argues, shifts "the reader's focus . . . to the fluid, permeable movement *across* and *between* borders," in part by representing a third space, which is a "space of possibility."[50]

While the story of the icy world beyond gender is significant within itself, the way in which Jewett extends this world into Dunnet Landing may be even more significant. Soon after hearing this story and just before traveling with Mrs. Todd to Green Island, "where mother lives," the narrator imagines that Mrs. Todd, "her enchantress," "would now begin to look like the cobweb shapes of the Arctic town" (34). The narrator imagines Mrs. Todd's metamorphosis into a creature from the land that gender forgot. It is as if the narrator, and probably Jewett, would like to reassert the world of female power and tradition, yet at the same time to dislodge them from a static and rigidly gendered realm. As the narrator imagines the matriarch transforming into the "cobweb shapes," it is as if her power radiates outward in glittering filaments.

Although the portrayal is more ghostly than biomorphic, the Arctic creatures Jewett creates may echo the strange, incredibly distant human ancestor, the "aquatic animal provided with branchiae, with the two sexes united in the same individual, and with the most important organs of the body (such as the brain and heart) imperfectly or not all developed."[51] Transposing the unimaginably distant time of human origins into an ever-elusive yet ever-present space, Jewett makes it continually possible to imagine humans as less gendered creatures. As a spatial horizon rather than a distant past, the image of humans as ungendered becomes a possibility for future evolution as well as a portrait of origins. Jewett's earlier novel, *A Country Doctor* (1884), in fact, imagines women evolving out of gender restrictions. But before I discuss this novel it is important to consider the late nineteenth-century feminist response to Darwin.

Darwin's work presented both possibilities and challenges for feminist thought. On the one hand Darwin tells us that our original ancestors were not differentiated by sex. This story of human origins can support feminisms that diminish or deny the significance of sexual difference. On the other hand, in *Sexual Selection in Relation to Man,* Darwin contends that man has evolved into a superior creature through his struggle to possess the female. Man, according to Darwin, is "more courageous, pugnacious and energetic than woman and has a more inventive genius."[52] Such declarations did not go unnoticed. Antoinette Brown Blackwell, in her 1875 *The Sexes throughout Nature,* refutes Darwin's assertion that the process of evolution resulted in man's superiority over woman. She argues, instead, that the different sexes of each species maintain "an approximate equilibrium and equivalence of forces."[53] While she certainly acknowledges difference between the sexes, she also claims that there is "a wide sense in which it may be said that the feminine and the masculine, with their opposed tensions and polarities of forces, are combined in every organism."[54] Furthermore, in the "inorganic world" the distinction between the sexes is without meaning, since "these elements and these forces are continually changing sides, entering into indefinite rearrangements in conjunction with other forces. Thus what might be distinguished as masculine in one case, would become feminine in the next."[55] Indeed, many pages later Blackwell performs her own social alchemy by demonstrating that intellectual work is crucial for the development of women and that "cooking and sewing . . . both belong more properly to the masculine function."[56] Even as she works within the categories of masculine and feminine, she dislodges and transforms them by demonstrating that sexual difference in nature is not a firm ground of hierarchical opposition, but instead a field of equivalences that shift and evolve.

Sarah Orne Jewett's 1884 *Country Doctor* portrays nature in a somewhat similar manner, as a place where gender roles are not enforced and where women can "evolve" into undomesticated creatures. By the time Jewett wrote this novel, the backlash against the woman's movement was being waged by scientists. "The Woman's Rights Question Considered from a Biological Point of View," which was published in the *Quarterly Journal of Science* in 1878, asserts that natural selection has resulted in the superiority of male mammals, concluding: "We have, therefore, in fine, full ground for maintaining that the 'woman's rights movement' is an attempt to rear, by a process of 'unnatural selection,' a race of monstrosities—hostile alike to men, to normal women, to human society, and to the future development of our race."[57] W. K. Brooks, in *Popular Science Monthly,* seeks to demonstrate a "fundamental and constantly increasing difference between the sexes"[58] and warns that "ignoring or obliterating the intellectual differences between [women] and men must result in disaster to the race," since "it is a natural law that the parts which the sexes perform in the natural evolution of the race are complemental to each other."[59] Lester Ward, writing in 1888, notes that "for the last twenty years" such comments have "constantly" appeared in "our best scientific literature."[60] Jewett's *A Country Doctor* responds to this backlash by reiterating that Nan Prince, the young woman who rejects marriage and becomes a physician, was created by entirely natural forces.

Nan, left without a mother or father, lives first with relatives and then with Dr. Leslie, an intelligent, compassionate, country doctor. Several characters shake their heads at Nan's upbringing, complaining that she was "left to run wild."[61] They say she is "as wild as a hawk," "belongs to wild creatur's . . . just the same natur," remains as "wild as ever," and runs "as a chased wild creature does."[62] Dr. Leslie, however, a well-read "scholar and thinker" modeled on Jewett's own father, approves of Nan's upbringing, saying that "she has grown up as naturally as a plant grows, not having been clipped back or forced in any unnatural direction. If ever a human being were untrammeled and left alone to see what will come of it, it is this child" (102). Even though her aunt argues that Nan's decision to become a physician is "unnatural" because a "woman's place is at home" (282), Nan's "untrammeled" development suggests that other women's domestic confinement is, in fact, what is "unnatural." Indeed, beside Nan, a fearless, gay, "wild thing," Miss Eunice seems a "hindered little houseplant" with her roots confined to a "familiar prison" (303). As Sherman puts it, the direction of Nan's "natural" growth is "not the domestic centripetal, inward and confining, but centrifugal, outward, and expansive."[63] Donovan reads the novel as another retelling of the Demeter-Persephone myth in which nature is a "matriarchal sanctuary" that Nan must leave behind for "new realms of patriarchal knowledge,"[64] but nature is identified neither with the world of the mothers nor with that of the fathers; rather, it exists as a third space, a place where Nan can liberate herself from gendered scripts. The turning point in the plot occurs, for example, when Nan "disappear[s] among the underbrush, walking bareheaded with the swift steps of a creature whose home was in some such place as this . . . going first through the dense woods and then out into the sunlight," to finally arrive at the "river-shore" where she throws herself upon a "low-growing cedar" and is struck with the realization that she must study medicine (164–65). This decision represents more than a mere career choice, since it entails the rejection of marriage, motherhood, and a domestic life. That Nan makes this pivotal decision in the "wild," in a place far from the "main road," exemplifies how nature serves as a space for gender resistance. Jewett poses nature not only as a physical space of transitivity, but also as a rhetorical space. The novel's stunningly repetitive rhetoric about "nature," the "law of nature," and the "natural" consistently argues that Nan—and women like her—should be allowed to evolve unencumbered by gendered norms.

The character of Dr. Leslie provides a vehicle for intellectual debate about Nan's development. Such debates constitute a sizable portion of this novel. Even though Dr. Leslie is the sole defender of Nan's seemingly "unnatural" development, the novel endorses his radical, but always convincingly argued, positions. Moreover, since this is a novel, after all, the plot, which charts Nan's rejection of marriage and development into a strong, useful country doctor, clearly supports Leslie's theories. Leslie is remarkably unconcerned that Nan shows no interest in marriage. Arguing with his friend Mrs. Graham, who is shocked that Leslie would encourage Nan to pursue a life outside of marriage, he explains that "Nan's feeling toward her boy-playmates is exactly the same as toward the girls she knows" (137). He rejects the idea of a single "law of nature" in favor of "the law of *her* nature," which is that "she must live alone and work alone" (137, emphasis added). As Donovan argues, the novel resists "the normalizing discipline of sexology, affirming instead the right of women to follow their own 'deviant' bent."[65] Jewett affirms the right to deviancy, however, by employing R. v. Krafft-Ebing's rhetoric from the *Psychopathia Sexualis,* which repeatedly explains that "unnatural" sexual inclinations seem utterly "natural" to the homosexual. Krafft-Ebing notes, for example, that "their own appears to them the natural act, and that permitted by law as *contra naturum.*"[66] Just as Leslie invokes "the law of *her* nature" against any monolith, the narrator revels in Nan's "untamed wildness" and challenges the reader to "understand that a nature like Nan's must and could make and keep certain laws of its own" (270). The "law" of Nan's nature exempts her from marriage, motherhood, and a life of domestic confinement. Moreover, by foregrounding Nan's "natural" development toward her vocation, the novel dismisses sex as a determinant: sex bears no relation to the "fitness" of an individual for his or her profession. Dr. Leslie, for example, vows that he will help Nan to "work with nature and not against it" by encouraging her to follow her own nat-ural inclinations to become a physician. He insists that it is irrelevant "whether it's a man's work or a woman's work" if it is her work (106).

Donovan argues that the organic metaphors in this novel espouse a "concept of nature . . . derived from the organicist Romantic theory pro-moted by Emerson and Margaret Fuller: that people, like plants, are born with inherited designs or entelechies and that the individual must be al-lowed to unfold as this predisposition dictates."[67] Although this Romantic nature certainly thrives within the novel, it does so in a rather hybrid form. That is, the novel unites this conception of nature with the nature of evolution, allowing Jewett to refute the "scientific" arguments about woman's inferiority and the rigidly determined role that prevailed during this period. Dr. Leslie's ruminations near the end of the novel exhibit Nan as a particular type of woman that has naturally evolved. He considers her representative of "the class of women who are a result of *natural progres-sion* and *variation*" (335, emphasis added). His terminology echoes, quite precisely, that of evolutionary theory. Rejecting the notion that the " 'woman's rights movement' is an attempt to rear, by a process of 'unnat-ural selection,' a race of monstrosities," *A Country Doctor* affirms that Nan and other women like her have evolved from an entirely natural process. Moreover, the novel partakes of the assumption that evolution means continual "progress" in order to portray Nan as exemplary of a liberatory future for women. When Nan tries to explain to her aunt why she refuses to marry George, she says that she "can *look forward* and see something a thousand times better than being his wife, and living here in Dunport keeping his house, and trying to forget all that nature fitted me to do" (321, emphasis added). The rather didactic narrator supports Nan's deci-sion, arguing that all women do not possess "certain qualities [that] are required for married, and even domestic life," but, rather than "attribut-ing this to the disintegration of society, it must be acknowledged to be-long to its progress" (332). The novel ends triumphantly, as both God and nature are called upon to witness and commend the aspirations of this forward-looking protagonist: "The soft air and the sunshine came close to her; the trees stood about and seemed to watch her; and suddenly she reached her hands upward in an ecstasy of life and strength and gladness. 'O God,' she said. 'I thank thee for my future' " (351). Notwithstanding the thanks given to God, it is the discourse of evolution that allows the novel to forge feminist futures.

After the publication of *A Country Doctor,* the debate over the implica-tions of Darwinian theory for the late nineteenth-century woman's movement continued. Exuberantly noting that "evolution has no limits," Lester Ward's 1888 "Our Better Halves" stresses that man's evolution depends on the evolution of woman since woman "*is* the race and the race can be raised up only as she is raised up."[68] Ward supports this position by arguing that "the female sex is primary in point both of origin and of importance in the history and economy of organic life."[69] What is most paradoxical about his argument, however, is that it turns on reading the sexless as, ultimately, female. He explains that "there is a great world of life that wholly antedates the appearance of sex—the world of asexual life—nor is the passage from the sexless to the distinctly male and female definite and abrupt."[70] Yet Ward immediately translates this world of sexless life forms into sexual categories, stating that "so far as sex can be predicated of these beings, they must all be regarded as female."[71] Although Ward assigns these creatures a sexual category in order to argue that the female sex is primary, it is important to note his fascination with the "great world of life that wholly antedates the appearance of sex." Similarly, even though Eliza Burt Gamble in her 1893 *The Evolution of Woman* sets out to prove that "the female among all the orders of life, man included, represents a higher stage of development than the male," she is intrigued by the time when "sex has not been developed . . . the two sexes have not been separated":

> Within this little primeval animal, the progenitor of the human race, lay not only all the possibilities which have thus far been realized by mankind, but within it were embodied also the "promise and potency" of all that progress which is yet to come, and of which man himself, in his present undeveloped state, may have only a dim foreshadowing.[72]

Although Gamble does not overtly proclaim what would be unthinkable, it seems that peering back toward our most distant ancestor—a creature who was not divided by sex—allows her to imagine a future that is nearly unimaginable—a future in which sexual categories may not be relevant.

One of the most interesting counterattacks on Darwinian feminism is Grant Allen's 1889 "Woman's Place in Nature," which responds to Lester Ward's contention that "woman is the race" by asserting that in humans, "as biological fact, the males are the race; the females are merely the sex told off to recruit and reproduce it."[73] This particular proclamation is rather predictable. What is fascinating, however, is that Allen's argument about males and females as biological entities dissolves into the demarcation of physical space: "All that is distinctively human is man—the field, the ship, the mine, the workshop; all that is truly woman is merely reproductive—the home, the nursery, the schoolroom."[74] This metonymic mapping grants men the vast spaces of the field, the mine, and the seas, while women's territory is circumscribed to the domestic or the nearly domestic. The sexed body, in fact, is read as such through surveying the spaces that constitute its domain.

When sexual division becomes indistinguishable from spatial division, the transgression of spatial boundaries becomes a means for contesting the very nature of sexual difference. Several of Mary Wilkins Freeman's stories, especially those from *Six Trees* (1903), diminish the divisions between the sexes by fusing nature and domestic space. These stories may be somewhat of an anomaly in Freeman's vast body of work, which certainly cannot be read in a monolithic way, especially since, as Elizabeth Meese argues, it is "textually inscribed" with "the interplay of feminism and antifeminism."[75] While Martha Cutter reads Freeman's work as consistent, in that it rejects all constraining stereotypes of woman by critiquing "the two most prevalent images"—the "Domestic Saint" and the "New Woman"— several other critics have found Freeman strangely contradictory when it comes to feminism.[76] Freeman's representations of nature are equally perplexing, in that nature is often associated with "a separate women's value system and a separate women's culture,"[77] yet in *Six Trees* nature is depicted as a force that erodes gender by making the male characters more "feminine" and the female characters more "masculine." The structure of the book itself calls attention to gender, as it begins with three stories about male protagonists, then tells two tales about female protagonists, and finally culminates in a story that breaks with this pattern—a story that questions the very origins of sexual difference.

The first story in *Six Trees*, "The Elm-Tree," tells of "old David Ransom," who flees to an elm tree because he has lost his home and his wife. His neighbor finds him looking forth "from the beautiful arms of the great tree as a child from the arms of its mother": "He had fled for shelter to a heart of nature, and it had not failed him."[78] Like Christmas Jenny's hybrid home, but without the "monstrous" edge, the tree unites nature and the domestic. Despite the invocation of the maternal, the tree is not gendered but disruptive of gender—the first two pages of the story insistently refer to this mother as a "he." The next story, "The White Birch," begins with a birch tree who has lived with several "sisters," but who is now alone and feels as if "something was gone" (45). When Joseph Lynn is jilted by his young fiancé Sarah, he comforts himself by caressing this tree, becoming, in effect, one of the tree's lost "sisters" and thus softening her sense of loss (65). Though he had planned to move his house closer to the road for Sarah, he is relieved that "the poor old house was not to be torn up by its roots like the clump of pinks, and set in alien soil" (64–65). Though the house stays in its place, the story gently uproots and intertwines nature and the domestic, male and female. The last story that focuses on a male protagonist, "The Great Pine," tells of a man alone in the forest who vents his frustrations by setting fire to a tall pine tree, but then stamps the fire out in order to rescue the tree. This "seemingly trivial happening" "tuned him to a higher place in the scale of things" (79), leading the narrator to ponder: "Who shall determine the limit at which the intimate connection and reciprocal influence of all forms of visible creation on one another may stop?" (80). Even as the story sublimates this question into a moral or spiritual matter, the question still reveals the hand of Darwin, bearing as it does upon the possibility that there is in fact "no limit" to the "intimate connection and reciprocal influence" of humans and nonhumans. Significantly, the influence this tree has on the man is to make him more "feminine." Returning to the family he abandoned ten years before, the man—who we now learn is named Dick—encounters his wife's second husband and their young children living in his home. Dick's wife and her mother have died and his daughter single-handedly struggles to take care of her younger siblings and step-father. Though Dick announces to his daughter that he is her "father," he immediately becomes a kind of mother, making corn-cake and porridge and attending to the needs of the sick husband. He also toils in the woods, the field, and the garden, but Freeman stresses his domestic work: "He washed and ironed like a woman. The whole establishment was transformed" (96).

The next two stories in *Six Trees* transform women into creatures who are less bound by gender. Martha, the joyless spinster in "The Balsam Fir," begins the story in great need of such a transformation. She has retreated from the world to such an extent that she seems literally untouched by it: "no mortal had ever seen a speck of grime upon Martha Elder or her raiment" (108). Pinched, vigilant, and self-denying, Martha stands as an unappealing exemplar of female selflessness: "there may have been something about the very fineness of her femininity and its perfection which made it repellent" (106). In a rather sudden turn of events, however, Martha rushes outside to stop a man from chopping down one of her trees. The passion of this moment transforms her. She snatches the ax away from the man "by such an unexpected motion—threatening to kill him if he steps nearer to her tree" (120). The man promises not to harm the tree and retreats, grumbling that "old maids" are "worse than barbed wire" (124). Martha awakes the next morning to find the fir balsam coated with ice—"transfigured, wonderful" (124). The glittering, radiant tree becomes a Christmas present in and of itself, convincing Martha "of her in-alienable birthright of the happiness of life" and encouraging her to assert that "whatever I've wanted I'm goin' to have" (126). Sarah Dunn in "The Lombardy Poplar" undergoes a similar transformation. At the start of the story Sarah, "the only survivor of a large family," "had resigned herself to living out her colorless life alone" (132–33). Even the company of her cousin, who is also named Sarah, seems to constrict rather than expand the parameters of her life, since Sarah is identical to Sarah not only in name but also in appearance. When cousin Sarah is given the clothing of Sarah's deceased twin sister Marah, the resemblance becomes "perfect." Even their minds seem identical, judging by their conversations, which were "a peaceful monotony of agreement" (137). This monotony contin-ues until Sarah affirms that a certain poplar tree "seems like my own folks," and cousin Sarah is horrified by this "sacrilegious" and eccentric notion (145). Cousin Sarah insults the tree, saying it is homely and "just stays, stiff and pointed, as if it was goin' to make a hole in the sky," and concluding that "[i]t ain't a tree. It's a stick trying to look like one" (147). Sarah's defense of the tree then transforms her:

> The tree seemed to cast a shadow of likeness over her. She appeared straighter, taller; all her lines of meek yielding, or scarcely even any-thing so strong as yielding, of utter passiveness vanished. She looked stiff and uncompromising. Her mouth was firm, her chin high, her eyes steady, and, more than all, there was over her an expression of in-dividuality which had not been there before. (148)

Sarah takes on the phallic form of the tree, asserting her own staunch sense of individualism—an individualism that in her community would certainly be the sole province of men. No longer fading into her colorless life, Sarah boldly proclaims her own presence by wearing a bright red dress, even though "[n]o woman of half her years, and seldom a young girl, was ever seen in the village clad in red" (164).

Although the stories in *Six Trees* embody some transcendentalist no-tions about nature's power to transform and emancipate individuals, as Robert M. Luscher argues, to read them as mere reiterations of Emerson-ian doctrines is to ignore the book's critique of gender. To read "The Bal-sam Fir" and "The Lombardy Poplar" as depicting the growth of "self-reliance," as Luscher does,[79] for example, is to ignore that the heroines' bold acts of self-assertion are accomplished when they seize symbols of male power—the ax and the phallus. Moreover, the final story in the col-lection, "The Apple Tree," enters into the debate over human origins, portraying humans as creatures who, in their natural state, exist unencumbered by gender polarities. "The Apple Tree," set in a Darwinian landscape, thus serves as an implicit commentary on the plots of the previous five stories, elucidating why it is that nature has the power to release individuals from the tight grip of gender.

The narrator introduces Sam Maddox's home in a revealingly ambivalent way. Though Sam and his family live under an apple tree that was "utter perfection," this is no prelapsarian Eden (174). Sam's "shameless," "sordid," home, with "every detail of squalor" in full sight to the passerby, was actually "provocative of physical discomfort to a sensitive observer" (172). The passerby's revulsion, induced by the sight of humans dwelling within the dirt and chaos of a "natural" state, echoes the disgust that evolution provoked. As Beer notes, "Many Victorian rejections of evolutionary ideas register a physical shudder."[80] Yet after arousing the reader's revulsion, Freeman begins to critique it, telling how the passersby expected the air to be "contaminated" but "in reality the air was honey-sweet; for there was no crying evil of uncleanliness about the place, and in the midst of the yard was a whole bouquet of spring" (173). Though not an orderly, tidy place, the Maddox home is graced by the beauty, fragrance, and abundant apples of the tree—the consumption of which brings pleasure without censure. Whereas eating the Edenic apple resulted in a more rigid distinction between the sexes, the Maddox children who dwell under this apple tree are unmarked by gender and nearly indistinguishable from their natural environment.

> Four more children pervaded the yard, their scanty little garments earth-stained, their faces and hands and legs and feet earth-stained. They had become in a certain sense a part of the soil, as much as the weeds and flowers of the spring. Their bare toes clung to the warm, kindly earth with caressing instinct; they grubbed in it tenderly with little, clinging hands; they fairly burrowed in it, in soft, sunny nests, like the hens. They made small, inarticulate noises, indicative of extreme comfort and satisfaction, like the young which are nursed and coddled to their fill. There was very little strife and dissension among the Maddox children in spite of their ill-repute and general poverty and wretchedness. (175–76)

The children—who are never distinguished by their sex—enact a Darwinian genealogy. The first sentence not only "stains" them with earth but breaks their bodies into component parts—"faces and hands and legs and feet." After that they become like nonhuman creatures, with clinging toes and grubbing hands, burrowing, nesting, and making animal-like noises. The feminist possibilities latent within this Darwinian image of human origins become clear when the story contrasts the Maddox clan with Sarah Blake, who is a "driven, compulsive housekeeper, unhappy herself and the cause of unhappiness in others."[81] In sharp contrast to the blissful Maddox children, who nest in the earth, Sarah labors furiously to maintain clear demarcations of domestic space, expelling the dust that ventures in through the open windows. As if to underscore the thematic import of the first five stories, the final story posits a stark opposition between the properly domestic—with its rigid demarcations between inside and outside, male and female—and a "natural" realm where human and animal, male and female, mix and blur. This story's hybrid temporality—it is both the culmination of the volume and an evocation of a distant era—fractures a linear sense of time, fusing the future with the past. The Darwinian landscape of *Six Trees* is simultaneously a portrait of human origins, a projection of evolutionary "progress," and most importantly, a space for the critique of sexual difference itself. Although many looked to Darwin for evidence of woman's "natural" inferiority, Freeman, Jewett, Gamble, and Blackwell drew on evolutionary theory to argue that the messy, mutating domain of nature does not foster contained, immutable (sexual) difference. In rather ingenious ways, they demonstrated that the nature of evolution can be a hospitable habitat for feminism.

Chapter Three: The Undomesticated Nature of Feminism

Mary Austin and the Progressive Women Conservationists

In no national movement has there been such a spontaneous and universal response from women as in this great question of conservation. Women from Maine to the most western shore of the Hawaiian Islands are alive to the situation, because the home is woman's domain. She is the conserver of the race. Whatever affects the home, affects the very life of the Nation.

Margaret Russell Knudsen

It is a common weakness of human nature to think of itself as idealistic when it is merely unimaginative.

Mary Austin, *Young Woman Citizen*

At the start of the twentieth century, during a time of racism, xenophobia, and gender anxiety, when women such as Margaret Russell Knudsen of the progressive conservation movement were exalting white women's mission to conserve natural resources in order to protect "the home" and enshrine "the race," Mary Hunter Austin saw nature not as a repository of resources for household use but as an undomesticated, potentially feminist space. Austin, social critic, feminist, and nature writer, challenged the "Municipal Housekeeping" ideology of the women's progressive conservation movement, which adhered to a utilitarian conception of nature and promoted women's domestic skills as their qualification for conservation work. Austin disentangles women from domestic ideologies by invoking nature and releases nature from the grip of utilitarianism by casting it as a woman. In *Cactus Thorn* and in other stories in which the desert appears as a seductive mistress, Austin takes the historically entrenched image of a feminine nature and turns it against itself, contesting discourses that position women and nature as resources for exploitation. Austin's startling creation of a sexual but not maternal land offers women a figure of identification outside the law by depicting nature as a force that resists mastery.

Austin's desert mistresses seem particularly unruly and heretical when set against the gospel of efficiency and the exaltation of the home then sweeping the country. "Efficiency" impelled both the methodical mastery of nature through conservation (as I explore in the next section) and the management of the home through the emerging field of domestic science. Domestic science was one answer to the "problem" of the home, which became a major political issue at the turn of the century. As many women sought to expand or dismantle the domestic sphere, writers, clergy, and politicians railed about the sanctity of the home. The early twentieth century's glorification of the home, however, was motivated not only by a moralistic backlash against women's advancement and the disruption of gender roles, but also by capitalism's demand for consumers. The 1920s witnessed the ravenous appropriation of feminism by individual consumerism,[1] as marketing and advertising firms spent "one billion dollars to promote private domestic life and mass consumption" in 1920 alone, exerting tremendous pressure on women's magazines to espouse a consumer-oriented domesticity.[2] Even before the appropriation of feminism by consumerism had become so pervasive, Jeannette Eaton had warned that the woman's magazine, which "has glorified the workbasket and the egg-beater and has infinitely stretched woman's belief in the miracles which may be wrought with them," is the "one sure antidote to feminism."[3]

The glorification of the home was—not surprisingly—inextricably bound to the glorification of motherhood. What is perhaps most remarkable about Austin's feminist perspective is the extent to which she was able to counter the omnipresent rhetoric, ideology, and politics of motherhood in which she was immersed. As Molly Ladd-Taylor states, during the Progressive Era, "Virtually every female activist used motherhood rhetoric, and virtually every male politician appealed to motherhood."[4] Teddy Roosevelt insisted that "woman must bear and rear the children as her first duty to the state"—lest "the whole social system collapse";[5] the National Congress of Mothers, devoted to maternal ideals, not gender equality, boasted nearly two hundred thousand members; and the maternalist social reformers intervened in the domestic practices of immigrant women in order to naturalize the threat of cultural diversity and to ensure that good, Americanized citizens would issue from these homes.[6] Though many women activists sought to radically redefine the domestic realm, they frequently invoked maternal ideals to secure a political voice as "public mothers."[7] Jane Addams, for example, celebrated women's motherly talents both within the family and outside the family as an important resource for social reform. Charlotte Perkins Gilman glorified motherhood even as she denaturalized women's responsibility for housework and child rearing and advocated taking the kitchens and nurseries out of houses in order to free mothers to be "world-servant[s] instead of house-servant[s]."[8] In contrast to Gilman, Addams, and other early New Women of her generation, Austin turned from maternal ideals in order to interrogate predominant notions of womanhood and the nature of gender. But unlike feminist modernists such as Djuna Barnes and Gertrude Stein, who were also overturning the "naturalness" of gender, Austin did not repudiate the "natural" by depicting " 'unnatural' worlds and unstructured situations beyond the threshold of conventional order."[9] Instead, Austin contested the conservative arguments that the free-spirited, independent, single, New Woman was "unnatural" by allying a feminist subjectivity with a masterless nature. Countering the stalwart ideologies of motherhood, the home, and woman's "natural" role, Austin created an antidomestic feminism by traveling to the "natural" world, invoking nature as a crucial imaginative space for the cultural work of feminism.

Austin's depiction of nature radically departs from the earlier tradition of women writers that Annette Kolodny describes in *The Land Before Her: Fantasy and Experience of the American Frontiers, 1630–1860*. The earlier writers created an alternative mythology of the frontier that "focused on the spaces that were truly and unequivocally theirs: the home and the small cultivated gardens."[10] Unlike these frontier women, who imagined their gardens as extensions of domestic space, Austin traveled toward a natural realm precisely because this space was *not* already designated as "truly and unequivocally" hers and thus was not already colonized by the domesticity that she sought to elude. Whereas the later generations of frontier women Vera Norwood studies (including Austin's contemporaries) "struggle with the conflicting values of domesticity and respect for the natural environment,"[11] Austin delights in the desert as a place to cast off constricting domestic values. For Austin, nature serves as a place of possibility, a space of disidentification from rigidly gendered cultural scripts.

An extremely prolific writer whose topics traversed religion, war, pacifism, American literature, Native American culture, and the nature and nurture of genius, Austin has been best known for her nature writing and most recently for her feminist work, but the relation between nature and feminism in her writing is difficult to decipher. Many early critics, such as Vernon Young, whose comments exemplify the male academy's reception of Austin, willfully denies any connection. While he bestows high praise upon Austin's nature writing, especially *The Land of Little Rain,* he finds her feminism intolerable, accusing her of "an obsessive repugnance toward the male animal."[12] More recently, Marjorie Pryse has characterized Austin's nature writing as profoundly gendered, claiming that "Austin's mode of narration defines" *The Land of Little Rain* "as a woman's text. What matters to her is the land, not the defeat of the land."[13] Just because a plethora of Euro-American male narratives promote the mastery of nature does not mean that white women as a group will conceptualize nature in less domineering terms. Indeed, Margaret Russell Knudsen proudly proclaimed in 1909 that "woman" had been the impetus for man's domination of nature: "For her sake, for home and happiness, he undertook to subdue the wilderness."[14] It is important to remember that Knudsen, like other female conservationists of Austin's time, espoused a utilitarian view of nature, while some male environmentalists, such as John Muir, condemned utilitarianism. Thus, Austin's anti-utilitarian representation of the land hardly comes naturally; rather, it results from Austin's attempts to resist, rework, and reimagine the discourses of nature and womanhood in which she was immersed. The progressive conservation movement, which was contemporaneous with Austin's early writings, offers significant insights into the discursive landscape of Austin's work.

The conservation work of the women's clubs, which had successfully promoted animal and forest preservation and reforestation since the mid-nineteenth century, flourished during the Progressive Era. Although the achievements of the women's progressive conservation movement have been largely ignored by most conservation historians, their impact was strong.[15] These women educated the public about conservation, lobbied politicians, published in conservation journals, promoted the "Audubon-net" (an alternative to hats decorated with the feathers of endangered birds), and engaged in direct action, such as when Mrs. D. M. Osborne of Auburn, New York cut down telephone poles and scared away the telephone workmen who trimmed her trees without her permission.[16] Backed by the numerous and well-organized women's clubs, they successfully pushed for environmentally protective legislation. Titles such as Lydia Adams-Williams's report, "A Million Women for Conservation," published in *Conservation,* the official organ of the American Forestry Association, radiate pride in the women's sheer numerical strength.[17]

Like other club women, the progressive women conservationists gained their political voice by advancing the ideal of "Municipal Housekeeping," "which justified women's right to correct social problems through the relationship of public work to domestic work."[18] In "Conservation—Woman's Work," for example, Adams-Williams calls on Joan of Arc, Josephine, and Queen Isabella to argue that women's "intuitive foresight," "power to educate public sentiment," and history of conserving and preserving money and other resources in the home make them most capable of conserving natural resources.[19] Similarly, Mrs. Overton G. Ellis argues that "conservation in its material and ethical sense is the basic principle in the life of women" because daily they succeed in such feats as "making yesterday's roast into today's hash."[20] Like other conservationists of the time, including Gifford Pinchot, Roosevelt's director of conservation, who labeled the forest as a "manufacturing plant for wood," the women conservationists were utilitarian.[21] Nature held little or no value in and of itself—nature was valuable only insofar as it provided resources for the home and the family. As Ellen Foster, the National Secretary for the Daughters of the American Revolution, asked at the First National Conservation Congress: "Why do I care at all about forests and streams? Because of the children who are to be naked and bare and poor without them in the years to come unless you men of this great conservation work do well your work."[22]

From 1909 to 1912 representatives from various women's clubs participated in the national conservation congresses along with leading male conservationists and government officials.[23] An examination of the speeches at these conventions reveals not only that the female conservationists used a separate-spheres ideology to justify their work, as Carolyn Merchant has argued, but also that despite some of their more sincere intentions, their work was impelled by the desire to "conserve" not only natural resources, but also racial purity, class privilege, and retrogressive notions of womanhood.

Although the club women accomplished an enormous amount of conservation work, the ideal of "conservation" was often used as a means for advancing innumerable and seemingly unrelated causes. Women like

Adams-Williams were serious and effective conservationists, but many club women attending the national conservation congresses created rather far-fetched metaphors and analogies in order to promote their cause as "conservation." For example, the committee against child labor asks, and answers:

> Now, why have we formed this committee against child labor? Because just as surely as a big tree is worth more than a growing slip, so a man is worth more than a child. That is a wonderfully commercial way to state it, isn't it? It is not only that we love the child and want him for ourselves, but it is because we know he is worth more to the country, if he is allowed to grow up.[24]

Even though stating it "commercially" sarcastically appeals to the men, the sarcasm doesn't alter the statement. The rhetoric of maternal care so prevalent in these documents here slips away, exposing how the upper class appropriates and seeks to manage lower class children, emphasizing how they, like trees, are resources for the wealth of the country. The tenuous stretch of this analogy suggests that "conservation" had come to have a great ideological power. Indeed, W. J. McGee declared in 1909, "Now conservation has become a cult," and Mrs. Overton G. Ellis observed that the term 'conservation" had "recently come to be a part of every vocabulary."[25] Oddly enough, participants in the conservation congresses promoted a multitude of "conservations": conserving food, conserving the child, conserving the home, conserving the peace, conserving morals, conserving "true womanliness," conserving "the race," and conserving "the farmer's wife" were all advanced as part of the same cause. Senator Clap even offered to "carry out the Conservation of time by omitting a speech."[26] But the overuse of the word "conservation" seems more than a tedious joke on the conference's appellation. Those seriously concerned with the conservation of natural resources, such as Marion A. Crocker, the head of the Department of Conservation in the Federation of Women's Clubs, were forced to try to wrest back the ever-proliferating term "conservation." By the Fourth National Conservation Congress, the utterly unconservative use of the term had become more than tiresome to Crocker because it actually threatened the conservation of resources:

> Conservation is a term so apt that it has been borrowed and made to fit almost all lines of public work, but Conservation as applied to that department bearing its name in the General Federation means conservation of natural resources only, and that is a field so vast that we have

found it all that can well be handled under one head without a chance of neglecting the very principle for which the Conservation movement was established.

Crocker warns that if we do not learn to "use but not abuse" nature, "the time will come when the world will not be able to support life, and then we shall have no need of conservation of health, strength, or vital force, because we must have the things to support life or else everything else is useless."[27] Why did the discourse of conservation have such potency and plasticity? The craze to conserve betrays the white, middle- to upper-class desire to preserve, maintain, and even cling to privilege and position in the face of social unrest. Nine million people had immigrated to the United States during the 1880s and 1890s alone. The labor surplus drove wages down and the turn of the century surged with union organizing, protests, and strikes.[28]

In her speech at the Second National Conservation Congress, Mrs. Matthew T. Scott displayed "conservation's" rhetorical entanglements as she nodded toward the conservation of natural resources while promoting an even more urgent cause.

> We, the mothers of this generation—ancestresses of future generations—have a right to insist upon the conserving not only of soil, forest, birds, minerals, fishes, waterways, in the interest of our future home-makers, but also upon the conserving of the supremacy of the Caucasian race in our land. This Conservation, second to none for pressing importance, may and should be insured in the best interests of all races concerned; and the sooner attention is turned upon it the better. [Great applause.][29]

Demanding the conservation of her own exalted position, Mrs. Scott promotes the "right" of future white homemakers to the supremacy of their race. The nationalistic will to conserve was fed not only by the mania for racial purity but also by certain women's determination to remain solidly on the pedestal, safe from the threat of the New Woman. Mrs. Scott enlightens us:

> For it is woman who is the divinity of the spring whence flows the stream of humanity—nay, she is the source herself. To her keeping has been entrusted the sacred fount. In her hands rests the precious cup, the golden bowl of life. Holier than the Holy Grail itself is this chalice glowing ever, with its own share of the divine fire, its own vital spark from the altar of Almighty power.[30]

Of course "woman" here does not designate any female body, but only the refined white ladyship. Interestingly, even though it is the Social Darwinist, hereditary justifications for racial purity that found her argument, when she describes actual reproduction she whitewashes the distasteful realm of sexuality with the soaring rhetoric of spiritual mission, thus removing white women even further from the field inhabited by those ever-multiplying dark and foreign bodies. The white women present themselves as the "natural" conservers, but they would not claim a "closeness" to nature because the sexual female body, long debased by its association with the natural, belongs only to those other women a few rungs lower on the evolutionary ladder. Notwithstanding Crocker's reprimand for straying so far afield from conservation proper, the discursive network of "conservation" reveals that—despite some of the women's sincere intentions—linking the ideals of "woman" with progressive conservation unleashed retrogressive forces. Since the women exalted to protect the hearth and oversee "municipal housekeeping" were white and middle to upper class, the rhetoric of this "difference" feminism could only forge connections between nature-as-resource and woman as ethereal WASP. The "feminism" of the progressive conservationists was not merely allied with but constructed from the ample "raw materials" that racism, xenophobia, and the capitalist demand for resources afforded. Furthermore, although invoking the potent ideal of "the home" undoubtedly strengthened not only the women's arguments for conservation but also their own role as "conservers," it bound "woman" ever tighter to the domestic. Although Austin's work is hardly free from racism, it does envision a feminist relation to the natural world that neither consumes nature as a household resource nor conserves "woman" within the domestic.

Born in 1868 in Carlinville, Illinois, Mary Hunter was never enamored with the joys of domesticity.[31] Her fifteen-year-old brother's ascendance to family ruler after their father's death made her a feminist at a young age. The infamous egg incident exposed the injustices of patriarchy to Austin. Revolted by even the sight of a soft-boiled egg, Mary requested that hers be cooked a minute and a half longer. Her brother objected, saying, "Somehow you never seem to have any feeling for what a HOME should be." Austin claims that learning that "a different sort of boiled egg was more than a female had a right to claim on her own behalf" was the kind of incident that "drove many girls of Mary's generation from the domestic life."[32] Austin did not, however, soon escape family life. After graduating from college, she joined her family in their new homestead in California, where she became intrigued by Indian cultures and enthralled by the land. Three years later she married Stafford Wallace Austin and had a daughter, Ruth. Her marriage proved unsatisfying and her domestic life nightmarish, as she was unable to accept or care for her mentally retarded daughter. While Austin attempted to write, her house became a ruin. Her neighbors, shocked by the mess, would clean her house, feed Ruth, and sometimes even bring Mary food. After leaving her husband and eventually placing her daughter in an institution, Austin lived the rest of her life as a "woman alone," supporting herself by teaching, lecturing, and writing. She traveled in Europe and lived in an artists' colony in Carmel, writing in her Paiute "wickiup" up in a tree. She was deeply influenced by the work of Charlotte Perkins Gilman and affected by other feminists and radicals she encountered in New York. Dividing her time between New York and California from 1911 to 1925, Austin met Emma Goldman, Elizabeth Gurley Flynn, Margaret Sanger, Bill Haywood, and Lincoln Steffens, and she became active in various feminist and leftist struggles.

In 1925 Austin settled in Santa Fe, visiting Willa Cather and Mabel Dodge Luhan, collaborating with Ansel Adams, championing Indian arts, and fighting for Indian rights. She called herself a "fierce and untiring opponent of the colossal stupidities, the mean and cruel injustices, of our Indian Bureau."[33] She met Theodore Roosevelt while opposing the Indian Bureau's attempt to prohibit Indian music in the schools. She also fought the Indian Bureau's schemes to terminate Indian dancing and served as president of the Spanish Colonial Arts Society. Contact with Native American cultures allowed Austin to create a feminist connection to nature that did not enshrine "feminine" values of home and hearth, as it encouraged her to understand nature in a way that challenged the premises of utilitarian motives.[34] As she learned, for example, "how Indians live off a land upon which more sophisticated races would starve, and how the land itself instructed them . . . the whole basis of her social philosophy and economy altered."[35] In keeping with her new philosophy, Austin campaigned against the construction of Boulder Dam, which would divert an enormous amount of water to rapidly developing southern California, because she opposed California's "cult of bigness" and thought the water belonged in smaller communities that epitomized her ideal of folk cultures living in harmony with the land. She thought the Boulder Dam controversy should be resolved by heeding "the Pueblo's regard for the limited resources of the earth and their acknowledgment of the land as a masterless entity."[36] Needless to say, those in charge did not embrace her position.

While Benay Blend sees Mary Austin's work as drawing upon while re-

vising the ideals of the progressive women conservationists, I contend
that Austin rejects them. Blend (incorporating Rudnick's work) argues
that Austin "took elements of Municipal Housekeeping from Eastern
Clubwomen and enlarged the traditional concept of home into a 'house
of earth' which included all outdoors."[37] Rudnick sees Austin, like Mabel
Dodge Luhan and Alice Corbin Henderson, as "mythologizing the entire
natural world as home."[38] Rudnick's argument that viewing the natural
world as home "radically revis[es] both terms" is persuasive, but I think
Austin attempted to create a counterdiscourse to domestic ideologies, not
a revision or expansion of them.[39] Austin sought in nature a place that was
not domesticated and that did not domesticate women. Unlike the
women conservationists, Austin does not promote women for their
mothering or housekeeping skills, nor does she subordinate the land to
the needs of the bourgeois household. No utilitarian ground, Austin's
land pulsates spiritually, aesthetically, and erotically. Sometimes Austin
celebrates the borderland as a place to think beyond the confines of gender; sometimes she couples women and nature through mutual strength
and resistance to male domination. Often, by picturing the land as a mistress, Austin creates a feminine land that conjoins women and nature not
as victims but as powerful allies. As a whole, her work does not put forth
a systematic, internally cohesive vision of the relation of feminism to nature. However, her many approaches seem aimed at the same goals: to
"disidentify" women from domestic ideologies with the help of nature
and to release nature from the grip of utilitarianism, often by envisioning
it as an unruly woman.

In *Lost Borders,* a collection of stories set in the California desert,
Austin portrays heroines such as the Walking Woman and various desert
mistresses who defy the prevalent ideals of womanhood that the progressive women conservationists, among others, promoted. The heroines she
creates are all the more notable for their rarity, since, as Austin explains,
many women are unable to take on the immensity of the desert.

> Did I say somewhere that women mostly hate the desert? Women, un-
> less they have very large and simple souls, need cover; clothes, you
> know, and furniture, social observances to screen them, conventions to
> get behind; life when it leaps upon them, large and naked, shocks them
> into disorder.[40]

The desert that captivates Austin is a terrain that seduces men but does
not appeal to most Euro-American women, who require domestic
niceties. The desert is not only vast but disturbingly bare—having no

need of the kind of vestments that would shield feminine vulnerability. Echoing Dickinson's "What Soft-Cherubic Creatures—/These Gentle-women are,"[41] Austin deflates domestic ideals while wryly admitting that the heroines she presents, the women of the borders, do not represent the majority of women, nor even most white women in the West. In order to find a space in which to forge another, undomesticated identity for women, Austin begins by painting nature itself as a woman. Of course, depicting nature as feminine is not exactly novel, as Kolodny's *The Lay of the Land* attests. Kolodny describes the dual trope of the land as mother and seductress that has populated the American male's literature and imaginary. For John James Audubon, for example, "the natural world was not only the Mother offering her bounty, but also, in some way, the seductress, 'afford[ing] ample inducements to the new settler,' inviting him to mine her coal, cut her timber, and paint her beauties."[42] Austin's mistresses—endowed with agency and resistance—hardly invite such treatment.

For example, in the first essay-story of *Lost Borders*, "The Land," Austin imagines the desert as a sensual yet impregnable woman.

> Mind you, it is men who go mostly into the desert, who love it past all reasonableness, slack their ambitions, cast off old usages, neglect their families because of the pulse and beat of a life laid bare to its thews and sinews. Their women hate with implicitness the life like the land, stretching interminably whity-brown, dim and shadowy blue hills that hem it, glimmering pale waters of mirage that creep and crawl about its edges. There was a woman once at Agua Hedionda—but you wouldn't believe that either.
>
> If the desert were a woman, I know well what like she would be: deep-breasted, broad in the hips, tawny, with tawny hair, great mass of it lying smooth along her perfect curves, full lipped like a sphinx, but not heavy-lidded like one, eyes sane and steady as the polished jewel of her skies, such a countenance as should make men serve without desiring her, such a largeness to her mind as should make their sins of no account, passionate, but not necessitous, patient—and you could not move her, no not if you had all the earth to give, so much as one tawny hair's-breadth beyond her own desires. If you cut very deeply into any soul that has the mark of the land upon it, you find such qualities as these—as I shall presently prove to you. (159–60)

Between the description of women's hatred for the desert and the detailed portrait of the desert as woman, Austin omits the story of an actual woman, carving an elusive space for unrepresented, undetermined (and as the narrator contends, unbelievable) female subjectivity. This open, fantasmatic space fades into the portrait of the desert, painting the desert itself as a feminist subject. No passive resource to be exploited, the desert becomes an alternative model for women's self determination and strength: "you could not move her, no, not if you had all the earth to give, so much as one tawny hair's-breadth beyond her own desires." The metaphor suggests the possibility for a new relation between women and the land where the land as a woman, but not a wife or mother, embodies an alternative identity for women, an identity unlike that of the women who "hate with implicitness the life like the land," and unlike the women Kolodny describes, who want to create a domestic sanctuary in the wilderness. Austin's portrait shuns the impulse to "civilize" as it celebrates the beauty and self-determination of the landscape as woman, offering possibilities for identification outside the constricted, domesticated female roles. Indeed, several critics have noted that this desert portrait resembles Austin herself. Yet, even here, in this gendered portrait, Austin resists the confines of gender, as she concludes the chapter by stating that "any soul"—male or female "that has the mark of the land upon it" embodies these qualities.

Lest jealousy of the desert as the "other woman" prevent women from enjoying the liberatory potential of her trope, Austin rewrites Kate Chopin's 1894 "The Story of an Hour," in which a woman, after being told of her husband's death, rejoices over her new freedom only to die suddenly when her husband appears at the door. Austin's tale critiques marriage, as Chopin's story does, but it also dramatizes an ironic alliance between wife and mistress. Austin begins "The Return of Mr. Wills": "Mrs. Wills had lived seventeen years with Mr. Wills, and when he left her for three, those three were so much the best of her married life that she wished he had never come back" (181). Mr. Wills was a dependable clerk in the East, but after moving West with his family he is unable to withstand the "lures" of the desert, its "glittering fragments of fortune or romance" (182). Mr. Wills leaves his family to go prospecting and soon enough "the desert had got him" (184). No female victims here: Mrs. Wills realizes her own strength and provides for her family better than her husband had. "She was not pining for Mr. Wills; the desert had him—for whatever conceivable use, it was more than Mrs. Wills could put him to—let the desert keep what it had got" (185). Although Mrs. Wills wonders what the desert could possibly want with her husband, she is more than happy to relinquish him to her. Celebrating women's strength and self-sufficiency, the story retells Rip Van Winkle from a feminist perspective, as Melody

Graulich argues: "While 'Rip Van Winkle' implies that women inhibit men's freedom and stifle their characters, 'The Return of Mr. Wills' asserts that men inhibit women's independence and stifle their growth."[43]

Mr. Wills suddenly returns three years later, settling "on his family like a blight" (186). Ironically, the church refuses to recognize the nature of Mr. Wills's affair with the desert. Mrs. Wills laments:

> . . . the only practical way to separate the family from the blight was to divorce Mr. Wills, and the church to which Mrs. Wills belonged admitted divorce only in the event of there being another woman . . . The minister himself was newly from the East and did not understand that the desert is to be dealt with as a woman and a wanton; he was thinking of it as a place on the map. (186)

Austin delights in the desert's wanton disruption of family life. Usually critical of the domestic women of the West, here Austin admires Mrs. Wills's strength and gives her the desert as an ally: at the end of the story, Mrs. Wills's only hope lies in her steadfast belief that the desert will once again seduce her husband away.

That Austin's erotic landscapes diverge from her otherwise dismissive treatment of sexuality underscores the significance of the cultural work that those landscapes undertake.[44] For by painting the land as a sexual female, Austin could not only forge an antidomestic identity for feminists, she could also subvert utilitarian conceptions of nature. For example, in *The Ford*, a long novel detailing the machinations of water-developing schemes in the West, Austin casts the land as a demanding—even domineering—mistress:

> For a man lives with his land as with a mistress, courting her, suiting himself to her humors, contriving as he can that her moods, her weathers shall drive for and not against him. And in time he becomes himself subject to such shifts and seasons. He cannot handle himself; he is to be handled.[45]

Taking control of her master, this mistress reverses the *Lay of the Land* narratives that feminize the land in order to conquer it. For Austin, the land, as enticing as it may be, always resists domination. As Lois Rudnick has argued, Austin, along with her Angla contemporaries in the Southwest, Alice Corbin Henderson and Mabel Dodge Luhan, "envisioned the land as masterless" and opposed the "Judeo-Christian imprimatur that man must rule, tame, and reform" the land.[46] Thus at the same time that the land-as-mistress embodies a model of undomesticated strength and self-determination for women, it also represents nature as a force that resists man's mastery. Although David Wyatt has argued that "Austin's career explores the connection between a woman's experience of maternity and her orientation toward place,"[47] I think Austin strove to create strikingly nonmaternal metaphors for the land. Unlike the well-worn trope of the land-as-mother that contains the land within patriarchal structures, the land-as-mistress presents nature as utterly untamed; she is outside the family and the law.

But before more of Austin's desert mistresses occupy center stage, it is important to consider how radically the female characters in her realist novels depart from such depictions. *Starry Adventure* and *The Ford* present starry-eyed, nature-infatuated men—but pragmatic, resolute New Women. *Starry Adventure,* which charts Gard's love for the New Mexican landscape, suggests that his lust for women springs from their resemblance to nature: "Queer how attractiveness in women always appealed to men as something they had seen in nature, slim bodies like trees, the rose of her face, the dove's look, the little hills of her breasts."[48] Despite Gard's desire for mystical nature-women, Austin provides him with tough, not at all dove-like New Women to love and marry. Similarly, the female characters in *The Ford* would never be mistaken for earth mothers: Kenneth and Anne's mother detests frontier life, Virginia is a suffragist and radical, and Anne becomes a hard-headed real estate developer. No doubt the different genres—realist novel versus nature story—partially account for the striking differences in Austin's representations of "woman." However, it seems to me that the strong, unromanticized, New Women of her novels self-consciously mark out the dangers of the very feminist philosophy that Austin travels toward: though she seeks in nature an undomesticated space for feminism, she realizes that connections between "woman" and "nature" risk evoking mystified revelries of the weak and the will-less.

Throughout her work Austin persistently and creatively contests portrayals of nature that render it as an empty resource. Such contestations not only reconceptualize nature for its own sake, but also allow her to forge feminist alliances with a nature that is not a background, resource, or pile of lifeless matter. Kenneth, a character in *The Ford,* realizes in a moment of clarity and humility that he lives in a world in which "lands, waters, the worth of women, had no measure but in a man's personal reaction," and, moreover, that such solipsistic estimations lack any ontological substance and violently reduce women and nature to "[t]oo small a measure."[49] Acknowledging that the land acts on its own terms, not those prescribed by the myopic estimates of men, Anne, the real estate agent in *The Ford,* proposes that ownership of the land should be determined not by capital, but by affinity: "Say a certain piece of land will grow prunes or potatoes; then you've got to have prune people or potato people."[50] As wacky as Anne's perspective is (one imagines a nation populated by onion people, pumpkin people, pea people, etc.), it insists that the land is not an utterly malleable resource but a force of its own.

Austin conceptualizes the power of the land in *The American Rhythm,* a book of literary theory and "Amerindian Songs Reëxpressed from the Originals" that must have raised many a skeptical eyebrow. She presents a fascinating, if unconvincing, argument that American poetry emanates out of the American landscape, as her rather vague theory of the "landscape line" attests: "It is this leap of the running stream of poetic inspiration from level to level, whose course cannot be determined by anything except the nature of the ground traversed."[51] In addition to grounding poetic form, the landscape effects a nationalism that has little to do with race:

> Where two or three races have successively occupied the same land, they will plainly show in their art and policies the influence of the land, its color and contours, winds, mountains, climates. It is even possible to guess from the songs of an unknown country whether it is open desert, or tree-covered, with sharp, heaven-climbing hills.[52]

Whether or not this is possible, Austin's theory endows nature with a substantial influence over culture. Indeed, if a people battle the land instead of adapting to it, "[i]n the long run, the land wins. If the people does not adapt itself willingly and efficiently, the land destroys it and makes room for another tribe."[53] Prefiguring recent postmodern theories of nature, Austin understands nature as an actor, not as a passive, malleable resource, as an influence on culture, not as culture's raw material. Since the land has been persistently coded as feminine and since Austin herself frequently employs the trope of a female nature, her insistence on the land as an actor with heretofore unrecognized yet nonetheless vigorous significance carries feminist implications.

In Austin's cartography the undomesticated desert provides a fertile zone for feminism. While Austin's late novella *Cactus Thorn* portrays the desert as a failed feminist utopia, an early story from *Lost Borders,* "The Walking Woman," paints it as an elusive one. These two narratives represent two poles, a battle between genders and a battle against gender itself: in *Cactus Thorn* women and nature are allied through their parallel exploitation and consequent desire for revenge, whereas in "The Walking Woman," the desert offers women a space beyond the constrictions of culture and gender.

Cactus Thorn seems disconcertingly anachronistic. Written in 1927, it could easily be dropped into the frame of contemporary ecofeminism. Like Susan Griffin's *Woman and Nature,*[54] *Cactus Thorn* illuminates the parallels between the exploitation of women and the exploitation of nature. Read now, it even seems like a sardonic response to Kolodny's *The Lay of the Land* in which after the land has been laid—and not to her liking—she strikes her revenge. Ferris Greenslett of Houghton Mifflin rejected the novella because "the hero's defection and his subsequent murder by the lady are not made absolutely convincing," but Melody Graulich suggests that *Cactus Thorn,* which remained unpublished until 1988, was rejected because editors found it too "radical."[55] Even if it was "dashed off" with a "minimum of effort," as Augusta Fink claims, this ninety-nine-page novella has a swift pace and an immediacy that Austin's more realistic but baggy novels lack.[56] *Cactus Thorn* tells a feminist morality tale; the stark plot about the "battle of the sexes" takes on a resonance mythic enough to withstand the heavy symbolism. Grant Arliss, a rising leftist political star, goes West to search for "a measure of freedom" and renewal because "the fire had gone out of him" (7, 18). In order to succeed politically he needed "that elusive quality of self-inflation called inspiration." His flame is rekindled not only by the desert but also by Dulcie (named after Agua Dulce, a spring), who embodies both the water necessary for survival and the burning seductiveness of the land. Once Arliss takes what he wants from Dulcie and the desert, he abandons them to return to his political career in New York and to marry Alida Rittenhouse, the daughter of a powerful senator who could further his career. When Dulcie arrives in New York and finds Grant engaged to someone else, the moment that the novel so insistently foreshadows arrives. She kills him. Since Grant has told no one in New York about Dulcie, she returns to the West, never even a suspect in the murder.

The novella is told from Grant's perspective; this form of narration mirrors the cultural work that Austin undertakes: we see Dulcie and the desert through male eyes, but the daggers and thorns transform that vision. Grant's perspective conflates Dulcie with the desert, as Grant barely sees her as a "separate item of the landscape" (3). She also embodies the fire that Grant desires, which

> . . . leaped subtly almost to the surfaces of this pale brown girl, as if she were, like the land, but the outward sheath of incredible hot forces that licked him with elusive tips before they dropped to the crackle of twigs under the kettle on the bare sand. Turning to gather a handful of fuel, he found the thin flame-colored film of a cactus flower almost under his fingers. Before the girl's sharp, deterring exclamation reached him, he drew back his inexperienced hand, wounded with the cactus thorn. (8–9)

Wanting to be lit but not burned, wanting the flower but not the thorn, Grant is wounded. If this scene does not provide enough ironic foreshadowing, Dulcie later rescues Grant from a snake by killing it with her "dagger like a thorn," explaining to him that "snakes were so much more likely to be found in the neighborhood of waterholes" (50). Indeed. When Dulcie arrives in New York and Grant informs her he is engaged to someone else, he "felt her arms go about him and a sudden surprising pain in his side like a thorn" (98).

The cactus thorn of the title unites not only the strength and self-protectiveness underlying the seemingly frail beauties of nature, but Dulcie's dagger and her vengeance. Though Austin tells a tale of "exploitation," the image of the cactus thorn derails a victimization narrative. *Cactus Thorn* seems to retell Austin's earlier story "Agua Dulce," part of *Lost Borders*, in which a coach driver tells his passenger the story of how he "took up with an Indian woman," camping at the beautiful watering hole, Agua Dulce (198). During a windstorm he gets sick and Catameneda, his Indian lover, helps him make it to the next watering hole. When he recovers, he finds her dead and discovers that she had given him all the food and water. Both narratives suggest utopian possibilities of love in the wilderness, and play with the metaphor of "sweet water" in the desert. That Austin replaces the Indian woman in "Agua Dulce" with a white woman suggests that Austin's feminism was indebted to Native American women. By the time she writes *Cactus Thorn*, she envisions Dulcie as a creature who, like Catameneda, not only can thrive in the desert, but can enjoy it as a realm of sexual freedom. Despite these similarities, the novella replaces martyrdom with vengeance, transforming the heroine from a victim to a victor, as Dulcie in the end kills Grant, not herself.[57] Furthermore, that Grant was killed by the "cactus thorn" of the title dramatizes the desert's prickly sovereignty.

Even though Grant's conflation of Dulcie and the desert render them resources for his own consumption, the novella insists on the desert as a place of feminist possibility, a space beyond social structures. Dulcie and Grant live together in an abandoned Italian villa that has been reduced to a mere campground for thirsty desert wanderers. The transplanted villa, utterly unfit for the environment, doesn't thrive there, warning of human hubris that disregards nature. The villa also stands (or doesn't) as a distinctly modernist image of the collapse of culture. Decaying, out of place, this metonym of high European culture suggests similar feminist images of modernism. In H.D.'s "The Walls Do Not Fall," for example, the ruins where the roof has fallen and "there are no doors" symbolize the freedoms and possibilities of "voyagers, discovers/of the not-known,/the un-recorded" for those who "know no rule/of procedure."[58] The old values and systems collapse, allowing for the possibility of something new, something possibly less antagonistic toward women. As the villa crumbles, the vast desert that surrounds them teaches Dulcie "never to make anything up," a denouncement of the social as mere fabrication, which grounds her desert-inspired feminism (11). Dulcie critiques marriage and other social structures when she explains that her friends were unhappy because they had "made-up ideas that a husband ought to be this and a wife ought to be that. Well, it was *all* like that to me; society and religion and politics" (46). For Dulcie, the desert exists beyond these illusory and constricting conventions. The desert, for example, allows Dulcie to cast off her drunken husband, who "exploited" her, and live as she wishes, without criticism from townspeople. Despite his desert sojourn, however, Grant's political "idealism" remains myopic and antifeminist; he becomes annoyed when Dulcie would " 'lead the subject back to sex,' when it so clearly had to do only with economics" (40), and when he and Dulcie camp together in the deserted villa, Grant "sniggers" at her vulnerability, thinking of "the lowest sort of use man has learned to make of woman" (37). Even while denouncing politics, Austin claims the desert as a site for expanding the conventional limits of the political, as Grant, the supposedly radical politico, briefly enjoys free love among the ruins but is unable to comprehend Dulcie's far-reaching utopian philosophy.

Before writing *Cactus Thorn*, Austin had envisioned Dulcie's philosophy of desert life unhampered by the constrictions of marriages, households, and towns. When Austin describes the land of *Lost Borders* she invokes nature as a realm beyond the social in order to imagine a feminism that does not promote a feminine ideal, but instead, offers the possibility of transgressing the boundaries of gender itself. Austin introduces the terrain of *Lost Borders* with "The Land," where the boundaries disappear and the land becomes "inextricable border ranges": "Out there, a week's journey from everywhere, the land was not worth parceling off, and the boundaries which should logically have been continued until they met the cañon of the Colorado ran out in foolish wastes of sand, and inextricable border ranges" (155). Far from barren, these "foolish wastes of sand" generate a geographic disruption of cultural borders. The land of *Lost Borders* does not merely describe a physical place, nor does geography symbolize a human condition. Instead, the land engenders a way of being in its inhabitants. In "Regionalism in American Fiction," Austin describes two criteria that regionalist fiction must fulfill: "the environment entering constructively into the story, and the story reflecting in some fashion essential qualities of the land." The region can become "another character," or an "instigator of plot."[59] As landscape becomes a character, with the power to affect plot, the nature/culture distinctions weaken and the generic lines between story and nature-essay disappear. The pieces in *Lost Borders* transgress genre boundaries, as sometimes they are meditative nature essays, sometimes descriptive travel tales, sometimes fleet, well-plotted short stories.

What interests Austin about the land beyond the borders is how the landscape itself dispels cultural order, "the law and the landmarks fail together" (156). "Out there where the borders of conscience break down, where there is no convention, and behavior is of little account except as it gets you your desire, almost anything might happen, does happen, in fact, though I shall have trouble making you believe it" (156). Without the constrictions of conscience or convention, the land beyond the borders offers freedom. Austin paints the desert as an almost Nietzschean land beyond morals, in the Wild West tradition of self-reliance.

> Clear out beyond the Borders the only unforgivable offense is incompetence; and conscience, in as far as it is a hereditary prejudice in favor of a given line of behavior, is not [the] sort of baggage to take into the wilderness, which has its own exigencies and occasions, and will not be lived except upon its own conditions. (167)

Beyond the borders one must accept the wilderness on its own terms and it's best to travel light, without the weight of conscience. Austin's desert is miles away from the moralistic and utilitarian rhetoric of either of the progressive conservation movements. By warning of its sovereignty, Austin's desert acts as an antidote to the fervent rush to domesticate nature by enshrining the hearth in the wilderness.

Lost Borders concludes with the "Walking Woman," an expansive ending to these geographical tales: she'll continue walking the land even as we finish. The narrator begins her story by expressing her wish to meet the mysterious Walking Woman, about whom she has heard many contradictory things: that she was "comely," that she was "plain to the point of deformity," that she limped, that she walked miles and miles (256–57). Moreover, although the young woman traveled alone and camped with strangers, she "passed unarmed and unoffended" (256). (The narrator speculates that her "unladylike" demeanor protected her.) According to Faith Jaycox, the narrator pursues the Walking Woman as an "alternative female subjectivity," giving the text a "psychological urgency" as the narrator seeks to determine whether "that alternative must be forcibly reinscribed within conventional discourse as 'insane,' 'deformed,' or 'lame.' "[60] The final image of the story suggests the Walking Woman eludes such reinscription, as the narrator runs down to where she has passed and sees the "track of her two feet," which "bore evenly and white" (262). As Graulich suggests, this final image implies that "the Walking Woman's trail is one worth following."[61]

Following the Walking Woman's trail leads us to a liberatory, self-reliant feminism embodied by the Walking Woman's life story, a story that she tells to the narrator. One momentous event occurs while she is saving a flock of sheep from a storm, working with a man as his equal "without excusing, without any burden on me of looking or seeming. Not fiddling or fumbling as women work" (259). She then loves this man and has a child by him, but the child dies. Neither having nor wanting marriage or a home, the Walking Woman seems to embody an antidomestic feminism that Austin reaches for in the desert, a feminism that rejects the rules of marriage and the "legitimacy" of children.

> She was the Walking Woman. That was it. She had walked off all sense of society-made values, and knowing the best when the best came to her, was able to take it. Work—as I believed; love—as the Walking Woman had proved it; a child—as you subscribe to it. But look you: it was the naked thing the Walking Woman grasped, not dressed and tricked out, for instance, by prejudices in favor of certain occupations; and love, man love, taken as it came, not picked over and rejected if it carried no obligation of permanency; and a child; *any* way you get it, a child is good to have, say nature and the Walking Woman; to have it and not to wait upon a proper concurrence of so many decorations that the event may not come at all. (261–62)

Austin's defensive tone ("But look you") demonstrates her anxiety at the reception of this portrait that endorses sex and childbearing outside of marriage. The narrator, the "I" here, approves only the Walking Woman's ideas about work; she backs away from her position on love and children. The Walking Woman's prominent place in this collection, however, and the way she epitomizes the territory beyond the borders, suggests that the Walking Woman represents a feminist ideal for Austin—even if it is an ideal she cannot openly commend.[62] As Nancy Cott notes, "Sex outside of marriage in the 1910s was outlawry," a transgression that could potentially erase the "boundaries between the 'pure' and the 'fallen' woman."[63] Traversing the land, staying in motion, the Walking Woman "walk[s] off all sense of society-made values," including those that would delineate between the "pure" and the "fallen." Traveling in directions that would somehow leave behind or unravel the workings of social construction, the Walking Woman dwells where the desert burns life down to a naked, fundamental meaning, unobstructed by unnecessary judgments, decorations, and demands. To those who would diminish the New Woman's feminist praxis by dismissing her as a by-product of urban decadence, Austin retorts with a "New Woman" whose feminism emanates from the desert landscape itself.

Of course Austin's vision of the desert as "outside" the social is yet another "social" construction of nature that partakes of historically persistent mythologies.[64] The land outside of "civilization" occupies a central place in American mythology of the West. This mythology, however, has been a predominantly masculinist one: manly men escape the annoyances of prettified culture and head to open spaces where they can finally breathe free. Countering the woman-centered domestic novel, Westerns "either push women out of the picture completely or assign them to roles in which they exist only to serve the needs of men."[65] Taking her position in this showdown of gender and genre, Austin intrudes on the male domain of the Western, celebrating its antipathy toward the domestic even while populating the desert with women.[66] Although Austin claims the desert as a feminist space, she does not inscribe it as female, but instead uses the Western myth of a nature beyond culture to elude domestic enclosure and to breach the boundaries of gender itself. Thus the Western desert—utterly undomesticated ground—allowed Austin to disidentify from rigidly gendered subject positions.

The Walking Woman loses her former name once she starts walking, as continual movement eludes the entrapment of identity. The narrator is convinced that "she never told [her name] because she did not know it herself" (257). Freed from her identity, the Walking Woman also troubles gender designations, wearing "short hair and a man's boots" and having "a fine down all over her face from exposure to the weather" (257). The narrator even becomes highly puzzled about how the woman touches her, as the story flirts with the possibility of transgressing the borders of desire: "[A]s often as I have thought of it, I have thought of a different reason, but no conclusive one, why the Walking Woman should have put out her hand and laid it on my arm" (261). Setting her brief encounter with the Walking Woman in the past enables the narrator to describe both an earlier time when she longed to meet her and a later period when the Walking Woman haunts her memory, framing the actual meeting between more enduring times in which the Walking Woman exists as provocatively apocryphal.

Cactus Thorn and the figures of the land as mistress take the historically entrenched image of a feminine nature and turn it against itself, contesting discourses that position women and nature as resources for exploitation. Austin's creation of a sexualized but not domesticated land offers women a figure of identification outside the law and depicts nature as a force that exceeds and resists mastery. As much as she promotes a feminism allied with an anti-utilitarian nature, however, Austin also challenges ideals of the feminine, preferring instead to disrupt the rules of gender by picturing a land beyond the borders.

> For the law runs with the boundary, not beyond it; it is as fast to the given landmarks as a limpet to its scar on the rock. I am convinced most men make law for the comfortable feel of it, defining them to themselves; they shoulder along like blindworms, rearing against restrictions, turning thereward for security as climbing plants to the warmth of a nearing wall. They pinch themselves with regulations to make sure of being sentient, and organize within organizations.[67]

The limpet, a mollusk that clings tightly to a rock when disturbed, embodies the human need for laws, systems, security. It cleaves to its very scar on the rock, an image of the destructiveness of its need. The limpet symbolizes how the "boundary" between civilization and wilderness constitutes both the limits and the underpinnings of human law: "For the law runs with the boundary, not beyond it." Traveling beyond the law reveals the politically constructed nature of the borders themselves, an insight which can perhaps loosen the grip of the law on the territory within. At a time when many women were "organizing within organizations" that preserved— even petrified—"woman" within the home, Austin was prying the limpet from its scar on the rock and journeying toward undomesticated ground.

Part II
Nature as Political Space

Chapter Four: Emma Goldman's *Mother Earth* and the Nature of the Left

Emma Goldman has a baby to provide for. I have a sample of the baby with me—it is called Mother Earth. *It is a lusty one and very young in years, but brimful of vim and vigor. I trust all of you will avail yourselves of the opportunity of helping to provide for it and thus encourage its mother to continue to give you nothing but the Truth which will make you free.*

Fred Young, 1915

Emma Goldman's "birth" of the journal *Mother Earth* plays off the contradictory conceptions of nature that compel this chapter and the next. Mother Earth—"brimful" of social values—promises truth, freedom, and abundance. Lurking behind this utopian portrait, however, is the notion that the maternal body is natural. As a force for social change the "lusty" "vim and vigor" of nature validates and energizes, but as a reproductive drive it is menacing, denying women freedom, agency, and self-determination. During the early twentieth century a strange assortment of social movements, characters, and texts all struggled to articulate nature with their aims, engaging in a "contest of mapping" that sought to secure nature as a cultural ideal. Yet when the battles over birth control began, the expansive political field of nature collapsed into the female body, where it became a concentrated site for dramas of feminist agency. Nature, in the early twentieth century, was a highly politicized space—both the ground for demarcating the contentious claims of the body politic and the site for asserting that women's bodies are themselves political.

Even while several feminist texts dramatize nature as something horrifically coterminous with the female body (as the next chapter will explore), many women on the left strategically employed the conception of nature as an ideal world apart. From Emma Goldman's creation of herself and her journal as *Mother Earth* to Agnes Smedley's *Daughter of Earth*, leftist women used "nature"—a space untouched by political inequities yet already saturated with cultural ideals—as a way of promoting the working class. Similarly, Marxist-feminist theorists Mary Inman and Rebecca Pitts pose nature as a liberatory space apart from the lock-step "manufacturing" of women, suggesting that gender itself is a product of capitalist culture, not nature. While feminists envisioned nature as a utopian space offering the potential for a less oppressive, less unjust culture, others fled to nature to reentrench their dominant positions. For example, many early twentieth-century conservationists and wilderness enthusiasts—epitomized by the popular exploits of "Nature Man"—sought to colonize the wilderness as a space for the (re)assertion of a brawny, white, bourgeois manhood. Staging their maneuvers in the wilderness, under the cover of a supposedly apolitical nature, these men naturalized their claims to power. Tillie Olsen's *Yonnondio* and Fielding Burke's *Call Home the Heart*, however, insist that these demarcations of nature are, in fact, political, as they respond to these mappings by staking out their own working-class claims to nature.

Emma Goldman's Insurgent *Mother Earth*

The monumental cultural potency of motherhood encouraged turn-of-the-century women to take up, rather than turn from, this category; by expanding "motherhood" to encompass women's role in the public sphere, women enlarged their territory and gained a public voice. By the late 1920s, however, motherhood "had come to be seen as 'at odds' with feminism and female autonomy," as feminists and maternalists clashed over the potential effects of the Equal Rights Amendment.[1] Ellen Key's work reveals, most strikingly, how motherhood and feminism could come to be "at odds." Ellen Key, an advocate of free love, argued for women's liberation on the grounds that motherhood would benefit the public sphere: "It was just in order that motherliness should be able to penetrate all the spheres of life that woman's liberation was required."[2] But Key's exaltation of motherhood was no mere expedient ploy to procure freedom for women. She worried that woman's participation in political life would cause her to neglect her home. Moreover, dismayed that some women were bearing only a few children, or—even worse—no children at all, Key feared that woman's liberation had inveigled them to reject motherhood, their highest calling.[3] Whereas Key glorified actual biological motherhood, Goldman reveled in its metaphorical potential. Forging the figure of "mother earth," who cares not for the bourgeois household, but for the people *en masse*, Goldman promoted a "motherhood" that would displace the domestic with the more broadly political.

In March 1906, Emma Goldman, along with her coeditor Alexander Berkman (recently released from prison), published the first issue of *Mother Earth*, a journal that persisted for twelve years. Goldman introduced the journal with a story of the same title, beginning the fable by lamenting: "Man issued from the womb of Mother Earth, but he knew it not, nor recognized her, to whom he owed his life." Instead, man's "egotism" led him to the "dreary doctrine that he was not related to the Earth" so should look toward the "Great Beyond" and be "tormented by that priest-born monster Conscience."[4] Despite Man's ingratitude, delusions, and follies, the earth, an ever-munificent mother, continued to give of herself.

> Yet she renewed herself, the good mother, and came again each Spring, radiant with youthful beauty, beckoning her children to come to her bosom and partake of her bounty. But ever the air grew thick with mephitic darkness, ever a hollow voice was heard calling: "Touch not the beautiful form of the sorceress; she leads to sin!"[5]

That the "good mother" earth is taken for a temptress collapses the polarity of the transcendent maternal ideal and the soiled fallen woman, opening up divergent spaces for sexual, but not denigrated, female subjects and allowing Goldman to endorse the principle of free love by sexualizing the bounty of the earth and naturalizing the pleasures of the female body.

The sexually enticing Mother Earth also appears in an editorial describing how the New York police crashed a meeting and seized the magazine. Goldman's ironic account claims that the very irresistableness of *Mother Earth* (not its "threat to society") ignited the police action: "But even detectives are human; they are not immune against the temptations of the fair sex—no wonder they could not withstand MOTHER EARTH; they took possession, as the Romans did with the Sabine women; and as the possessors they forbade all others to enjoy her charms."[6] Understandably, the police desire Mother Earth, but they have no right to deny her pleasures to others. The seizure of the magazine by the state parallels the exploitation of the earth by the greedy few. Significantly, the conflation of the abundant earth with the desirable female body situates the nexus of value not in the realm of capital, patriarchy, or state power but in an anti-capitalist, female, and anarchistic space which offers equal access to all.

At the end of Goldman's founding fable this space is captured, as Mother Earth, who in her American incarnation had seemed "vast, boundless, full of promise," falls prey to those who would shackle her.

> Mother Earth, with the sources of vast wealth hidden within the folds of her ample bosom, extended her inviting and hospitable arms to all those who came to her from arbitrary and despotic lands—Mother Earth ready to give herself alike to all her children. But soon she was seized by the few, stripped of her freedom, fenced in, a prey to those who were endowed with cunning and unscrupulous shrewdness.[7]

The story concludes by proclaiming that *Mother Earth* will appeal to "those who long for the tender shade of a new dawn for humanity free from the dread of want, the dread of starvation in the face of mountains of riches. The Earth free for the free individual!"[8] The utopian celebration of Mother Earth as a realm of freedom, not necessity, allows Goldman to indict social structures as instruments of bondage and deprivation. Moreover, the charge that the rapacious few have stolen Mother Earth from "all her children" not only appeals to the cultural ideal of motherhood but also to the equally powerful ideals of nature and the "natural."[9] The slippage between the name of the journal and the earth itself allows Goldman to appeal to the ethical, populist authority that the "earth" lends, while legitimating the journal's radical ideas by securing them within assumptions about the "natural" role of mothers. Furthermore, the utopian stance of Mother Earth engenders a trenchant perspective for social critique. Goldman asks:

> Must the Earth forever be arranged like an ocean steamer, with large, luxurious rooms and luxurious food for a select few, and underneath in the steerage, where the great mass can barely breathe from dirt and the poisonous air?[10]

The trope of society as an ocean steamer reveals that the status quo distribution of wealth is not only unjust, but is disturbingly *unnatural*, since the beneficent mother would never condone this treatment of the "great mass" of her children. Painting social injustice as unnatural directly challenges the resigned acceptance, borne of our immersion in the social structure, that economic inequities—however extreme—are themselves "natural." Unlike the bottom-heavy steamship, anarchism, according to Goldman, works with rather than against natural law, guaranteeing "to

every human being free access to the earth and full enjoyment of the ne-
cessities of life."[11]

Depression-era writers echoed Goldman's portrayals of Mother Earth.
Tillie Olsen's *Yonnondio,* for example, which I discuss more extensively in
the next section, condemns capitalism by dramatizing how it perverts the
cultural ideal of "mother" earth. Instead of giving birth to her children,
she devours them. When a crazed miner tries to drop a child down a mine
shaft, it is because he believes that the mine "only takes men 'cause she
ain't got kids. All women want kids." Hoping to deliver the miners from
this rapacious mother, he attempts to "fill" the "ol' lady" with a child.[12]

While it forwards the journal's politics, the title "Mother Earth" also
forges a distinctly female position of power for Goldman herself. As Margaret C. Anderson declares in the Tenth Anniversary issue of *Mother
Earth,* "Emma Goldman is Mother Earth." She continues:

> There are spirits who can be described in exquisite images of stars,
> trees, rivers, hills. There are others for whom you need bigger concep-
> tions—earth, sky, sea. But for Emma Goldman you must reduce to the
> largest concepts—you can only say land, water, air. In this way
> MOTHER EARTH, as a name, has a significance, an appropriateness,
> quite beyond what its founder imagined when she chose it.[13]

Despite Anderson's contentions to the contrary, Goldman was not oblivi-
ous to the way in which the journal's majestic title reflected back on herself. In the opening comments to many issues of the magazine, Goldman
playfully uses "Mother Earth" to refer ambiguously to herself and the journal. Rather than attempting to elude the potent discourses of motherhood, Goldman plays up the trope of mother earth to broaden the reach of
"mothering" far beyond domestic space, indeed, encompassing the entire
globe. Goldman, the woman who was jailed for declaring that "women
need not always keep their mouths shut and their wombs open,"[14] rearticulates the socially sanctioned power of "mothering" into a distinctly female force for social justice, as the following illustration suggests.

The cover of the tenth anniversary issue of *Mother Earth* portrays a
woman, nude from the waist up, protecting a baby in her arms, while glar-
ing up and over her shoulder defiantly (see Figure 1). Within the rhetoric
of the journal the figure can be read in several overlapping ways. First, the
image represents Mother Earth herself, as her curving body suggests the
shape of a globe. Her ample breast and her large, strong hand cover and
protect her child, emblematic of all her children, from the oppression and
injustice waged by those above them. *Mother Earth* the journal under-

Figure 1. Tenth Anniversary issue of Emma Goldman's *Mother Earth*, March 1915, cover.

takes the same struggle as her namesake, as the journal and the mythical figure blend into and sustain each other. Furthermore, since it was common to describe *Mother Earth* as Goldman's "baby," this illustration can also be read as a portrait of Goldman protecting her journal from the many assaults it had to endure. Interestingly, since the "mother" in this portrait shifts from the earth, to the journal, to Goldman herself, Goldman is not linked to the earth via a corporeal fecundity, but rather by the journal—emblematic of political struggle and intellectual work.

Even though Goldman's use of "mothering" plays off of the notion of motherhood as women's requisite role and exemplary virtue, her metaphorical use of mothering delivers women from the need to become actual mothers, as it expands the scope of the term. Goldman becomes a powerful mother figure by mothering a journal, not a child, and, by means of the slippage between herself and the title, becomes through her political (not domestic) work the "mother" of all the people she fights for.[15] Like Jane Addams and other settlement-house women, Goldman articulated a role for "public mothers"; yet unlike them, Goldman defined the public mother as a sexual, powerful, and insurgent being, thus evicting the lingering Victorian pieties of motherhood and replacing them with a playful but nonetheless revolutionary spirit. The image of earth as female, and as maternally female, especially, often underwrites a biology-as-destiny script for women, but Goldman places biological mothering in the background, promoting a feminized force for social struggle by casting Mother Earth as a revolutionary. In short, Goldman employs a feminine image of nature to naturalize a revolutionary vision of a just society and to forge an insurgent, not reproductive, identity for women.

Landscapes and Laborers: Mapping Nature as a Political Space

When Ralph Waldo Emerson laments that "you cannot freely admire a noble landscape if laborers are digging in the field hard by," he intends to illustrate the discord between "man and nature." His complaint, however, demonstrates how the discord between "men" shapes different conceptions of nature. In the early twentieth century, preservationist discourses, Nature Man, the masculinist wilderness movements, Marxist-feminist theory, and such novels as Josephine Johnson's *Now in November,* Agnes Smedley's *Daughter of Earth,* Tillie Olsen's *Yonnondio,* and Fielding Burke's *Call Home the Heart* wage class, race, and gender struggles by drawing, contesting, and making visible the boundaries of nature. Rather than analyzing the politically charged disputes over "wilderness," "nature," or the "natural" in terms of a contest of meanings, I here bracket cultural semantics in order to examine a "contest of mappings." To examine nature's vertiginous discursive travels in terms of a "contest of mappings" means to chart how various political identities struggle to align themselves with nature—a nature that they map in such a way as to enable such alignments. If, as Jennifer Daryl Slack puts it, "identities, practices, and effects . . . constitute the very context within which they are practices, identities or effects,"[16] nature, a plurality of criss-crossing spaces, is paradoxically constituted by the very practices and identities that reach toward it as an exterior and separate space.

As outlined in the previous chapter, the utilitarianism of the progressive conservation movement was the prevailing view of nature at the start of the century; however, several other competing discourses about nature also characterize the early twentieth century, including ecology, aesthetic conservationism, and the macho wilderness cult. The period between the wars, specifically, witnessed the beginnings of ecological science, as crucial key terms like "ecosystem," "niche," and "food chain" were created, which led to the conception of nature as an interdependent holistic system.[17] Albert Schweitzer and Alfred North Whitehead conceived of an ethics consistent with ecological science, while Aldo Leopold began developing his "land ethic," which claims that "a thing is right when it tends to preserve the integrity, stability, and beauty of the biotic community. It is wrong when it tends otherwise."[18] In the 1920s, a growing number of aesthetic conservationists, or "nature lovers," who wanted to protect natural beauty and wildlife not only gained popular support but garnered influence among the conservation community, even at the federal level. One result of these developments was the National Park Service.[19]

Notwithstanding the significant achievements of the early twentieth-century environmental movements, many of the flights "back" to nature were bound up with white, middle- to upper-class anxiety about control.[20] Donald C. Swain, for example, argues that support for the National Park Service was secured by a national "urge to preserve the American heritage" that reached "fever pitch" partly because related pathologies—anti-immigration policies, the rise of the KKK, and the Red Scare—plagued the American body politic.[21] The need to preserve nature was often advanced, implicitly or explicitly, as evidence for the need to preserve the dominion of white, upper-class males. In William T. Hornaday's 1913 *Our Vanishing Wildlife: Its Extermination and Preservation,* for example, nature validates the middle- to upper-class white male's naturalized "rights" to control his territory. Three chapters of Hornaday's book target specific villains, marked by gender, race, and class: "Extermination of Birds for Women's Hats," "Slaughter of Song Birds by Italians," and "Destruction of Song-Birds by Southern Negroes and Poor Whites." In the latter chapter, Hornaday expresses his horror that "[i]n the South, the negroes and poor whites are killing song-birds, woodpeckers and doves for food."[22] Hornaday remains untroubled by these groups' needs for food—to the contrary, their very need for food makes them unworthy of the "sport" of hunting.

> No white man calling himself a sportsman ever indulges in such low pastimes as the killing of such birds for food. That burden of disgrace rests upon the negroes and poor whites of the South; but at the same time, it is a shame that respectable white men sitting in state legislatures should deliberately enact laws permitting such disgraceful practices, or permit such disgraceful and ungentlemanly laws to remain in force![23]

A "sportsman" need not kill birds for food, and when he does kill birds, he only kills "game" birds. The designation of some birds as "game," however, depends on tautological and arbitrary traditions: those are the birds that "sportsmen" kill. Appealing to racial and class designations of the "sportsman" and "gentleman," Hornaday urges those in charge to bring "their" territories under control. Hornaday's arguments depend on an implicit demarcation of "nature" that sets the pastoral against the savage, the upper class against the lower. By painting pictures of swarthy, bloodthirsty Italians and relating (often in dialect) the slaughter and ravenous consumption of birds by "negroes" and "poor whites," he mires racially marked and lower class bodies within a barbarous nature that virtually cries out for authoritative control. The pastoral nature that the "sportsman" and "gentleman" inhabit, however, is orderly—indeed civilized—"game" birds are courteously hunted while ethereal songbirds grace the air.

During the Depression, when many were anxious about the need for social control, President Roosevelt called on Congress to create the Civilian Conservation Corps, which organized two million men into several thousand camps to work to preserve natural resources. Roosevelt's 1933 request to Congress reveals that part of the motivation for this program was to ensure social stability.

> We can take a vast army of these unemployed out into healthful surroundings. We can eliminate to some extent at least the threat that enforced idleness brings to spiritual and moral stability. It is not a panacea for all the unemployment but it is an essential step in this emergency.[24]

The "healthful surroundings" of nature promise to cleanse the "vast army of the unemployed" in order to bring not only "spiritual and moral stability" to them, but also, one can infer, to help bring social stability to the country in a time of social upheaval. Perhaps Roosevelt believed, along with H. F. Osborne, that "[n]ature teaches law and order and respect for property."[25] A letter Robert Fechner wrote to Roosevelt three years later reveals more about the government's attitudes toward the unemployed. "I, therefore recommend that *this program of conservation work among men and natural resources* be adopted as a permanent part of our national governmental activities."[26] Interestingly, lower class men become conflated with nature itself when Fechner represents both as objects of "conservation work," the resources that the government needs to control. Illuminating how the mirror of production frames identical reflections of nature and the worker, Jean Baudrillard explains that Enlightenment rationality and capitalist production split nature into a " 'good' Nature that is dominated and rationalized (which acts as the ideal cultural reference) and a 'bad' Nature that is hostile, menacing, catastrophic, or polluted." Labor is then merged with these two poles of nature: "When exploited, labor power is good: it is within Nature and is normal. But once liberated, it becomes menacing in the form of the proletariat."[27] The Civilian Conservation Corps transported the menacing proletariat—quite literally—to the location of the "good Nature."

Whereas the worker was transported to the "good" nature in order to render him innocuous, more privileged males fled to the wilderness in order to reassure themselves of their power to dominate. Theodore Roosevelt's turn-of-the-century sentiments prefigure later back-to-nature trends. He worried that the American (that is, the white American *male*) "was in real danger of becoming an 'overcivilized man, who has lost the great fighting, masterful virtues.' "[28] While insisting that American women must, as their patriotic duty, bear at least four babies, Roosevelt saw the wilderness as the place that could transform some of those babies into men. The wilderness, a veritable breeding ground for American machismo, promoted "that vigorous manliness for the lack of which in a nation, as in an individual, the possession of no other qualities can possibly atone."[29] The male ability to dominate the wilderness served not only as an apt metaphor for "domestic" relations but for international politics as well, reflecting American imperialism during Roosevelt's era.

Donna Haraway argues that conservation, eugenics, and even museum exhibitions were all "prescriptions against decadence, the dread disease of imperialist, capitalist, white culture."[30] The fear that "vigorous manliness" was in danger would persist for decades and would motivate several back-to-nature movements. Boy Scouts, for example, sprang up across the country; their handbook, first published in 1910, sold seven million copies in only thirty years. The number of wilderness enthusiasts burgeoned, expanding from a "relatively small group of romantic and patriotic literati to become a national cult."[31] In 1913 the country was captivated by Joseph Knowles, the "Nature Man" who, (supposedly) naked and bereft of tools or shelter, retreated into the Maine wilderness for sixty days, during which time he somehow managed to slay a bear and make clothing from its skin. Knowles was welcomed back to civilization as a celebrity; he became a vaudeville hit, sold paintings of wild animals, and penned his account of his experience, *Alone in the Wilderness*, which sold three hundred thousand copies. Evidently, the public's desire to believe him outweighed the dubiousness of his story. When a newspaper exposed him as a fraud, "a vociferous denial arose in reply: quite a few Americans in 1913 apparently wanted to believe in the authenticity of the 'Nature Man.'"[32] Later, Knowles attempted the "experiment" again, this time accompanied by Elaine Hammerstein, a "society leader" dubbed "Dawn Woman." But alas, Dawn Woman returned to her "sissy boudoir" after a mere seven days because, in Knowles's words, "She just couldn't take it."[33]

As eccentric as Nature Man seems, he exemplifies the trend toward using the wilderness to rigidify rough-hewn ideals of masculinity. Robert Marshall, for example, not only illustrates the "refined, urban" backgrounds of many wilderness promoters, as Nash points out,[34] but—as Nash fails to notice—Marshall also typifies the wilderness promoters' masculine bent. Marshall feared that (feminine) "sentimentalism" would taint (male) encounters with the wilderness—the wilderness which should, ideally, serve as a rugged male refuge far from the "coddling of civilization" that enervates them. In "The Problem of the Wilderness," Marshall denounces the emasculating effects of the "*effete* superstructure of urbanity"; praises "America's most *virile* minds," which withdrew to the solitude of nature; and advocates physical or mental "adventure," which demands "*breaking into unpenetrated ground.*"[35] Reacting to similar anxieties as those of Marshall, the woodcraft movement and the Boy Scouts were determined to manufacture manly men, as Mark Seltzer explains: "The craft of making men was the antidote to anxieties about the *depletion* of agency and virility in consumer and machine culture."[36]

The threat of machine and consumer culture helps explain why certain men fled to *nature* to reassert their virility, but I think their flight was also a reaction to feminist and leftist assaults on their power. Concurrent with raging feminist and class struggles for increased social power, this "love" of wilderness betrays a white, mainly middle-to upper-class male anxiety about weakness and a drive to demonstrate and reassure men of their potency and authority. Reacting to women's encroachment into the public sphere, men fled into the wilderness, a place ostensibly "outside" of the political domain. Thus, the wilderness becomes an ideal place to play out—even while repressing—their political anxieties.[37] In 1904, for example, *The Century Magazine,* in "We Americans and Other Animals," praised the back-to-nature movements for their "wholesome and conservative influence," which reassured that "in spite of the alarming growth of sinister influences among us, the heart of the people is sound at the core."[38] This mapping aligns nature with the robust "heart of the people" (begging the question of who qualifies as part of "the people") while exteriorizing, distancing, and minimalizing various political struggles. As Judith Butler argues, "the recourse to a position . . . that places itself beyond the play of power, and which seeks to establish the metapolitical basis for a negotiation of power relations, is perhaps the most insidious ruse of power."[39]

Feminists rarely leave such deleterious mappings of nature uncontested. Intruding upon the middle- to upper-class masculine domain of nature, Agnes Smedley claims an idealized but gritty earth for the working classes while Mary Inman and Rebecca Pitts make nature the habitat of feminist subjects. Fielding Burke and Tillie Olsen take a slightly different approach: they make the invisible demarcations of nature visible, dramatizing that however neutral they seem, the class-based boundaries are hardly "beyond the play of power."

Paradoxically, Inman and Pitts bolster their social constructionist arguments by appealing to what is "natural." Inman's "Manufacturing Femininity," originally published as part of a series in *People's World,* argues that it is not "woman's nature, but her environment," that causes her to become a "chambermaid" rather than an "engineer." Women are "manufactured," not born; because they are influenced by their physical surroundings, it is "*natural* that they should so react."[40] Inman draws a parallel between social construction and industrial production, explaining that women,

> . . . like members of other subject groups, such as workers and Negroes, have had part of their behavior cut to a particular group pattern and forced upon them, often from birth . . . Deliberately manufactur-

ing characteristics by this artificial process is neither more natural nor mysterious than the deliberate manufacture of sauerkraut.[41]

Since oppressed subjects have been artificially produced, freedom lies somewhere beyond the oppressive social system, in a more "natural," less mechanistic realm.

Likewise, in her 1935 essay for the *New Masses,* "Women and Communism," Rebecca Pitts argues that "the tragedy of womanhood is not biological at all—but *social*"[42]—yet she supports this contention by appealing to nature. Pitts argues that because women are forced to choose between work and marriage, the woman who chooses marriage is driven to be " 'normal' with a vengeance . . . absorbed, that is, in a highly personal, self-regarding manipulation of sex"—which is hardly "natural": "[T]he 'normal' adjustment is just as false—just as empty a shadow or reality—as any of the varieties of rebellion. The 'normal' is approved for purely statistical reasons; but the term carries no implication whatever of the *natural* or organically *right.*"[43] Even while arguing that biology is not destiny, Pitts appeals to the "*natural* or organically *right*" to envision and endorse a womanhood beyond the social construct that she denounces. Pitts may be less contradictory than she seems, since she theorizes nature in such a way as to transcend the opposition between nature and culture. Criticizing D. H. Lawrence's "identification with 'nature' in a mindless, sensual darkness," she contends that the "men of the future will not follow Lawrence in his rejection of mind and society; they will, on the contrary, see Nature risen to supreme self-consciousness *in the human community.*"[44] By arguing beyond the dualities of body/mind and nature/culture, Pitts can explain that woman's "nature" has been socially constructed and—at the same time—can deploy the value of "the natural" to carve out a position for women that does not destine them solely for reproduction. For Pitts, as for Sedgwick, Jewett, and Austin, the natural serves as a realm apart from what has already been so rigidly socially scripted; it serves both as a space of possibility and as a validation of those possibilities.

While Pitts's theories map nature as a potentially feminist space precisely because it is beyond gendered scripts, in Josephine W. Johnson's 1935 Pulitzer prize winning *Now in November* (1934), the experience of nature is itself profoundly and enduringly gendered. In this strikingly poetic, pastoral novel of a young farm girl's coming of age, economic realities and aesthetic revelries are sharply divided along gendered lines. For the females the woods "seemed all answer and healing and more than enough to live for," whereas the male "transcendence over nature . . . appears a regrettable evil."[45] Marget, the narrator, regrets her father's merely economic relation to the land and his lack of aesthetic sensibility: he "couldn't see the masterpiece of a maggot or be satisfied with the shadow of a leaf."[46] In retrospect the narrator admits that she and her sister were blind to the "heaviness" of their father's economic responsibility, which, like that of other indebted farmers, is Sisyphean: They labor by "crawling along the ruts and shoving [their] debts ahead like the ball of dung-beetles. Worse off than the beetles themselves who can bury their load and be done."[47] Since both the 1920s and the 1930s were plagued by severe postwar agricultural depression, for farmers, "survival" was hardly a matter of frolicking about in the nude and slaying bears barehandedly; survival was an altogether quotidian struggle. Although Johnson, who grew up on a farm near St. Louis, Missouri, sympathized with farm laborers and was arrested in 1936 for "encouraging cotton field workers to strike,"[48] *Now in November* does not map nature in such a way as to align it with the working class. Despite the fact that within this novel natural metaphors (such as the dung beetles) sometimes push along economic insights, the gendered opposition between the pragmatic male attitude toward a nature that must be worked and the romantic female love of nature for itself prevents the novel from engaging in struggles over the constitution of nature. In an elegiac mood, the novel reminisces about a feminine, childhood affinity with nature, but fails to link gender differences with feminist subjectivities or cartographies. Rather, pragmatism and romanticism stand as seemingly eternal polarities that obscure political demarcations of "nature."

Agnes Smedley's 1929 *Daughter of Earth,* by contrast, enlists a romantic conception of nature to further class struggles. Marie, the protagonist and narrator, paints lower class men as "close" to nature by musing upon her illiterate father's affinity with the earth:

> There was nothing in a book for him; but even a hole in the ground became filled with romance. He kept his eyes, not upon the stars, but upon the earth; he was of the earth and it of him. He dug in the earth, he hugged the earth, he thought in terms of the earth ... He was digging not just a hole in the ground, but uncovering marvelous things, all that lies in the earth. That I knew because I knew him, for I was my father's daughter.[49]

Enduring an otherwise bleak existence, and denied the cultural escape of books, Marie's father takes his mystery and romance from the earth itself. Marie knows that he is not just digging but "uncovering marvelous things" of the earth because she is her father's daughter—recalling the title of the novel itself, *Daughter of Earth,* and thereby endowing this passage with a force that it otherwise would not have. Perhaps what is most remarkable about this passage is that it would even appear in this novel. Like most radical women's novels of the 1930s, *Daughter of Earth* (despite its title) focuses almost exclusively on social revolution and does not concern itself much with nature. *Daughter of Earth,* written in a straightforward, unadorned style appropriate for the uneducated workers from whom Smedley comes and about whom she writes, is so overburdened with documenting the many brutalities that her people endure, so determined to fight gender and class oppression, that it would seem the novel has no time for romantic ruminations on nature. Marie's abused mother starves to death. Her aunt chooses prostitution over the worse abuses of marriage. Her young brothers are given to a "brutal" farmer who not only worked them "like animals from dawn to darkness" but beat them.[50] Later, one brother is forced to fight in the war for rich men, while the other dies, "his mouth and eyes" "filled with mud" while digging a ditch "like a rat in a sewer."[51] Miners die because their lives are worth less than the coal they shovel. Dire poverty, company stores, police brutality, rape, and political imprisonment all fight for attention in this novel. In the midst of such a landscape as this, the passage that marvels at "all that lies in the earth" is rare and all the more notable for its rarity.

The nostalgic and idealized portrait of her father's intimate connection to the earth, however, may not be as out of place as it would seem, since it serves to "ennoble" an otherwise wretched class, to underline their humanity and worth, by aligning them with an idyllic nature. Thus these seemingly apolitical aesthetic reveries may forward the political causes of the novel, not detract from them. Significantly, Smedley, who knew and corresponded with Emma Goldman, echoes Goldman's insistence on the rights of all people to the earth. When an Indian nationalist asks Marie if she can understand "what it means to love the very soil of your country," she answers:

> "Love my country, Sardarji—do you mean the soil? Yes, I love that. I love the mountains of the West. And I love the deserts. But what most people mean by country is the government and the powerful men who rule it. No. I do not love them. But the earth—yes. This is our earth. Or—it must one day be."
>
> "What do you mean?"
>
> "I mean all of us who work and live and suffer. It must belong to all—not just individuals."[52]

Although this novel is surprisingly frank about sexual politics (it recounts rape, prostitution, and abortions), *Daughter of Earth,* unlike *Call Home the Heart, Quicksand,* and *Weeds,* does not portray reproductive freedom as women's power over the "nature" of their own bodies.[53] Since Smedley draws on a romantic idea of nature to endorse principles of human justice, it would be difficult for a less lofty, more corporeal characterization of nature to cohabit the same text. Furthermore, since not only female, but lower class bodies of either sex, have long been debased by their "closeness" to the natural world, Smedley must remap this ideological terrain, displacing such denigrating proximities in order to align the working class with an idealized earth. Like its predecessor *Mother Earth, Daughter of Earth* reaches toward a vast, implicitly just nature as an ally for the people who may be socially marginal but are nonetheless solidly "of the earth."

Visible Boundaries: The Politics of Trespassing

As disparate as they are, the muscle-flexing wilderness movement, Pitts's and Inman's Marxist-feminist theory, and *Daughter of Earth* all represent nature as a place beyond the social. Even Pitts, who argues against a nature/culture dichotomy and sees nature as inclusive of human community, envisions the natural as a space of possibility outside the flawed social structure. For Pitts and the others, the very positioning of nature as "outside" the social endows it with political purchase. But the politics of "nature" are more complex than that. For the very constitution of nature as outside of politics becomes contested when the boundary between the two is traversed. Judith Butler explains how the "political" is always constituted by an "outside."

> In other words, the very domain of politics constitutes itself through the production and naturalization of the "pre-" or "non" political . . . Here I would like to suggest a distinction between the constitution of a political field that produces *and naturalizes* that constitutive outside and a political field that produces and *renders contingent* the specific parameters of that constitutive outside.[54]

A political field that "naturalizes the constitutive outside" erases its own production, while a political field that "produces and *renders contingent* the specific parameters of that constitutive outside" allows for political struggle that contests the boundaries of the political itself. Contingent boundaries are themselves zones of political contestation, and the traversing and shifting of these boundaries affects structures of power.

For Tillie Olsen and Fielding Burke nature becomes political precisely through a traversing of boundaries. Olsen, a feminist and a long-time activist in the labor movement, wrote *Yonnondio* in the 1930s.[55] This novel remained unfinished but was supposed to have combined two genres of proletarian fiction: the strike novel and the novel of political conversion to communism. In one scene of *Yonnondio*, which would seem quite irrelevant to either political genre, the malnourished Anna takes her children in search of greens, attempting to heed the "Wheel of Nutrition," which suggests "One Serving: Green Leafy Vegetable Daily."[56] Deborah Rosenfeldt argues that this scene "is less a vision of political and economic revolution" than one of "humanistic optimism" about the survival of the "drive to love and achieve and create."[57] Grounded in class-marked territories, however, this scene projects an implicit political argument about who has access to nature. In search of nutritious food, Anna and her children wander into alien territory where "lawns, flower beds, and borders, children on bikes" announce a solid economic status.[58] Anna recognizes that her only role within such a neighborhood would be as a domestic laborer, noting that this "would be a good neighborhood to ask for launderin work."[59] Her child's nervously reiterated warnings, "*Ma this isn't the way,*" and the "high wire fences" and "borders" they encounter shroud the scene with a sense of trespassing. As the family ventures through the suburban gardens to a fenced-off but abandoned yard, however, the prose erupts into a stream-of-consciousness lyricism: "the old worn fragile bliss, a new frail selfless bliss, healing, transforming. Up from the grasses, from the earth, from the broad tree trunk at their back, latent life streamed and seeded."[60] As they gather greens and become enraptured by flowers, and as the sickly Anna becomes so transported that her children hardly recognize her, nature's blissful transformative abundance entirely dispels the sense that the family does not belong here. Echoing Goldman's munificent Mother Earth, who naturalizes "radical" ideals of social justice, this utopian moment naturalizes the working-class mother's right to provide for her children, even when that entails transgressing class-marked boundaries. This family's claim to nature's nutrients and raptures contests the borders they had to cross by arguing for a more just redistribution of nature. Expanding the grounds of working-class protest, the novel contests the constitutive boundaries that mark off "nature" as an apolitical territory.

Fielding Burke, the pseudonym for Olive Tilford Dargan, was born in 1869 to two school teachers in Grayson County, Kentucky. In 1916, after her husband's death, Dargan moved to the mountains of North Carolina, where she farmed and studied mountain lore. Dargan never joined the Communist Party, yet she actively supported communists and called herself a "vivid red."[61] The protagonist of *Call Home the Heart* becomes involved in the cotton mill workers' strike in Gastonia, North Carolina, which took place in 1929.[62] Although Dargan visited Gastonia while the strikes were occurring and described her visit as exhausting, it is unknown whether she was personally involved in the strikes. Fear of political harassment may be responsible for the many lacunae in our biographical knowledge of Dargan, as three different times Dargan's papers were destroyed by fires that she may have set herself.[63]

Like *Yonnondio*, Fielding Burke's *Call Home the Heart* demonstrates that nature is a political territory, even though reviewers, ironically, divided the novel into sections about nature and sections about politics, praising the portions about nature as properly apolitical art and censuring the political portions as nonartistic propaganda. According to Sylvia J. Cook, several reviewers of the first edition asserted the novel "shifted from art to propaganda as the setting changed from rural to urban, only to be redeemed into art again by the final return to nature."[64] The settings of the novel do roughly correspond to the pattern that reviewers noted, but the novel's aims and concerns are consistent. Nature, in fact, may be a more important topos within the "political" portions of the novel, since these sections dramatize its demarcation along class lines. Like Anna in *Yonnondio*, Ishma takes her child out in search of a bit of nature within the town. She discovers a beautiful park with tall trees and green open spaces, only to find that it is not only fenced off, guarded, and prohibited to the public, but is the property of a mill owner. The gatekeeper gives her daughter a shameful "stolen flower" before they proceed to the public park, offering "no flowers, no shrubs, no fountains," just some "thin woods with their few stunted trees."[65] Nearby, the mill workers' houses lie between strips of flat, briar-covered land, graced by the stench of stagnant waters. As in *Yonnondio*, the nature to which all should (naturally) have access is stingily denied to the working classes.

Ishma attends a communist lecture asserting that the earth, "the home of humanity, the land that feeds us, that gives us our material and our foundations," is the people's first birthright.[66] The earth, when free from the grudging reach of capitalism, gives generously of such gifts. But when capitalists colonize the earth, they steal nature from the people, denying them the stuff of life itself. Ishma tries to persuade Derry, the communist physician, that nature is no luxury, but crucial for survival, when, in the midst of the strike, she insists that the sickly and malnourished children need to be sent to the country:

> "There are about forty children that ought to be sent out to the country somewhere—on the farms, or up in the mountains—"
> "Don't jump so fast daughter."
> "They'll die down here."
> "Bread—bread—bread. We'll not let them die of starvation at least."

Derry continues to argue that they can't expect union funds, which come from the pockets of poor workers, to "give our children a change of climate."[67] (Derry's argument appears hypocritical later, when, in the midst of the strike, he retreats for a week to enjoy a "farm cure.") Ishma's plan to take children into the mountains displaces nature as a bourgeois object of aesthetic enjoyment (carefully framed apart from the political), characterizing nature instead as a healthy *environment* upon which survival itself may literally depend. Similarly, both *Yonnondio* and *Daughter of Earth* contrast farm life with the threatening environments of the mines, slaughterhouses, and other industrial locations.[68] In *Call Home the Heart,* even after Ishma retreats from the mill workers' struggle by returning to the mountains, she envisions her mountain as a place to fortify workers' children. She tells her husband, "I was thinking about a lot of little kids that I'd like to bring up here in the summer—every summer. I'd like to give them plenty to eat and turn them loose on the mountain to get strong."[69] Like the Civilian Conservation Corps, which aimed to place the unemployed in "healthful surroundings," Ishma's plan stresses the healing potential of natural environments, but in this case the workers' children are to be strengthened for class battle.

Despite the fact that most studies of American representations of nature ignore class, the texts discussed here reveal how struggles over class, as well as gender and race, shape the imaginary terrain of nature. As divergent territorial battles are waged to secure its discursive potency, "nature"—impossible to map—is constructed as a plurality of criss-crossing, overlapping political spaces. The very constitution of nature as the outside of culture, as a field free from social struggle, serves to mask the class-marked terrain of nature and ward off questions of who has access to nature as a resource, a healthy environment, an aesthetic or muscle-flexing playground. Writers such as Burke and Olsen contest the very constitution of nature as an apolitical category by blatantly trespassing on class-bounded territories. Conversely, Goldman, Smedley, and the Marxist-feminist theorists use the constitution of nature as "outside" for their own purposes; exterior to the hierarchical status quo, the earth serves as a space in which to imagine another, more just society and to promote the "naturalness" of that alternative. America's strong pastoral tradition certainly influenced how these writers recruited nature for radical causes. Yet their work is less interested in the nature that they gesture toward and more concerned with the social systems they turn away from. For Goldman, Inman, and Pitts, the use of nature as a space to imagine more just human relations denaturalizes predominant subjectivities and systemic inequities by highlighting their social construction and denying them an ontological "naturalness."

This illusion of ontological "naturalness," or similarly, in Ernesto Laclau's terms, this "objectivity," is achieved when "the traces of the original contingency" fade.[70] The discourses of the progressive women conservationists (discussed in the last chapter), the preservationists such as Robert Marshall, and the popular wilderness cults all, albeit in quite different ways, establish their proper "ownership" of nature via antagonisms of race, class, or gender, the traces of which, the excluded "lower" terms, are then concealed, enabling the identities and claims of the powerful to seem natural, "objective," or unproblematically present. For example, the drive to manufacture men as "rugged individuals" obscures gender, race, and class—even as it relies on them to constitute the American "individual." By staking their own explicitly gendered or class-based claims to romantic, fortifying, and otherwise "good" natures, and by traversing and thus making visible the borders of class, Burke, Olsen, and Smedley reveal the contingent relations that constitute and demarcate the desirable nature.

If, as Cary Nelson argues in *Repression and Recovery,* political poetry has been devalued due to "to our own resistance to (and fear of) a literariness that is socially engaged, politically critical, and committed to change,"[71] then literature about nature has been esteemed for precisely the same reasons. Nature, supposedly bearing universal truths, has long served as an honored literary topos in part because of the way it is constituted as a disembodied theme, floating free from historical contingencies, social involvement, or political struggle. Nevertheless, the "contest of mappings" in the early twentieth century dramatizes how the nature/culture divide is always political, as nature becomes a space for social struggle, a space to be mined precisely for its supposedly apolitical, naturalized cultural authority. Nature provides a kind of cultural authority because it is positioned as a world apart, unsullied by human motivations and the changing contingencies of history. Culture maps nature simultaneously onto and against itself; nature serves both as boundary and as bounded space, as an outside that constitutes the terrain of the inside. While Burke and Olsen challenge the class-marked designation of nature as apolitical and reveal the contingency of those boundaries, some feminist theory and fiction in this period strategically invokes the exteriority of nature in order to forge a space for the possibility of another culture not so recalcitrantly determined by capitalist inequities and the relegation of women to a domestic sphere. In this sense, nature has served as a crucial space for the cultural work of feminism. That this space is paradoxical should be no surprise, since, as Gillian Rose argues, the "subject of feminism" "depends on a paradoxical geography in order to acknowledge both the power of hegemonic discourses and to insist on the possibility of resistance."[72]

Chapter Five: Reproduction as a Natural Disaster

Breed, little mothers,
With a faith patient and stupid as cattle,
Breed for the war lords,
Offer your woman flesh for incredible torment,
Wrack your frail bodies with the pangs of birth
For the war lords who slaughter your sons!

Lucia Trent

Where can one flee, where find refuge? . . . Space is nothing but a
"horrible outside-inside."

Gaston Bachelard

Lucia Trent's caustic call for women to breed is a far cry from Emma Goldman's playful birth of *Mother Earth*. Nature, for Trent, is hardly a revolutionary utopian space, but that which wracks women's flesh with pain, making them kin to the "patient and stupid" cattle. Nature is even more dramatically the villain in Edith Summer's Kelley's *Weeds*, Nella Larsen's *Quicksand*, and Fielding Burke's *Call Home the Heart*. In these novels, nature robs women of all self-determination, engulfing them in the "weeds" and "quicksands" of reproduction. The political landscape of the early twentieth century motivated feminist writers to combat the nature that was waged against them. At roughly the same time that birth control was condemned as "unnatural" and E.R.A. proponents were labeled as "barren," the New Woman, who threatened the status quo, was similarly disciplined, defined as "physiologically 'unnatural,' the symptom of a diseased society," in order to reaffirm "the legitimacy and the 'naturalness' of the bourgeois order."[1] Given that the "natural" was summoned to discipline feminist subjects and deny women reproductive control, it is hardly surprising that nature and the natural would be particularly volatile sites within women's texts. As struggles for reproductive freedom rage, "nature" becomes a particularly vexed, fervidly contested site in women's writings. Thus "nature," dense with contested meanings, becomes a discursive nexus for feminist attempts to establish agency, self-determination, and reproductive control.

Feminist rearticulations of nature draw on predominant categories and are no less contradictory. While Rebecca Inman and Mary Pitts, for example, portray nature as an anti-essentialist realm of freedom, in *Weeds* and *Quicksand* nature becomes essentialist with a vengeance as it reduces the protagonists to breeding bodies. Despite some ecofeminists' affirmations of a "closeness" between woman and nature, during the period when women battled for reproductive freedom, nature was frequently portrayed as feminism's foe—especially when such "closeness" erupted into natural disasters. Helga, for example, feels no cheery bond with the nature that consumes her in a "quicksand" of endless reproduction; nor does the protagonist in *Weeds* appreciate the duplicitous nature that seduces her only to betray her with the horrors of childbearing. At the same time that feminist and leftist writings were drawing on nature as an "outside" territory that endorsed alternative social possibilities, several women's novels dramatized this liberating "world apart" as collapsing into and colonizing the female body. Space becomes nothing but a "horrible outside-inside." In both Edith Summers Kelley's *Weeds* and Fielding Burke's *Call Home the Heart*, nature offers the young female protagonists an escape from domestic drudgery. But when girls become women, the nature that exists as a liberatory field outside of the domestic manifests itself within their bodies, and, paradoxically, renders them the very nucleus of the domestic realm as child bearers.

Even as nature and the natural are saturated with cultural ideals, a less lofty conception of nature lurks in the background, linking female, lower class, and racially marked bodies with an abject and will-less nature. Stuart Hall explains that some associations, though not "given for all time," are "difficult to break" because "the ideological terrain of this particular social formation has been so powerfully structured in that way by its previous history."[2] The centuries-old Western associations between working-class and racially marked bodies and a denigrated nature facilitated the popularity of eugenics movements and the Social Darwinist chain of being—making it extremely difficult for those on the left to sever such links. Edith Summers Kelley's *Weeds* and Nella Larsen's *Quicksand,* for example, do not distance their heroines from these ideologically tenacious conceptions, but, rather, present reductio ad absurdum narratives that call for reproductive control via (in Irigaray's terms) a kind of "mimicry" or disruptive excess. On the other hand, Fielding Burke's *Call Home the Heart* reinstates nature as a racially stratified terrain, as the white protagonist gains refuge in her pastoral mountains only by projecting a corporeal "nature" onto a black woman's body.

The very proximity of the maternal body to "natural" forces often catalyzes antinatural, antimaternal feminisms. During the same period when the novels discussed here were attempting to combat the procreative "nature" of women's bodies, lesbian and bisexual women writers parodied the widespread condemnation of themselves as freakishly "unnatural" by writing modernist fictions that "repudiat[ed] the 'natural.'"[3] By imaginatively liberating themselves from the constrictions of the "natural," these lesbian modernist texts mark the heterosexist horizons of the novels discussed here, which struggle against the discourses of the "natural" from within. Despite these horizons, such feminist narratives perform significant cultural work by protesting against the "nature" of women's bodies. Though Paula Rabinowitz is somewhat critical of the way in which the figure of the mother dominates the work of several radical writers of the 1930s, arguing that "without a corresponding aesthetic and political culture of feminism, they remained stuck in traditional renderings of femininity,"[4] representing the female body as overwhelmingly maternal need not be retrogressive, as many women's narratives reproduce the maternal body—with a vengeance—precisely in order to deliver women from the natural disaster of reproduction.

It is significant that the novels discussed here articulate their feminist positions through and against the discourses of nature, since one of the most potent arguments against birth control was the charge that it was "unnatural." Even certain contingents of the free love movement, such as the pre-Marxist, romantic socialists and feminists, trumpeted reproduction as women's "natural"—and thus requisite—role.[5] Many articles in *Birth Control Review,* including the editorial "Unnatural?"; "Is Birth Control Unnatural," by W. J. Robinson, M.D.; and "How Nature Gets Even," by Margaret Sanger; attack the denigration of birth control as "unnatural" by arguing, variously, that most human activities are "unnatural"; that the unnatural is not necessarily bad; that birth control is not unnatural, but merely a more "intelligent" use of nature; and, most dramatically, that "Nature" itself proves, by way of "revenge," the necessity of birth control.[6] In the African American journal *The Messenger,* J. A. Rogers critiqued the idea that "nature" imposes strict boundaries on women's "liberalization" by making her responsible for bearing children.[7] African American birth control advocates not only contended with the more diffuse arguments that birth control was "unnatural," but also, more specifically, argued against the (Marcus) Garveyites, who warned that "birth control interfered with the 'course of nature' and God's will."[8]

Two *Birth Control Review* cover illustrations portray opposite responses to the charge that reproductive control is unnatural. The ornate cover of the August 1921 issue depicts a nude woman and child relaxing under a pastoral tree, which curves, globe-like, in perfect harmony with the mother's back (see Figure 2). The mother's graceful body dwarfs the barely visible, distant town, with its prominent church steeple and presumably conservative social mores, while nature, aesthetically rendered, protectively encircles the mother and child, offering them a haven quite apart from the diminutive town. Whereas this illustration invokes a romantic conception of nature to support women's reproductive self-determination, another cover illustration portrays a more "base" nature to advance the same goal. Stephen Siding's sculpture "Captive Mother," shown on the cover of the October 1921 issue, depicts a globe-shaped mother whose hands are bound behind her back. The already-fat infant drinking from the mother's breast forces her to curve lower to the ground, pulling her even closer to the base soil (or the soiled base) (see Figure 3). Unlike Goldman's Mother Earth, who glares defiantly up and over her shoulder, the "Captive Mother's" gaze is restricted to a narrow two-foot expanse consisting of the body of her child and the ground into which both their bodies sink.

Before discussing the feminist fictions that, like these cover illustrations, draw on various conceptions of nature to argue for reproductive self-determination, I will briefly outline the history of modern birth control movements. Unlike nineteenth-century feminists, who promoted "voluntary motherhood" through abstinence as the way for women to gain control over reproduction, several feminist activists of the early twentieth century advanced women's rights to both sexual pleasure and reproductive freedom.[9] From 1910 on, Emma Goldman lectured that birth control was imperative for women's sexual liberation and freedom from marital bonds. The feminist and socialist birth control movements between 1914 and 1920 promoted sexual freedom but also asserted "that birth control could alleviate much human misery and fundamentally alter social and political power relations, thereby creating greater sexual and class equality."[10] Many working-class women were well aware that the

BIRTH CONTROL
REVIEW
INTERNATIONAL NUMBER

AUGUST, 1921   25 CENTS

Figure 2. Cover of *Birth Control Review*, August 1921.

wealthy had better access to birth control. When Margaret Sanger worked as a nurse during 1912, working-class women told her, "It's the rich that know the tricks, . . . while we have all the kids."[11] When the labor papers publicized Sanger's pro-birth control journal *The Woman Rebel* in 1914, Sanger claimed that she received "over 10,000 requests for contraceptive information."[12] During the 1930s, as Trent's poem "Breed, Women, Breed" indicates, birth control for working-class women became an explicitly political issue, since in capitalism, reproduction, like production, ultimately profits the bankers, the war lords, and the mine owners.[13]

Although the push for birth control originated in radical movements,

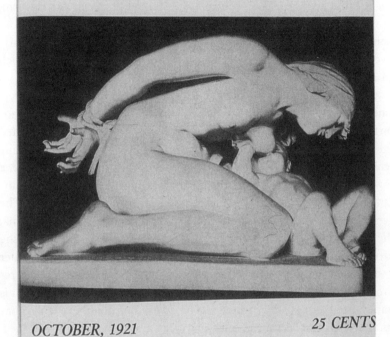

Figure 3. "Captive Mother," by Stephen Siding, cover of *Birth Control Review*, October 1921.

by the 1930s birth control had become "professionalized," as the medical establishment appropriated it as their domain. This meant not only that women's self-determination became mediated by a (male) physician, but that working-class women had far less access to birth control because they had far less access to private doctors.[14] Even so, it would seem that working-class women's desperate need for birth control impelled them to overcome these obstacles, since by the end of the Depression "more effective contraceptive use outside the white middle class was mounting."[15] The upper classes did establish some clinics for poor women, in part because the eugenics movement "transform[ed] a charity into a political cause" as it sought to discourage the "unfit"—such as the poor or African Americans—from reproducing.[16] Margaret Sanger's contradictory position epitomizes the tortuous history of reproductive politics. Sanger originally promoted birth control as a method of liberating the lower classes from exploitation, but after 1920 she advocated birth control in order to "protect the rest of society from the prolific alien poor and 'unfit.' "[17] That such justifications for birth control were steeped in racism and classism, however, did not prevent African Americans and the working classes from demanding reproductive control. The complicated terrain of the early twentieth-century birth control movements shapes the ways in which women's novels of that period represent nature.

Call Home the Heart unambiguously demonstrates that the impoverished working classes, whether rural or urban, had a desperate need for birth control. "Every year" Ishma's sister Bainie, for example, "presented the tolerant household with a new baby; and every year saw the family scale of living running lower."[18] "[R]apid child-bearing" makes Genie, a town woman, an invalid who, the doctor warns, will either die or go insane within six months if she cannot stop bearing children (179–81). The very plot of the novel turns on the lack of reproductive control, as Ishma, the protagonist, leaves her husband and her mountains, both of which she loves, because she "couldn't go on living like an old cow. Fodder in winter and grass in summer and a calf every year" (393). Associating rampant reproduction with animality, Ishma echoes her community's belief that it is nature itself that enslaves women as breeders. Her mother reiterates nature's decree that "A gal she must marry, an'a wife she must carry" (20), and her brother tells Ishma she must resign herself to her fate since "[a] man can walk off any time, but a woman kain't. God, or Nature, or something we kain't buck against, has fixed it that way" (149). As we will see later, though Ishma does buck against this Nature by fleeing from the mountains, its ideological energy refuses to disappear.

Paradoxically, nature is both the force that confines women to breeding and a liberatory space outside the domestic. Ishma, who lives with her impoverished family in a small cabin, is for six days of the week "merely a family possession, giving herself so effectually that no one suspected she was giving," but on Sunday she escapes to the hilltops in order to "replenish . . . her fount" by drinking in the beauties of the mountainside (1). The pastoral elixir offers relief from the endless, domestic drudgery that is exacerbated by her sister's ever-increasing brood of children. Most dramatically, echoing Emma Goldman's identification with

Mother Earth, Ishma's self becomes boundless when it disperses into the expansive realm of nature:

> Fields, woods, cliffs, peaks, unbaffled waters and far horizons, were not merely her background. She was of them, and would always be. Their essence was with her like a spatial self wherever she went. It was this that once made Derry Unthank ask her if it didn't hurt her to into little houses. "You can't possibly get all of yourself inside, Ishma." She had laughed and asked, "What do I leave out?" "Why," he had said, "a mountain or two, some miles of deepwood, and at least one waterfall." (232).

Bounded by neither the outlines of her body nor the claustrophobic walls of domestic space, Ishma's "spatial self" grants her a liberatory, limitless subjectivity. Whereas in *Hope Leslie* nature offers a haven for feminist subjects who wish to escape narrow domestic spaces, here the feminist subject herself becomes the boundless space of nature, delightfully depicted by a "mountain or two" which crashes against the doorways of "little houses."

Moving beyond both her own corporeality and the walls of the domestic, Ishma's expanding "spatial self" parallels the way in which the novel transfigures biological motherhood into mothering as revolutionary work. Throughout the early part of the 1930s the left had viewed motherhood "as draining, debilitating, and ultimately dangerous for the workers' struggle: because perpetual motherhood consigned a family to greater poverty, the woman-as-mother might not be consistently militant in her class solidarity."[19] *Call Home the Heart,* first published in 1932, transforms motherhood, depicted as a hindrance to revolutionary struggle, into vital work within the struggle, as Ishma is liberated from literal to metaphorical motherhood.

After she flees to town with Rad, leaving her son and her husband, Britt, Ishma gives birth to Vennie, Britt's child. Vennie, a terribly nervous, sickly girl, makes overwhelming demands on Ishma, who feels entrapped by her:

> But what did Vennie matter? Was her life to be forever bound up in a child's? Was her horizon always to be Vennie's horizon? Was she never to reach the world? . . . Now she had felt that she had again come a long, hard way, and before her, filling her road, was a little stunted child, doomed from her birth to insignificance. She had heard people say that they were fulfilled in their children, but for her the mother's sacrificial gesture could have no meaning. (231)

A mere two pages later, in a surprising deus ex machina, a car hits Vennie and kills her. The novel does not chastise Ishma for wishing her own child dead; it presents the death as fortunate, as right, because "[d]ear little Vennie had been consuming out of all proportion to her significance" (243). Later Ishma's friend Derry, a communist and a physician, expresses his relief at Vennie's death: "I'll tell you what I used to think of when I'd see you laboring with Vennie. An Amazon sentenced for life to pick up chips" (327).

Though the novel offers "rational" justifications for Vennie's death, it seems that the cultural force of motherhood cannot be so easily dispensed with. The scene in which Ishma wishes for her child's death and the scene in which a car kills Vennie—two incendiary narrative moments—are sequestered by a revealing passage in which nature "mothers" Ishma: "Nature, whose child she was, took her back. The breast offered was thin and unbounteous, but it served. In her mountain days the earth that had given her bread had done more than feed body and spirit. It had made her part of itself" (232). This scene anticipates and refutes the charge that Ishma is "unnatural" for desiring her child's death. Most significantly, by calling in "mother nature," this scene also displaces the ideological energy of motherhood onto nature, momentarily freeing Ishma from that role. After Vennie's death, Ishma is free to work for the strike night and day, which she does, primarily by caring for the strikers and their children, thereby expanding "motherhood" into a revolutionary role. Freed from mothering one child, Ishma becomes the "great Earth-mother" (294–95), an embodiment of communism itself, the "great mother calling us to peace and plenty" (290). Just as Ishma's "spatial self" cannot be contained within the domestic, "mothering," as vital revolutionary work which links women to the spirit of communism itself, cannot be reduced to its merely biological meaning.

Although the novel successfully disarticulates motherhood from its reproductive and domestic moorings and rearticulates it with revolutionary social struggle, it fails to transform the nature that constitutes women's bodies as reproductive. Once Ishma learns the secret of birth control,[20] the novel performs its cultural work on the ideal of motherhood, not the biological script of childbearing. Nevertheless, although methods of birth control would seem to free Ishma from the "nature" of her own body, the novel stages a drama of agency that binds the denigrating nature to the denigrated race. The plot's final turning point, in which Ishma decides to flee from the mill town and return to the mountains (even though this means abandoning the strikers during the most difficult part of the strike), displaces the corporeal nature onto the body of a black woman—an ideological move with a shameful and tenacious history in American culture.[21] Gaffie Wells, trying only to express her gratitude to Ishma, who has just saved her husband from lynching, receives this ungracious portrayal and response:

> Gaffie Wells was very fat and very black. Her lips were heavy, and her teeth so large that one needed the sure avouch of eyes to believe in them. It was impossible to associate her with woe, though tears were racing down her cheeks. As her fat body moved she shook off an odor that an unwashed collie would have disowned.
>
> "Bressed angel, bressed angel ob de Lawd," she kept repeating, and with a great sweep enveloped Ishma, her fat arms encircling the white neck, her thick lips mumbling at the quivering white throat. "We'll all be in heaben togeddah! Sishtah! sistah! Yo' sho' got Jedus in you!"
>
> The fleshy embrace, the murky little room, the smoking ashes, the warm stench, the too eager faces shining greasily at the top of big, black bodies, filled Ishma with uncontrollable revulsion. She thought of a high, clean rock on Cloudy Knob, half covered with sweet moss and red-tipped galax. She shut her eyes and saw a cardinal flying over the snow. (383)

Ishma strikes Gaffie repeatedly, falls over, runs off, and catches a train to the mountains, all the while berating herself for her "beastly" behavior. Though Gaffie Wells, is, in Ishma's eyes, a horrific signifier of an engulfing maternal body, it is precisely this body that enables Ishma to gain her own "angelic" wings. Ishma escapes this claustrophobic entrapment of the flesh by imaginatively ascending to a "high, clean rock" where an ethereal cardinal soars over the snow—the redness of the bird highlighting the "whiteness" of the place. Acting out a drama of agency in which the subject and the other are mutually constituted as such, the novel transfers the low, corporeal nature that has long defined "woman" onto the black woman's body, which then serves as the ground against which the white protagonist marks her own transcendence. It is remarkably odd that within a novel replete with vivid accounts of the plight of striking workers and long discussions of communist theory, the body of a black woman would function as a crisis point. Yet this disturbing scene plays a pivotal role not only in the narrative structure but in the novel's negotiations of nature, the female body, and motherhood. Race may seemingly enter through the back door, but it is nonetheless disturbingly central to the novel's discursive negotiations of the "nature" of reproductive politics. Unlike *Call Home the Heart*, *Weeds* and *Quicksand* narrate tales of descent, not transcendent projection, as their protagonists struggle against the nature of corporeality from within.

Prior to writing the 1923 novel *Weeds,* Edith Summers Kelley lived at Helicon Hall in Englewood, New Jersey, the experimental community begun by Upton Sinclair which, among other benefits, featured communal kitchens and nurseries. After Helicon Hall burned down, Kelley lived in Greenwich Village, where she encountered various anarchists, feminists, and socialists. Kelley was friends with Floyd Dell, the editor of *The Masses,* a radical journal which defended Sanger's birth control activism. Emile Zola's *Germinal,* a naturalistic novel that *The Masses* serialized in 1912, may have influenced *Weeds.*[22] Kelley wrote *Weeds* while struggling to survive on a small farm in California with her husband and three children. Before farming in California, Kelley and her husband managed a seven-hundred-acre tobacco farm in Scott County, Kentucky, like the one in *Weeds.* Although the Kelleys were managers and not tenant farmers, they "lived in a tenant shack and despaired when drought or weeds threatened their crops."[23] Though college educated, Kelley spent most of her life in extreme poverty. Kelley, described as a nature lover who " 'never put a flower in a pot or had a caged bird,' "[24] created Judith, a "backwoods" girl whose affinity for nature gives her a "troublesome" wildness. Her animal-like, corporeal subjectivity enables her to dodge the tethers of gender.

> Judith was a lithe, active, slim little creature, monkey-like in the agility with which she could climb trees and shin up poles and vault over fences. Her bare, brown toes took hold like fingers. There was something wild and evasive about her swift, sinuous little body, alive with quick, unexpected movements, like those of a young animal.[25]

Kelley celebrates Judith's active, energetic, "wild" body that propels her into a realm of "natural" freedom, giving her a sense of kinship with barnyard creatures, birds, reptile, fishes, and even insects. As her "harmony with natural things" grows, Judith clashes with two powerful institutions of female social construction, "the school and the home kitchen" (25). A feral creature, Judith knows, instinctively perhaps, that these forces wish to domesticate and feminize her. Nature not only offers itself as a realm of freedom from the feminine, but provides a rich tapestry of aesthetic pleasures, as Judith's aesthetic sensibility is shaped by such things as "the big dragonflies with gauzy wings iridescently green and purple in the sunlight, that darted back and forth over the brook" (16). Such aesthetic representations of nature, however, do not merely decorate the novel's prose; they actually fortify the novel's feminist stance. Since Judith herself is not distinct from the natural world, by drawing on the ideals of aesthetic conservation, which argue that nature has value apart from its role in industrial production or the reproduction of the family, the novel can dramatize the significance of a feminist subjectivity that neither produces nor reproduces.

The novel echoes not only the representation of nature as aesthetic, but also the free love movements, as it couples sexual desire with what is natural in order to mark its approval of Judith's premarital and extramarital sexual pleasure.[26] Before she marries Jerry, they enjoy "a speedy, simple, natural courting, like the coming together of two young wild things in the woods" (102). After she marries, Judith becomes mesmerized by an itinerant preacher, ignoring his religious chatter "as a duck's down sheds water," but indulging in his desire: "With an ecstasy transcending anything that she had ever felt in her life, she yielded herself to his passion" (272). Oddly enough, this "dark-eyed stranger" does not receive much description or dialogue. Instead, Kelley displaces Judith's sexuality onto pages of reverie about the beauty and sensuality of the natural world, as the novel describes, in lush, enticing detail, the outdoor locales where she and the preacher meet. The music of bird songs, for example, rushes forth with orgasmic intensity.

> Then, soaring far beyond the compass of these humble singers, burst forth rapturously into such floods of melody that the sunlight seemed filled with a rain of bright jewels. With delirious abandon to love and joy, the music welled from their little throats, palpitatingly, delicate, piercingly sweet. The enraptured rush of it, the sudden turns of it, the mad surprises of it penetrated Judith's being and swayed her like the master passion of which they were the voice. (275)

Significantly, the absence of a subject in the first sentence leaves it unclear as to what, or who, "burst forth rapturously into such floods." While these ecstatic descriptions of the natural world endorse female sexual pleasure by linking it with what is "natural," the loaded diction in this passage— "abandon," "enraptured," "master passion"—intimates a sexual enthrallment that foreshadows Judith's maternal entrapment.

Duplicitous nature steals into the novel in a long scene that was cut from its original printing; contemporary readers of the Feminist Press edition may thus read what readers of the 1923 edition were denied. Kelley, angered by this excision, considered the birth scene essential to the novel: "I had never read in the works of a woman novelist—obviously a woman is the only one who could do it justice—an adequate description of childbirth, so I concluded that the job was waiting to be done by me."[27] Kelley's defense of the scene suggests that the editors may have denounced the scene as "unrealistic": "Though it is in no way exaggerated, it reads a bit that way, and some people would be inclined to deduce from it that the whole book is hysterical."[28] The expunging of this scene, a scene intended to be an "adequate description of childbirth" that is "no way exaggerated," suggests that the horrors of childbirth are unrepresentable, that they exceed the territory designated as literary—even when other works of "naturalism" (Upton Sinclair's work comes to mind) do not spare the reader.[29] Perhaps what was so threatening about Kelley's rendition of childbirth was that she portrayed abject, uncontrollable corporeality not from a safe distance, but from the inside out, dramatizing the subjectivity within.

Lest we read Judith's experience as extraordinary, her physician assures us that Judith's symptoms "are quite normal and natural." Despite his authoritative presence, he is unable to help Judith, counseling Judith's husband Jerry that "[w]e must leave nature to do it; and nature takes her own time" (341). Nature, the source of Judith's freedom and sexual pleasure, betrays her with the agony of childbirth.

> For her there was no longer any return from the ghastly No Man's Desert of pain into which she had been snatched by a strong, pitiless hand again and again for so many long hours. She was there now quite alone and cut off from all humankind. Out of it there led but one sinister canyon through which she must pass to come back to the world of men. All other ways were closed but this. Nature that from her childhood had led kindly and blandly through pleasant paths and had at last betrayed her, treacherously beguiling her into this desolate region, now sternly pointed her the one way out: the dread and cruel pass of Herculean struggle through tortures unspeakable. (344)

The unendurable pain of childbirth transforms the beauty, freedom, and sensuality of the natural world into mere ruses to entice women into this horrific predicament. Ironically, this passage underscores Judith's heroism in the face of solitary and onerous labor, dramatizing a momentary sense of agonistic agency that "nature" will eventually crush.

Childbirth as a revelation of the nature of women's bodies is so powerfully transformative that the ubiquitous references to animals that characterize Judith as energetic, rebellious, strong, and sexual become, in this chapter, horrific signifiers of an inescapable corporeality.[30] Jerry, her husband, becomes "terrified" by a

> sound that he had never heard before, a deep-toned, guttural, growling sound that ended in a snarl. It was not like that of an ordinary dog; but more as Jerry imagined some wild, doglike creature, inhabitant of lonely waste country, might growl and snarl over its prey. Could it be Judith who was making this savage sound? (343)

It is none other than Judith—Judith whose "gums were fleshed in the snarl like the gums of an angry wolf" (344). As she becomes more resigned to her fate, she seems less like a savage wild dog or wolf and more like a cow. " 'If she'd been a caow [*sic*], she'd a been dead long ago,' [Jerry] muttered; then started violently, shocked at his own comparison" (345). The description of the baby is even more shocking.

> It was over, and the doctor triumphantly held up nature's reward for all the anguish: a little, bloody, groping, monkey-like object, that moved its arms and legs with a spasmodic, froglike motion and uttered a sound that was not a cry nor a groan nor a grunt nor anything of the human or even the animal world, but more like a harsh grating of metal upon metal. It was a reward about the worthwhileness of which not a few women have had serious doubts, especially when first confronted with what seems to the inexperienced eye a deformed abortion. (348)

Nature betrays women once again, this time by "rewarding" them with less than adequate compensation for their labor. The sound the child emits, "like a harsh grating of metal upon metal," troubles the boundaries between human and machine, suggesting not only that reproduction is as abrasive and alienating as industrial production, but that in a "modern" industrial age reproduction is no more "natural" than mass production. The baby's metallic wail pierces through the discursive body of the text, rupturing the naturalistic fiction that reproduction is a natural (not cultural) disaster.

Not surprisingly, Judith is not eager to bear another child. "The women who liked caring for babies could call her unnatural if they liked. She wanted to be unnatural. She was glad she was unnatural. Their nature was not her nature and she was glad of it" (240). Boldly affirming an oppositional "unnatural" identity, however, does not in and of itself afford Judith the means by which to control her fertility. Despite her determination, she becomes seduced by the preacher and the bird songs and finds herself pregnant. Again she attempts to wrest control of her destiny by trying to abort the child with a knitting needle, herbal concoctions, and a vigorous horseback ride. All methods fail. After unsuccessfully trying to drown herself in a pond, she falls ill and the pregnancy is terminated. Echoing her nineteenth-century predecessors, she decides abstinence is her only option.

> She wanted no more children that she could not clothe, that she could hardly feed, that were a long torture to bear and a daily fret and anxiety after they were born . . . Too long she had been led along blindly. Now her eyes were open and she would be a tool no more of man's lust and nature's cunning. She would see her path and choose it. She would be mistress of her own body. (299–300)

Jerry, however, is less than enthusiastic about this plan. Because Judith's resolve makes her home life one of continual discord, she surrenders. She becomes pregnant with another child, one she wishes would die but instead "triumphs" over death. Judith then resigns herself to her fate: "Convincingly she had realized the uselessness of struggle . . . Like a dog tied by a strong chain, what had she to gain by continually pulling at the leash?" (330). Judith, portrayed as a tethered domesticated animal, ends the novel on this note of entrapped resignation, dramatically underscoring the novel's naturalism. Casting nature itself as the villain makes women's descent into childbearing the ultimate "naturalistic" subject, since naturalism depicts characters that are "conditioned and controlled by environment, heredity, instinct, or chance."[31] And what could be bleaker than biology as destiny?

Although Judith resigns herself to her fate as a "captive mother" and literally embodies a literary "naturalism," the novel seeks another conclusion outside its bounds by demonstrating the need for reproductive control. As a tale of an artist manqué, the novel argues that even more than poverty or lack of education, it is the lack of birth control that robs Judith of her creative potential. Furthermore, the title of the novel encourages us to compare reproductive control with already acceptable agricultural practices, by sprouting "weeds" into tropes of profuse, incessant, and wasteful procreation.

> The weeds grew with such lustiness and vigor that Jerry had to cultivate his corn and tobacco again and again to keep the plants from being smothered. As soon as one generation was laid low another came to take its place. The earth teemed with the seed of this useless but vigorous and persistent life. (213)

The farmer wages a constant, strenuous battle against the weeds that threaten his crop—but at least he has methods of control. Women, without birth control, have no means to arrest the lusty, vigorous weeds of reproduction. Whereas men, as farmers, may battle the nature that is "out there," women cannot; nature becomes the ultimate betrayer of women by offering them freedom and pleasure outside the domestic, only to steal into and take root inside their own bodies, commanding them from within.[32] *Weeds* seems to reproduce, in fictional form, the 1920 editorial in *The Birth Control Review* entitled "Unnatural?" which defends birth control by comparing it to agriculture, proclaiming that "at last" men and women "will plan their families with at least as much care as they plant their crop." Just as the farmer must exercise constant vigilance lest nature "rapidly reduce his garden to a wild tangle,"[33] woman must battle the weeds of unchecked reproduction.

Weeds, written after most of the prominent naturalist texts, represents in excess the very maternal body that naturalism sought to supersede. In *Bodies and Machines* Mark Seltzer argues that the "emphatically 'male' genre of naturalism" with its "appeals to highly abstract conceptions of force" replaces the maternal body with the machine in order to project generative yet autonomous male power.[34] Naturalism represents this power by defining masculinity against both woman and nature: "the anti-biological and anti-natural biases of naturalism involve . . . the transcendence of 'the natural' and 'the female' both."[35] But *Weeds* does not represent the monstrous maternal body as a mythical or abject figure that haunts the margins of male discourse. Instead, it inhabits this discursive space by representing it from the inside out—that is, from the perspective of Judith, a strong-willed protagonist raging against her entrapped embodiment. By representing Judith's struggles against her own corporeality, the novel fractures naturalism's conflation of woman and nature while dramatizing the need for *female* power that is not maternal. The uncontrollable weeds of reproduction not only upstage other naturalist horrors, but also threaten the gendered cosmology of naturalism itself.

Like *Weeds*, *Quicksand* chronicles one woman's descent into the corporeal quagmire of childbearing; this "quicksand," however, is saturated with racist ideology. Angela Davis explains that whites have labeled African American women as sexually wanton in order to justify rape and systemic sexual exploitation, while racist factions of the eugenics movement have sought to curtail African American reproduction.[36] Hurston and Larsen's novels both reflect the difficulty of representing African American women's sexuality against a racist historical context. What has perplexed many readers about Zora Neale Hurston's 1937 *Their Eyes Were Watching*

God is why the protagonist, though sexually active, never becomes pregnant. Hurston's novel, however, was written nearly ten years after Larsen's, during a time when birth control was more widely practiced and accepted. Rather than skirting the question of reproductive freedom, the novel embraces the possibilities birth control affords, creating a feminist narrative of self-possession that is contingent on Janey's understanding of her body. Early in the novel when Nannie asks Janey if she is pregnant, Janey not only assures her that she is not, but asserts her own ability to *know* that she is not: "Ah'm all right dat way. Ah *know* 'tain't nothin' dere."[37] While many readers are surprised that Janey enjoys sex without reproduction, many more are shocked by the ending of Nella Larsen's 1928 *Quicksand,* in which Helga Crane, the cosmopolitan, refined, educated, and aesthetically inclined protagonist, marries a rural pastor (a "fattish," "rattish yellow man") and is worn down by continual childbearing. Helga, more educated and worldly than Janey, lacks the knowledge and the means to prevent pregnancy. Hazel Carby argues that *Quicksand*'s tragic narrative confronts the way most African American women writers had displaced sexuality.

> Helga consistently attempted to deny her sensuality and repress her sexual desires, and the result is tragedy. Each of the crises of the text centered on sexual desire until the conclusion of the novel, where control over her body was denied Helga and sexuality was reduced to its biological capacity to bear children.[38]

Although I agree that *Quicksand* narrates a tragedy of sexual repression, I think it warns equally of the bitter fruits of sexual expression, since it is not Helga's repression that reduces her sexuality to childbearing but her lack of birth control. Moreover, the novel battles the forces that deny reproductive control to black women by contesting the religious dogmas that render the female body as naturally reproductive and the ideological forces that denigrate the racially marked body as a "savage," "primitive," and will-less natural entity.

Birth control was an extremely important issue in the early twentieth-century African American community. Many African Americans argued that limiting African American reproduction would help improve the health and economic status of the race, and several writers drew upon eugenics to support their views. W. E. B. DuBois contends, in a 1922 issue of *The Crisis,* for example, that "of all who need [birth control] we Negroes are the first."[39] Similarly, J. A. Rogers, in *The Messenger,* calls for "more cultivation of the species and less propagation of it."[40] *The Birth Control Re-*

view devoted several special issues to the African American community which included plays by Mary Burril and Angelina Weld Grimké. Many of Grimké's works, including the play *The Closing Door,* link the exigency of birth control to the horrors of lynching. As one character passionately cries out: "I—An instrument of reproduction!—. . . a colored woman—doomed!—cursed!—put here!—willing or unwilling! For what?—to bring children here—men children—for the sport—the lust—of possible orderly mobs."[41] Just as Trent sardonically enjoined women to "breed," Grimké urges African American women not to deliver babies unto lynch mobs. More broadly, however, between 1915 and 1945 African Americans tended to see birth control as crucial to a wide range of political issues, including "economics, health, race relations, and racial progress," and, occasionally, to feminism.[42] While *Quicksand* was certainly informed by such ideas, it does not articulate specific political arguments for the need for birth control, but instead contests the intersecting ideologies of religion, race, and class that render the black woman's body the corporeal manifestation of a denigrated nature.

When Helga marries Mr. Pleasant Green and follows him to "the tiny Alabama town where he was pastor to a scattered and primitive flock,"[43] the novel rapidly becomes *antipastoral,* exposing the confluence of religion and "natural law." *Quicksand*'s dystopic, even nightmarish, representation of the pastoral implicitly critiques Jean Toomer's 1923 *Cane,* which idealizes rural southern women as rooted in the natural preindustrial world they glide through. Karintha, for example, "as innocently lovely as a November cotton flower," gives birth in an unimaginably passive way: a "child fell out of her womb onto a bed of pine needles in the forest. Pine-needles are smooth and sweet. They are elastic to the feet of rabbits."[44] Karintha neither labors nor lingers; it is the narrator—not Karintha—who luxuriates in the sensual details of this scene, relishing the "smooth," "sweet" "pine needles" and the "feet of rabbits." Such aesthetic revelries push women into the silent, though beautiful, landscape. Devoid of subjectivity, women like Fern become the canvas for modernist musings, as "the whole countryside seemed to flow into her eyes."[45] No knowledge, insight, or awareness emanates from Fern's eyes; they are instead receptacles for someone else's pastoral visions. *Quicksand* exposes how the idealization of nature that Toomer invoked to elevate rural African American women actually impedes the development of a self-determined black female subjectivity. Though Helga (echoing Grimké) had previously argued that it is a "sin" to reproduce more "dark bodies for the mobs to lynch" (75), when Helga joins Green's "primitive" flock, such arguments seem to fade as the novel casts Helga's predicament as a battle between nature and reason, passion and will. The sensuality of the night, for example, offers itself as the only redeeming feature of her new life: "Emotional, palpitating, amorous, all that was living in her sprang like rank weeds at the tingling thought of night, with a vitality so strong that it devoured all shoots of reason" (122). Her sexuality, represented as excessively vigorous, foul weeds, overtakes her reason, as nature triumphs over female self-determination. Because she cannot desert her children, she is trapped with Mr. Pleasant Green in the maternal quicksand of an antipastoral nightmare. The novel ends ominously: "she began to have her fifth child" (135).

Helga's first encounter with the Reverend Green foreshadows her later fall into a "natural" corporeality. Helga meets the Reverend Mister Pleasant Green during a revival meeting, of which she is at first "contemptuous" yet "entertained," and then horrified, and then, strangely enough, converted (113). During the meeting Helga collapses against a railing only because she fears she is going to be sick, but the congregation, and then she herself, interprets this "fall" as religious conversion (113). The religious fervor of this "conversion" is depicted as a kind of demented, misplaced sexual energy, "with its mixture of breaths, its contact of bodies, its concerted convulsions, all in wild appeal for a single soul" (133). This bacchanalia, which catalyzes her marriage to the pastor, also implicitly condemns it by associating religious fervor with sexual fever, both of which steal Helga's self-determination. As the parishioners sing Hymn 111, the repeated line "Less of self and more of Thee" portends Helga's diminishment. Religion leads ultimately, not to spiritual uplift, but, ironically, to a fall into a "primitive" nature, as the women who celebrate Helga's conversion demonstrate, "crawl[ing] over the floor like reptiles, sobbing and pulling their hair and tearing off their clothing" (114). It is no coincidence that in both *Weeds*, and more pivotally in *Quicksand*, a preacher is the agent of the women's fall into childbearing. Though nature is represented as the villain in both novels (but much more so in *Weeds*), it is a "nature" conjured by culture. Indeed, the Reverend Mister Pleasant Green's appellation couples Christianity and the pastoral, suggesting the common conflation of "God's will" and "natural law." When Helga questions how other women manage pregnancy after pregnancy, which to her is "almost unendurable," the Reverend Mister Pleasant Green "gently and patiently" reminds her that it is a "natural thing, an act of God" (125)—nature and God being nearly synonymous. The reverend's flock reiterates the (religious) belief that endless childbearing is "natural" and accepts Helga only after she submits to this belief.

But the quicksand that engulfs Helga at the novel's end gains its strength not only from religious constructions of the "nature" of women, but also from the ways in which the "natural," the "primitive," and the "sexual" are overcoded with racial and class hierarchies. Though Helga criticizes Anne for her hypocritical class pretensions, demonstrated by her dislike of "all things Negro," Helga frequently invokes class to elevate herself above much of her race. Helga's aestheticism, for example, allows her to conceive of her body as an art object—"something on which to hang lovely fabric" (123)—rather than as a sensual, physical entity. It is not at all surprising that Helga would wish to distance herself from her body, given the tenacious racist ideologies that have defined the black woman in terms of a denigrated corporeality. Such ideologies prevent Helga from experiencing desire without disgust; while ecstatically dancing, Helga realizes, with shame, "that not only had she been in the jungle, but that she had enjoyed it" (59). Helga spins together music, dancing, sensual pleasure, desire—all that is not rational and controlled—as that which is of the "jungle" and the "savage." Corporeality may be intensely pleasurable, but, saturated with race, such constructions of the body also render it as violently abject, "blown out, ripped out, beaten out," and as will-less as "whirling leaves" (59). Throughout the novel, overlapping polarities of race, class, and gender render a series of terrains that, for the protagonist, are uninhabitable. Fleeing from one extreme zone to another, Helga finally finds herself in the quicksand where race, gender, and class meet in one strong vortex that drowns the subject in an excessive, "natural," and "primitive" corporeality.

Like *Weeds*, however, *Quicksand* represents this abject corporeality from within, inhabiting what has been repulsed and insisting on the subjectivity of what has been objectified. *Quicksand* can be read in terms of Luce Irigaray's ambitious aim: to jam "the theoretical machinery itself," rather than merely "elaborating a new theory of which woman would be the *subject* or the *object*."[46] The surprising and extreme conclusion works as a "disruptive excess" that seeks to explode the novel's constitutive binaries (black/white, female/male, rural/urban, South/North, educated/folk), which not only render every social landscape uninhabitable, but engulf the black, female body within a "primitive" nature. Rather than having Helga straightforwardly aspire to the elevated categories of this constellation, by positioning her as a "subject" in white, Western, and male terms, the novel takes on a much more difficult project—that of "jamming the theoretical machinery itself." By doing so, the novel presents more than a protest against the "nature" of women's bodies that reduces them to continual childbearing; it attempts to deconstruct the very categories that constitute some bodies as unbearably "natural" and thus forwards a radically inclusive argument for reproductive self-determination.

Quicksand and *Weeds* could be criticized for casting nature as the villain when the struggle for reproductive control is, of course, a political struggle. Yet this begs the question of how the "political" is constituted in the first place and ignores the ideological power that "nature" carries. Since "nature" is saturated with ideologies that define women in terms of bodily reproductive capacities and maternal roles, women's challenges to the "nature" of reproduction are hardly coincidental.[47] Prohibitions against birth control reinscribe the female body as a "natural" ground, a territory outside the domain of cultural intervention and human agency. No doubt prohibitions against birth control are related to anxieties about women's increasing political power during the beginning of the twentieth century, since women's control over the "nature" of their bodies threatens to diminish the foundation of women's cultural oppression, the supposed "natural" biological differences between the sexes.

By erasing the boundaries between an exterior nature and an interior psychic realm, and by portraying the abject, will-less, "natural" body from the inside out, both *Weeds* and *Quicksand* refuse to represent woman as either "subject" or "object," and thus, in Irigaray's terms "jam the theoretical machinery itself." By inhabiting the discursive space of the uninhabitable, abject, "natural" body, the texts blur the boundaries between inside and outside, body and mind, nature and culture, and thus seek to subvert the very dualisms that render the female body as natural matter. The protagonists' bodies are much like the (volatile) body that Elizabeth Grosz describes, hovering "perilously and undecidably at the pivotal point of binary pairs, neither—while also being both—the private or the public, self or other, natural or cultural, psychical or social."[48] Though it would seem that the protagonists are dying for a straightforward Cartesian "mastery" of their bodies that birth control would afford them and that Grosz critiques, the narratives demonstrate that the body is indeed a volatile borderline between these binaries, since public prohibitions against birth control constitute the permeable boundaries of the private self, making reproduction at once a natural—and cultural—disaster. Descending into the disastrously uninhabitable body, *Weeds* and *Quicksand* call for reproductive freedom, yet, unlike *Call Home the Heart,* they do so by disrupting the subject/object divide, rather than by marking their own subjectivity against the ground of an other.

While *Weeds* and *Quicksand* revolt against reproduction as a natural disaster, Margaret Atwood's *Surfacing* attempts to forge feminist alliances with nature—only to be derailed by the same persistent link between nature and procreation. Octavia Butler's Xenogenesis Trilogy and Marian Engel's *Bear,* on the other hand, transform the human relation to nature by depicting bodies that are neither determined by maternity nor disconnected from the natural world.

Part III

Feminism, Postmodernism, Environmentalism

Chapter Six: Playing Nature

Postmodern Natures in Contemporary Feminist Fiction

We won't play nature to your culture.
                    Barbara Kruger

The defiant voice of Kruger's photograph refuses the role of silent ground, passive resource, or abject matter. The woman's face, still as death, lies at an oddly inhuman angle, making this more a chiaroscuro landscape than a portrait (see Figure 4). The leaves covering her eyes obstruct her vision and seemingly deny her subjectivity. Yet the leaves evoke that very play to a newly self-conscious and parodic form; they turn her face into a mask that mocks the conventional association of woman with nature even while suggesting the subjectivity beneath the mask.[1] With no such declarative captions, Ana Mendieta's earth-body sculptures may be read as affirmations of the connection between the body of woman and the body of the earth, the vibrant flames and the smoldering fire insisting that neither of these bodies is inert (see Figure 5). But the smoke and flames also signal an explosion of the volatile associations between woman and nature, as the sculptures burn up the ground of gender itself. The work of Kruger and Mendieta suggests the possibilities for feminists to "play nature" in parodic, subversive, and otherwise postmodern ways that confront, destabilize, or transfigure the associations between "woman" and "nature." Playing nature as a mode of cultural critique and transformation is a risky act, however, as several contemporary novels dramatize. In Toni Morrison's *Song of Solomon* and Leslie Marmon Silko's *Ceremony,* women

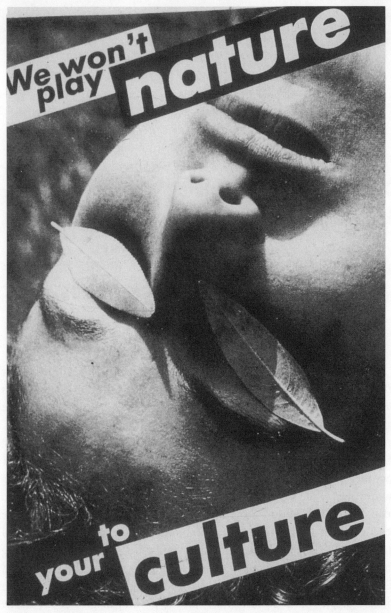

Figure 4. Barbara Kruger, untitled ("We Won't Play Nature to Your Culture"),
1983. Courtesy: Mary Boone Gallery, New York.

Figure 5. Ana Mendieta, untitled (from the Silueta Series), 1978, Silueta with Gunpowder in Iowa. Courtesy of the Estate of Ana Mendieta and Galerie Lelong, New York.

play Earth Mother to the questing male protagonists. In Margaret Atwood's *Surfacing*, the heroine renounces civilization, strips off her clothes, and becomes one with the elements. The protagonist in Marian Engel's *Bear*, originally written for an erotic anthology, falls in love with and makes love to a bear, herself becoming shaggy and ursine in the process. Do these fictions idealize the same "natural woman" that feminist theory has rejected? Do they reinvoke nature as a mute, feminine ground on which the ascendant male subject erects himself? Or do they, like Kruger and Mendieta's works, suggest possibilities for feminists to "play nature" as a postmodern political act?

As the Introduction outlines, the detrimental associations between woman and nature in Western thought have driven most feminists to extricate "woman" from the category of "nature." Motivated in part by the desire to combat essentialism, this strategy actually solidifies the very ground of essentialism because it reinforces the notion that nature is everything that culture is not. The feminist flight from nature fails to transform the terrain of struggle, leaving in place the very associations— with stasis, with passivity, with abject matter—that have made nature a hazardous terrain for feminism.

Postmodern feminisms and postmodern conceptions of nature offer a way out of this dilemma. Even though postmodern feminism works to denaturalize the concept of woman, it need not culminate in the severing of woman from nature. Such a refusal to "play nature" not only leaves the dichotomous nature/culture terrain intact, but forecloses possibilities for subversive significations of "woman." Judith Butler argues that "what women signify has been taken for granted for too long, and what has been fixed as the 'referent' of that term has been 'fixed,' normalized, immobilized, paralyzed in positions of subordination."[2] Precisely because "nature" has long functioned as a discursive anchor tethering woman into a subordinate position, it is crucial not only that feminist theory affirm the "constant rifting" over the category of woman as its "ungrounded ground,"[3] but that it cultivate the rifting of the category of nature. Rather than taking flight from nature, feminism can affirm multiple alliances and articulations, deconstructions and reconstructions of this discursive terrain. Feminist theories, politics, and fictions can travel beyond the false dichotomy of rejecting "nature" or valorizing the whole ideological package, can "play nature" with a vengeance by deploying discourses of woman and nature in order to subvert them, can destabilize the nature/culture divide while constructing feminist alliances with postmodern natures.

Playing Nature

Whether feminist critics embrace or reject "playing nature" seems to partly depend on a work's genre. Given the popularity and positive critical attention given to Margaret Atwood's *Surfacing,* on the one hand, and the academic-feminist denouncements of ecofeminism on the other, it seems that critics are, in general, more generous toward fictional performances. Rita Felski, for example, fences off fiction from theory to rescue the novels from their similarities with the "Romantic feminism" (Griffin, Daly, Rich) that she denounces as "theoretically naive" and "politically unsatisfactory": "While as a *political* and *theoretical* account of gender relations cultural feminism is problematic, as a *poetic* discourse it gives voice to a powerful experience of cultural dislocation."[4] To cordon off the fiction from the kind of scrutiny that Felski casts on the theory generates more problems than it solves, since many texts (e.g., Susan Griffin's *Woman and Nature*) or bodies of work (that of Adrienne Rich) cannot be divided neatly into theory or poetry. Ironically, opposing theory and poetry calls up the gendered dualisms of reason and emotion which play into the very nature/culture divide that is at issue here. Felski's divisions also echo the "double gesture" of strategic essentialism, which "generates a theory/practice split" by "associating essentialism with practice, and antiessentialism with an ultimate theoretical truth."[5] We need not operate within the terms of such a divide, however; Amanda Anderson contends that "theory need not be other than (and superior to) practice; ideally, it is practice itself as self-reflexive."[6] In this chapter and the next, I do not demarcate divisions between theory and practice, but instead examine the vexed relations between "woman" and "nature" as they are performed and contested within theoretical, fictional, and popular culture texts.

I begin by considering to what extent *Song of Solomon* and *Surfacing* can inhabit nature as an oppositional space without either irrevocably distancing nature from culture or strengthening deleterious associations between "woman" and "nature." My argument about *Song of Solomon* will turn on Pilate, who, despite her commanding presence, has been criticized as stereotypically feminine, lacking in heroic status:

> [W]hile she embodies Morrison's values, she is not the complete hero that Milkman is, for she lacks his recognition of meaning. By contrast to his final state, she seems intuitive, personal, and rather passive. This distinction is bothersome because it comes so close to the old active-man/passive woman stereotype.[7]

Although there is no way around the fact that Milkman is the questing hero of this novel, his quest affirms the constellation of values that Pilate embodies. The first time Milkman meets Pilate he is amazed that she could make him ashamed of himself, since she "was the one who was ugly, dirty, poor, and drunk"; yet the novel ends with Milkman realizing that he loved her because "[w]ithout ever leaving the ground, she could fly."[8] Milkman's quest and his changing attitude toward Pilate diachronically enact what the novel synchronically represents: a transvaluation of values that reverses gender and class hierarchies by celebrating Pilate and indicting Macon. Pilate, dwelling brilliantly at the same vortex of race, class, and gender that had consumed Helga in a quicksand of "natural" corporeality (see Chapter 5), transforms nature, a marginal space, into a "site of radical possibility, a space of resistance."[9]

Just as the novel shifts away from allusions to European fairy-tales and toward the clues that African and African American songs, tales, games, and place names provide,[10] it represents nature from an African American, not a Euro-American, perspective. Euro-Americans have long denigrated African American women as "animals," part and parcel of a nature devoid of any "redeeming dose of culture."[11] Despite the vicious ideologies that mire race within a fallen nature, African Americans have experienced nature, or more specifically the "wilderness," as a real and imaginary place of refuge. Melvin Dixon, in *Ride Out the Wilderness,* asserts that slaves viewed nature from a radically different perspective than that of their masters.

> Slaves looked upon nature and determined in their lore that the wilderness, the lonesome valley, and the mountain were places of deliverance . . . If America, as Leo Marx has argued, "was both Eden and a howling wilderness," slaves developed different ideas about the dichotomy between order and chaos. Slaves knew that as chattel they were considered part of the property and wilds of nature, which a smoothly functioning plantation could restrain.

Regarding "the 'garden' ideal of the plantation with understandable suspicion," slaves saw the "chaos" of the wilderness as a path to freedom.[12]

Just as the wilderness offered a space of freedom from plantation slavery, nature, in *Song of Solomon,* offers a utopian oppositional space, free from capitalism and its hierarchies of class and gender. The novel clearly demarcates a polarity of ideologically saturated spaces—Macon's patriarchal household and Pilate's matriarchal home. Macon practices and preaches: "Own things. And let the things you own own other things. Then you'll own yourself and other people too" (55). As Susan Willis notes, for Macon, "all human relationships have become fetishized by their being made equivalent to money. His wife is an acquisition; his son an investment in the future."[13] Macon's women live as "doll babies," obeying not only the father but the son, as they suffocate their days fabricating fake flowers. In contrast to the living "Dead" in Macon's household, the women in Pilate's home enjoy a prelapsarian nature, savoring sexual freedom; eating whatever they want, whenever they want; and living "pretty much as though progress was a word that meant walking a little farther on down the road" (27). Pilate's family livelihood stands in stark contrast to Macon's exploitative materialism: "With everyone working to separate berries from thorns, winemaking is not a means for creating surplus value, but a communal social activity whose natural raw material suggests, in Morrison's symbolic register, another link to rural agricultural society."[14] Pilate's home also suggests rural life. Even though Pilate and her family don't live in the country, their sidewalk (a mark of "civilization") is a full eighty feet from the house, and the yard is distinguished by "four huge pine trees," from which Pilate "got the needles she stuck into her mattress" (27). Fabulously, the house seems to grow out of the earth itself: its "basement . . . rising from rather than settling into the ground" (27). Like her home, Pilate is encoded as natural, chewing on pine needles, smelling "like a forest," playing enchanting music that reminds Macon of "fields and wild turkey and calico" (29). Milkman and Guitar become mesmerized by Pilate: "The pebbly voice, the sun, and the narcotic wine smell weakened both the boys, and they sat in a pleasant semi-stupor, listening to her go on and on" (40). The fields, the wild turkey, the pebbly voice, the sun, all situate Pilate's strength and freedom within a mythic realm of nature. Her ties to the power, the magic, and the beauty of the natural world elevate Pilate to dramatic—if not heroic—dimensions. Though she is certainly a kind of "earth mother," conjuring up Milkman's very life and (remarkably) giving birth to herself, she is hardly passive or mindless, but instead possesses formidable strength and wisdom. Pilate dwells not in the (fallen) nature that denigrates African American women, but in a space for feminist resistance, the "wilderness" of refuge and freedom.

Thus "nature" serves not only as an oppositional space but as a symbolic means of celebrating Pilate and the matrix of gender, race, and class positions she represents. As Patricia Hill Collins explains, empowerment entails "rejecting the dimensions of knowledge, whether personal, cultural, or institutional, that perpetuate objectification and dehumanization" and fostering the perspective of the subordinate group.[15] Nature, as a realm apart from the dominant culture's institutions, provides a place from which Pilate can embody an oppositional position and Morrison can symbolically reverse the valences of class, gender, and cultural hierarchies. Furthermore, associating Pilate with nature allows Morrison to distinguish black feminism from a white, bourgeois feminism and to repel the normative vision of the patriarchal household trumpeted by the Moynihan report.

Even though nature can endow Pilate with symbolic power because it is apart from the dominant cultural institutions, the novel does not amplify a nature/culture divide. In fact, in *Song of Solomon,* as in other works by Morrison, African American culture is itself rooted in nature, as the land "is not merely a place" but "one of the significant bases of the folk's value system."[16] When Milkman travels South, the landscape offers clues to his cultural heritage puzzle, as place names are an essential part of the songs, stories, and family history that he seeks. Just as Milkman's quest intertwines genealogy with geography, his hunt in Shalimar (a place unknown to the official "Texaco map") is at once a prototypical communion with nature and a kinship ritual that ties him to his "people" (280). Thus, even though nature functions as an oppositional space, it is not a world apart from culture—only from the dominant culture.

Despite the weighty presence of nature in the novel, the motif of flying would seem to exalt the ideal of transcendence. Michael Awkward, for example, reads the insertion of Hagar's death within the narrative of Milkman's quest as a critique of "phallocentric myth's failure to inscribe usefully transcendent possibilities for the female."[17] Yet the novel's conclusion subverts the very ideal of transcendence, as Milkman falls into the "killing arms of his brother," and Pilate flies "without leaving the ground." Such grounded flights suggest that the horizontal, not the vertical, trajectory of the novel as nature—a nature inscribed with the genealogies, stories, and rituals of the African American community—functions as a rich oppositional space.

Unlike *Song of Solomon,* which does not sever nature from culture, Margaret Atwood's *Surfacing* ends up representing nature as a romanticized and ultimately unapproachable realm. By self-consciously "playing nature," the heroine of Margaret Atwood's *Surfacing* dramatizes the potentials for alliances between feminism and environmentalism. Yet these political alliances, which attempt to combat the pernicious connections between "woman" and "nature," break under their weight.

Surfacing begins with a trip "back to nature." The unnamed protagonist returns to her childhood cabin in the woods, along with her lover, Joe, and another couple, Anna and David, to search for her missing father. While in the wilderness, the protagonist learns how American imperialism, capitalism, sexism, racism, and violence against animals reinforce each other. Whether they are actual "Americans" or Canadians who earn that alias through emulating their colonizers, the "Americans" destroy the land and its creatures for greed or the thrill of domination. Environmental injustices reflect and further social injustices, as Atwood compares the treatment of animals to the treatment of people ("Anything we could do to the animals we could do to each other: we practiced on them first"),[18] but especially to the treatment of women, as the bodies of women and animals suffer similar indignities. David notes that Canada was "founded on the bodies of dead animals," especially that of the beaver, which, significantly, has become "a dirty word" (46). As the men joke about putting a "split beaver" on the Canadian flag, the novel suggests that the bodies of animals and women have been the unacknowledged raw materials for the construction of the nation (141). The novel also dramatizes the representational violence waged on women and animals, when the protagonist and her friends find a heron "strung up like a lynch victim." Because "it couldn't be tamed or cooked or trained to talk, the only relation they could have to a thing like that was to destroy it. Food, slave or corpse, limited choices . . ." (138). The men's delight in discovering the heron—a perfect "subject" for their film, *Random Samples*—suggests that their callous representations are complicit with the violence of the original killing.[19] Later, when the men want Anna to "get naked" because they need a "naked lady with big tits and a big ass" for their film, David tries to persuade Anna with this less-than-enticing offer: "You'll go in beside the dead bird, it's your chance for stardom, you've always wanted fame. You'll get to be on Educational TV" (158–59). Side by side, the heron and the naked lady become objects for the male gaze. The title of the film, *Random Samples,* a code word for scientific validity, betrays how objectivity can objectify, how the "distance" of the supposedly impartial observer masks the desire for domination.

Through this wilderness sojourn in which she decodes such signs as the mutilated heron, the protagonist realizes how capitalism, imperialism, sexism, and the exploitation of nature form a matrix of domination. Unlike her friends, who understand but collude with these forces, for the heroine an intellectual comprehension is not enough. She declares: "[I]t was time for me to choose sides" (181). She decides to oppose the forces of domination completely; thus she sides with nature against them, attempting to "play nature" as a political act. She escapes from her friends and retreats into the surrounding woods. She washes herself in the lake, relinquishes her clothes, squats in the garden gnawing vegetables, and sleeps in a "lair near the woodpile" (208–29). Declaring that "[e]verything from history must be eliminated" (207), she indulges in a nature that is not only unsullied by history, but one in which language, an integral part of culture, is unnecessary because the creatures of nature enjoy an unmediated signifying presence:

> . . . the boulders float, melt, everything is made of water, even the rocks. In one of the languages there are no nouns, only verbs held for a longer moment.
>
> The animals have no need for speech, why talk when you are a word
> I lean against a tree, I am a tree leaning
> I break out again into the bright sun and crumple, head against the ground
> I am not an animal or a tree, I am the thing in which the trees and animals grow, I am a place. (212–13)

By perceiving boulders that "float, melt" like everything "made of water," and by glorifying verbs at the expense of nouns, the protagonist reaches toward an ontology not only of harmonious unity and relation, but of fluid boundaries that keep things in flux, in which even the boulders are actions, not objects; verbs, not nouns. In this utopian moment the heroine plays nature, even to the extent that she herself transforms into "a place."

But she doesn't remain a place for long. Not only does the protagonist realize she'll run out of food in the woods, but she is also politically motivated to return to culture: "Then back to the city and the pervasive menace, the Americans. They exist, they're advancing, they must be dealt with, but possibly they can be watched and predicted and stopped without being copied" (221). Thus, "playing nature" has given the heroine a newly politicized consciousness, which she will enlist upon her return to culture.

Despite this transformative experience, the last lines of the novel reveal a distance between the heroine and nature: "The lake is quiet, the trees surround me, asking and giving nothing" (224). Neither the lake nor the trees communicate to her; as the heroine heads for the city, nature is stripped of its semiotic power. Was she merely duped by the pathetic fallacy? A better way of understanding this estrangement is to focus on how the Romantic view of nature as an unsullied world apart ultimately distances nature. The heroine is either becoming a tree or heading back to the city in her car—the two extremes determine the territory. The heroine uses Nature as a consciousness-raising retreat—but, in the end, the novel abandons nature to silence. The novel takes the characters and the readers "back" to nature, lifting some ideological veils along the way, but the conclusion to this journey amplifies the division between humanity and nature—dropping the curtain on a victimized nature existing ever elsewhere. Despite the alliances forged between feminism and environmentalism, by depicting nature as a world apart, the novel becomes determined by the very matrix of forces it denounces, thus preventing a satisfactory conclusion for either "woman" or "nature."

Even though the silence at the end of the novel resounds with an ultimate distancing from nature, the all-too-holy alliance that the novel has forged between nature and women manifests itself in a narrative that underwrites heterosexuality and condemns reproductive freedom.[20] While she is "playing nature" the protagonist realizes she must reproduce to replace the child she aborted. Comparing abortion to hunting animals, the narrator regrets that she did not allow her body to serve as a (natural) sanctuary for the creature inside: "He said it wasn't a person, only an animal; I should have seen that was no different, it was hiding in me as if in a burrow and instead of granting it sanctuary I let them catch it. I could have said No but I didn't; that made me one of them too, a killer" (170).

Judith McCombs notes that the narrator's condemnation of abortion arises directly from her "pro-nature" stance: "Denial of birth had alienated her from nature; creation in her body connects her to all creation. The woman/nature myth is here explicit and life-linked."[21] Taking this myth to its logical political end, Patricia Jagentowicz Mills warns how the "pro-nature" stance of ecofeminists, which claims that " 'Nature itself knows best' or that 'Nature must become an end in itself,' " can endanger women's right to abortion.[22] This problematic affirmation of the "natural woman" not only valorizes procreation as a natural force but also underwrites a narrative of normative heterosexuality, since "woman" needs a man to breed with. Tellingly, after the protagonist has "played nature" she takes Joe out in the woods: "I'm impatient, pleasure is redundant, the animals don't have pleasure. I guide him into me, it's the right season, I hurry. He trembles and then I can feel my lost child surfacing within me, forgiving me . . ." (190–91). In this novel, teeming with split, severed, and butchered bodies, the protagonist recovers wholeness only through conception, creating a child that substitutes for the one she aborted. Sex in this scene is only for reproduction, not for pleasure (although Joe, we can surmise, took pleasure in the act). Oddly enough, she assumes animals don't enjoy sex; presumably they engage in it only because of a procreative telos. Thus "nature" not only classifies (female) sexual pleasure as irrelevant but underwrites a procreative heterosexual script. Even though the novel presents a mythic female quest, not a romance, Joe emerges at the end as an undeniably essential character—"The Man": "what's important is that he's here, a mediator, an ambassador, offering me something: captivity in any of its forms, a new freedom?" (224). The exigency of his masculinity apparently renders the nature of his offering irrelevant.

One could read *Surfacing* as a warning against female enthrallment into a Romantic nature, seeing the heroine as playing nature with a vengeance by pushing the ideologies of "nature" to their extremes as a reductio ad absurdum. Joe, as a merely phallic anti-hero, would then parody the ideologies of normative and procreative heterosexuality that "nature" endorses. Yet to read the ending parodically undercuts what the rest of the novel so forcefully presents: the heroine's politicized understanding of the parallel exploitation of women and nature. What the heroine and the novel fail to understand, however, is that retreating to an idealized nature only returns them to where they began. In other words, when the heroine sides with nature against the cultural forces of domination, she remains within a dichotomous and thus untenable territory, a territory that the novel fails to remap. Caught, unwittingly, in the ideological snare of nature, the feminist quest becomes a romance, culminating in procreation. In the end, nature is left silent and the heroine barefoot and pregnant.

While for *Song of Solomon* nature is a "site of resistance" precisely because it is interwoven with African American culture, for *Surfacing* nature is oppositional when it is a world apart. Idealizing the pristine wilderness is, at times, politically exigent; however, this conception of nature bears no small resemblance to nature as *terra nullius,* that which is semiotically empty, distant, and devoid of significance. The fact that *Surfacing,* a novel propelled by feminist and environmentalist intentions, concludes with an ideological landscape hostile toward them both demonstrates how extraordinarily difficult it is for feminism to affirm, promote, or take refuge in nature. The novels discussed next combat these difficulties in part by radically redefining nature. *Desert of the Heart* purges nature of its associations with a normative, reproductive heterosexuality, while *Ceremony* represents nature as an agent, not as passive matter. *Bear* and the Xenogenesis Trilogy create feminist epistemologies that counter the "objectively" dominant gaze epitomized by *Random Samples.*

Feminist Epistemologies of Embodied Knowledges

Octavia Butler's Xenogenesis Trilogy and Marian Engel's *Bear* enact feminist epistemologies that disentangle nature from the structures of knowledge that distance, objectify, and immobilize. Several feminist theorists have analyzed the connections between masculinist epistemologies and the domination of nature. Carolyn Merchant's *The Death of Nature* exposes how the scientific revolution penetrated and dominated a feminized nature. Jane Flax analyzes how Cartesian philosophy intermeshes "the desire to know . . . with the desire to dominate": "Nature is posited as pure otherness which must be conquered to be possessed and transformed into useful objects." Nancy C. M. Hartsock critiques "abstract masculinity's" dualistic stance of separation and opposition. Finally, Donna Haraway shatters the epistemological "god tricks" of objectivity, relativism, and totalism.[23] Attempts to posit alternative, feminist epistemologies have been met with critiques of their lack of scientific validity, or from other camps, of their insufficient postmodern credentials.[24] Though I do not have the space to examine debates over whether feminist epistemology is or is not postmodern, I would contend that insofar as various feminist epistemologies dislodge "woman" and "nature" as the ground for a transcendent masculinist subjectivity, they contribute to a postmodern feminism. What I would like to focus on here is the potential for "epistemologies of marked subjectivities," in Hartsock's terms, to strike at the very root of deleterious connections between nature, woman, and other others. Those tired but tenacious old dualisms of nature/culture, body/mind, object/subject have been trotted out time and time again to posit women and racially marked others as more bodily and hence "closer" to a debased nature. Instead of taking flight from the denigrated side of the dualisms, Butler and Engel radically reconceive the body and nature in such a way as to confound the dualisms themselves. They create fictions that enact feminist epistemologies of embodied knowledges, thereby countering the dominant paradigms of distance and objectification.

As I have argued elsewhere,[25] Octavia Butler's corpus holds profound implications for environmentalist philosophy and politics by its innovative interrogations of the links between nature, the body, and race. Butler's Xenogenesis Trilogy (*Dawn, Adulthood Rites,* and *Imago*) introduces the Oankali, an antidotal species who lives out feminist and Afrocentric epistemologies. The Oankali arrive amidst the ruins of a nuclear apocalypse—an apocalypse detonated by humans' deadly genetic combination of intelligence and hierarchical behavior. The Oankali embody forms of knowing that are inhospitable to hierarchies. Their values are consonant with the Afrocentric feminist epistemologies described by Collins, which favor "concrete experience" and the "capacity for empathy."[26] They have a corporeally based empathic ethic—they themselves feel any pain they inflict on an other. Furthermore, the Oankali perceive the world not through vision, which implies distance and abstraction, but through their sensory organs, which touch and taste genetic information. The Oankali do not distance, abstract, and categorize but instead, relish the intriguing particularities of each creature—human, plant, or animal. The Oankali perceive no chasm or hierarchy between humans and "nature"—they taste a delicious spectrum of life.

Since the Oankali seek continual evolution through trading genetics, they do not see difference as "other" so much as a valuable future aspect of themselves—selves which are continually transforming in, as Eric White aptly puts it, an "erotics of becoming."[27] Even as the Oankali set out to learn everything they can about human biology, history, and culture, they would be baffled by an epistemological divide between subject and object, since the "object" of knowledge is that which will transform their own flesh. Blurring the boundary between self and other, the Oankali embody Hartsock's "feminist standpoint," which, grounded in women's traditional labor, offers the "experience of continuity and relation—with others, with the natural world, of mind with body" as an ontological starting point for a less oppressive society.[28] The labor of the Oankali, in fact, is never instrumental, but is something remarkably akin to the labor of subsistence and child rearing, which, in Hartsock's theory, confuses mind/body and nature/culture dualisms. Communicating with their ship through their own body chemistry and with each other via direct neural stimulation, the Oankali experience no disjunction between mind and body, the material and the mental. In fact, when an ooloi, the third sex of the Oankali, gives its child its "inheritance," it transmits a deluge of cells, "genetic memories," a legacy that is as biological as it is cultural, via a process that is as sensual as it is cerebral.[29] Moreover, the Oankali embody "continuity and relation" to such an extent that their "space ships" and "environments" are not separate entities, but different forms of themselves. Their shuttles "were like extensions of Oankali bodies" and their tree-like ships, with walls of rippling flesh, enjoyed various forms of consciousness.[30] Since "ships controlled themselves," knowledge does not purchase mastery of another entity, but instead circulates in networks of pleasurable exchange. Lo, their earth-planted "environment" that will one day be a ship, is neither passive resource nor pristine wilderness. Lo learns and adapts, shares information and grows houses, food, and clothing for its inhabitants. "[P]arent, sibling, home"—Lo neutralizes the nature/culture divide as it would a toxin.[31]

Several critics have interpreted the Oankali as a less than utopian species. Frances Bonner claims that "there is nothing utopian about the societies in Xenogenesis"; Michelle Erica Green argues that the Oankali colonize the humans by reducing them to a "package of genes"; and Donna Haraway contends that "the aliens live in postmodern geometries of vast webs and networks" that are "hardly innocent of power and violence."[32] I would argue, however, that the Oankali—though not innocent—certainly emerge as an antidote to the humans, who are forever bickering, plundering, raping, maiming, and murdering. As a trilogy, the series transports us from a human perspective to one that is more and more Oankali; it begins with Lilith, the human who first mates with the Oankali, then focuses on an Oankali/human construct, then on a construct ooloi. Against the backdrop of a world devastated by a nuclear catastrophe resulting from hierarchical behavior, Butler portrays another way of thinking and being in which continuities and interrelations eschew hierarchies and affirm difference. Though power and violence can certainly take postmodern forms, the embodied knowledges of the

Oankali act as oppositional epistemologies which make nonsense of the dualisms that support the oppression of women, African Americans, and other socially marginalized groups. Moreover, the ontology of continuity and relation found in the Oankali and in Hartsock's feminist standpoint theory not only provides a paradigm for feminism and anti-racism, but also confirms, on a human plane, the ecological worldview of situated connectedness and constitutive interrelations.[33] By creating another species and another gender to embody this feminist, anti-racist ontology, Butler eludes the associations between women, people of color, and a denigrated nature even while valorizing a world in which nature is not "other" than culture.

An epistemology arising out of an experience of continuity and relation hardly upholds Enlightenment ideals of disinterested objectivity. The seeming neutrality afforded by distance and disembodied reason, however, has functioned only to veil a stance of domination in which the knowing subject masters a lifeless world. As Linda Holler puts it, "the denial of being *in* the world is historically and ontologically tantamount to the denial of the being *of* the world."[34] Rather than relinquish the concept of objectivity,[35] many feminist theorists have radically revised it, underscoring—not denying—the situated position of the knower and her relation to the "object" of knowledge. Sandra Harding proposes a model of "strong objectivity" that strives for a "reciprocal relationship between the agent and object of knowledge."[36] Evelyn Fox Keller distinguishes between "static objectivity," which severs subject from object, and "dynamic objectivity," which, like empathy, "grants to the world around us its independent integrity but does so in a way that remains cognizant of, indeed relies on, our connectivity with that world."[37] While the dominating practices of static objectivity are, appropriately enough, bound up with battle metaphors, Keller's epigraph from June Goodfield suggests love as a metaphor for dynamic objectivity: " 'Again I say the nearest an ordinary person gets to the essence of the scientific process is when they fall in love ... Sometimes you fall in love with a fireplace, or you fall in love with a tree, and I honestly think this is the nearest ordinary people get to the genuine experience of science.' "[38] Although love certainly poses hazards for feminist theorizing, the metaphor of loving connection adroitly contrasts with disembodied epistemologies that underwrite the blithe domination of the natural world. In Haraway's terms, such epistemologies proceed from the irresponsible "god tricks" of totalization and relativism that promise "vision from everywhere and nowhere equally and fully."[39] Opposing such transcendent vanishing acts, Haraway argues that "only partial perspective promises objective vision": "Feminist objectivity is about limited location and situated knowledge, not about transcendence and splitting of subject and object. In this way we might become answerable for what we learn how to see."[40]

Such radical redefinitions of objectivity, which refuse to sever subject from object, are played out in Marian Engel's *Bear*. In this abundantly spare novella, Lou, a librarian from the Historical Institute in Toronto, is sent to investigate and catalogue the Cary Estate, a new acquisition. To her surprise, the estate, located on an island in northern Lake Huron, comes with a bear. At first she finds "the idea of the bear joyfully Elizabethan and exotic," but when she sees him she is shocked with his actuality: "Bear. There. Staring."[41] Her ontological and epistemological ruminations begin: "Everyone has once in his life to decide whether he is a Platonist or not, she thought. I am a woman sitting on a stoop eating bread and bacon. That is a bear. Not a toy bear, not a Pooh bear, not an airlines Koala bear. A real bear" (34). She attempts to purge the popular culture misrepresentations from her expectations of bearness by assessing the "real thing." "She thought, you have these ideas about bears: they are toys, or something fierce and ogreish in the woods, following you at a distance, snuffling you out to snuff you out. But this bear is a lump" (34). Unsatisfied with her conjectures based on observation, she then asks him, "[W]ho and what are you?" (36). The bear doesn't respond; Lou's inquiry continues. The novella becomes an epistemological drama as Lou, dissatisfied with shuffling facts onto index cards, becomes intrigued by the possibility of coming into a deeper knowledge of the bear. She wonders, for example, what and how humans know about animals, especially bears:

> She had no idea what animals were about. They were creatures. They were not human. She supposed that their functions were defined by the size, shape and complications of their brains. She supposed that they led dim, flickering, inarticulate psychic lives as well.
>
> He, she saw, lay in the weak sun with his head on his paws. This did not lead her to presume that he suffered or did not suffer. That he would like striped or spotted pyjamas. Or that he would ever write a book about humans clothed in ursomorphic thoughts. A bear is more an island than a man, she thought. To a human. (60)

Although she speculates about bears' psychic lives, her inability to discern the bear's preference in pyjama patterns mocks the human desire to clothe the unknowable in the familiar, to envision the world in our own image. The bear is as puzzling as a human "clothed in ursomorphic thoughts."

Lou comes to know the bear not through philosophical ruminations but—like Goodfield's description of the scientific process—by falling in love with him. This is no pioneer tale in which the hero conquers the wilderness, which may mean, as Coral Ann Howells argues, that this is a quintessentially Canadian story.[42] At the same time, its embodied knowledges and its parody of romance novels paint *Bear* as particularly feminist. Indeed, as an epistemological quest, *Bear* acts out *Moby-Dick* as a grocery-store romance.[43] The rather outré cover of the Bantam edition of *Bear* announces its affinity with bodice rippers, as the bare-breasted heroine (nipples conveniently covered by long strands of hair) is sumptuously enveloped in the lavish fur of the bear towering behind her (see Figure 6). Casting a bear as the romantic hero certainly strikes a blow at the pretension of phallic exigency—unlike the heroine of *Surfacing*, Lou hardly requires a Joe.[44] But more importantly, perhaps, Engel's transposition reverberates with feminist and ecophilosophical implications. According to Janice Radway's categories, *Bear*, which ends with the bear ripping Lou's back, is a "failed" romance because the brutal hero is not transformed into a caring partner and the reader is deprived of a happy ending.[45] As a failed romance, however, the novel critiques the desire for an "ideal" romance, since the reader's common-sense belief that the bear certainly can't be transformed into something other than an animal exposes the pernicious parallel hope on which romance novels are founded, that "true love" will transform the brutal "hero" into a dream husband. Simultaneously, the importation of the standard romance plot, which for all its flowery trappings and overflowing bodices is a story of control, warns us against the desire to tame nature, since a happy ending for this romance would mean clothing the bear in spotted (or striped) pyjamas.

While it is much easier to capitalize on *Bear*'s parallels with mass market romances, its similarities with *Moby-Dick* are no less striking. Both *Bear* and *Moby-Dick* dramatize the obsession of the protagonist with one particular inscrutable animal—though in *Bear* love, not destruction, motivates the quest for knowledge. Both take epistemological quandaries to heart. And both juxtapose encyclopedic information about the animal with the plot. In *Bear*, as Lou catalogues Cary's books, random notes about bears fall out of the texts. The first, suggesting a connection between capitalism and instrumental knowledge, falls from the "*Penny Cyclopaedia* produced by the Society for the Promotion of Useful Knowledge" (42): "*In the Linnean system*, brown, beautifully curled, minute handwriting told her, *Ursus comes between Mustela and Didelphis. The order includes Arctos, the true bears; Meles,*

Figure 6. Jacket cover from *Bear,* by Marian Engel, 1977. Copyright 1977. Used by permission of Bantam Books, a division of Random House, Inc.

the badgers; Lotor, the raccoon . . ." (43). These notes, although hand-written, are distant, "scientific," disembodied fragments of information, falling seemingly from nowhere, mixing taxonomic and folkloric data about bears: *"The Laplanders venerate it, and call it the Dog of God. The Norwegians say, 'The bear has the strength of ten men, and the sense of twelve' "* (101).

As they drop out of various volumes, these fragments of cross-cultural data epitomize the "relativism" that, in Haraway's words, "is a way of being nowhere while claiming to be everywhere equally."[46] Such "god tricks" float the knower far above any concern for the object of knowledge, as Lou's visceral punctuation joltingly indicates.

> Out of the volume fell another message from God or Colonel Cary: *Among the Ainu of Japan, once, long ago, a bear cub was taken from its mother and raised at a woman's breast . . . At the winter solstice when it was three years old, it was taken to the centre of the village, tied to a pole, and, after many ceremonies and apologies, garroted with pointed bamboo sticks. Ceremonies were again performed, during which its surrogate mother mourned for it, and its flesh was eaten.* "Never," she cried. (115)

Lou's passionate, empathic response exposes the detached, "merely" descriptive voice of God or Colonel Cary, who never reveals his own position on bears but always keeps one tied up on his island. The contrast between the perspectiveless, bloodless notes and Lou's positioned quest for knowledge parallels Haraway's argument "against various forms of unlocatable, and so irresponsible knowledge claims" and for "situated and embodied knowledges."[47] Significantly, the free-floating notes take no responsibility for the tethering of the bear, as knowledge from nowhere remains happily heedless. On the other hand, Lou's epistemological drama, like Keller's dynamic objectivity, draws upon the knower's connectivity to the world, playing up the extent to which knowledge is situated, embodied, and always relational.

Before Lou's romance with the bear begins, her epistemological certitude about a creature she hardly knows affords her the delusion of control. She sums him up: "An unprepossessing creature, this bear, she decided. Not at all menacing . . . I can manage him, she decided" (36). Later, however, while Lou is classifying "a series of Victorian natural history manuals" (57), the bear disrupts this cold, meta-taxonomizing of nature by breaking into the house, coming up the steps, and plunking himself in front of the fire—asserting his "nerve" and his own knowledge. Lou is surprised that "[h]e knows his way" (58). This scene dramatizes Harding's "strong objectivity" in that it allows "the Other to gaze back 'shamelessly' at the self who had reserved for [herself] the right to gaze anonymously at whoever [she] chooses."[48] Appropriately, it is the bear himself who transgresses the subject/object divide and forces Lou's knowledge to become "situated": "Situated knowledges require that the object of knowledge be pictured as an actor and agent, not as a screen or a ground or a resource, never finally as slave to the master that closes off the dialectic in his unique agency and his authorship of 'objective' knowledge."[49] Although Howells contends that the bear becomes Lou's "sex object" because she "takes all the initiatives" and because Lou's "gratification . . . comes first,"[50] the bear is certainly an actor in their love play: he instigates their erotic relationship not only by entering the bedroom but by licking Lou's back. Lou's morning-after rumination also attests to the reciprocity of their relations: "what a strange thing to do. To have done. To have done to one" (107). No epistemological object to be simply "managed," the bear, himself an agent, transforms Lou into a more ursomorphic creature, as she becomes romantically enthralled by him. "She looked at herself in the female colonel's pier glass. Her hair and eyes were wild. Her skin was brown and her body was different and her face was not the same face she had seen before. She was frightened of herself" (125). Though these transformations may fade, the bear marks Lou permanently when he turns the tables and "manages" her. In a much commented-on scene, he "reached out one great paw and ripped the skin on her back" when she tried to copulate with him (131). Thus, the embodied, situated knowledge in this tale results in the "knower" being transformed by the "known," an epistemological scenario that seems particularly feminist in its positioned relationality, its insistence that knowledges have material effects, and its disruption of the categories of subject and object.

The novel's sanguine humor flows from such transgressions of the nature/culture divide in which nature, for all its bearish bulk, is no mindless brute materiality. The bear's sexual performance is beyond reproach, to be sure—but he's no sex toy. Lou, in fact, falls deeply in love with the bear. She eats with the bear, massages the bear's shoulders, reads with the bear's head in her lap, swims and plays games in the lake with the bear: "They lived sweetly and intensely together" (119). Take, by way of contrast, Lou's long-term affair with the Director of the Historical Institute, who "fucked her weekly on her desk while both of them pretended they were shocking the government and she knew in her heart that what he wanted was not her waning flesh but elegant eighteenth century keyholes" (93). The keyholes suggest the Director's objectification and nullification of Lou, un-

locking the beastliness of their affair. Thus, the novel transgresses boundaries between nature and culture not only by representing bestiality but
by portraying intraspecies sex as brutal and Lou's ursine affair as erotic,
passionate, and humane.

Many critics, seemingly uncomfortable with the novel's destabilization
of the walls between nature and culture, seek to erect firm barriers. Describing the scene in which Lou tries to have intercourse with the bear and
he claws her, Elspeth Cameron asserts, "Nature itself draws the boundaries; the balance is righted; sanity resumes." Howells argues that "finally
it is the bear who draws the demarcation line between them and shows
her what is forbidden by natural law."[51] Yet "natural law" is usually an oxy-
moron; cultures project onto nature the "laws" they want to find there.
Furthermore, that it is the bear, not the human, who draws the "ethical"
line between them, who makes the "moral" distinction, confounds any
conventional system of ethics and muddles the distinction between human and animal (the very distinction that "natural law" supposedly upholds). While Cameron and Howells underscore the boundary beyond
which sex between women and bears must not proceed, S. A. Cowan's interpretation of the conclusion erases Lou's sexuality altogether and affirms the "purity" of the natural order. The novel concludes: "It was a brilliant night, all star-shine, and overhead the Great Bear and his
thirty-seven thousand virgins kept her company" (141). Cowan reads:
"Purity has been restored to both Lou and the wilderness, as the allusion
to 'virgins' suggests."[52] A less moralistic and more ironic reading, however,
would connect the dots of the constellation so as to inscribe Lou's erotic
experiences, suggesting that though the thirty-seven thousand may still be
"virgins"—in a technical sense—they may well have, like Lou, enjoyed ursine cunnilingus. Significantly, whether one is judging virgins or landscapes, "purity" is valued as a blank, mindless space, the background for
the subject's erection. Rather than reading the scene in which the bear refuses to penetrate Lou as a long-awaited construction of a barrier between
human and animal, nature and culture, one can instead read it as a parody
of phallic centrality, deflating the "great cock" that was "majestically . . .
rising" (155).[53]

Though the situated knowledges enacted by Lou and the bear blur the
bounds between subject and object—thereby radically challenging the
category of nature—they also warn against the total collapse of boundaries between subjects. Lou, in the midst of her passion for the bear,
grasps for a kind of unity with him in a series of lyrical invocations: "Bear,
take me to the bottom of the ocean with you, bear, swim with me, bear,

put your arms around me, enclose me, swim, down, down, down with me. Bear, make me comfortable in your world at last. Give me your skin. Bear, I want nothing but this from you" (112). Of course, when applied to a bear these invocations parody the enthralled desire to be engulfed by the lover. This passage seems to reveal the danger zone or necessary limits of the metaphor of love as a feminist epistemology: romantic enthrallment has not only been destructive for women, but, paradoxically, if two entities become one through love, the relationship is no longer situated because it is no longer truly relational. Ascending to a singularity which ignores the "material/semiotic" actions of the "known," such a unity forfeits any sense of objectivity. If "objectivity" is about "intersubjectivity,"[54] objectivity requires more than one subject. Lou's plea "Give me your skin. Bear, I want nothing but this from you" reverberates with irony: her love, seemingly so different from the usual human responses to bears, would reduce him to just another familiar ursine icon—a bear skin (rug).[55]

What, in the end, does Lou finally know about the bear? Perhaps this is the wrong question to ask. In *Gender Trouble,* Judith Butler explains how such questions are themselves generated by the epistemology of distance: "The language of appropriation, instrumentality, and distanciation germane to the epistemological mode also belongs to a strategy of domination that pits the 'I' against an 'Other' and, once that separation is effected, creates an artificial set of questions about the knowability and recoverability of that Other."[56] Lou seems to reject the "artificial set of questions" about the bear as Other when she relinquishes Cary's notes on bears: "Over her collection of Cary's notes she hesitated. . . . But in the end, she put them in an envelope and left them in the desk drawer marked 'Cary's notes on bears.' She did not need them anymore" (139). More telling, perhaps, is the way in which she comes to describe the bear: "lover, God or friend. Dog too, for when she put her hand out he licked and nuzzled it" (134). Even though describing the bear in these familiar words may be like putting him in pyjamas, naming him in contradictory terms allows him to escape being circumscribed into a limiting definition, underscoring the extent to which he cannot be known. As Holler explains, it is impossible to know the "thing-in-itself" because there is no such thing—"[a]ll things stand in relationship to each other."[57] "Lover," "God," "friend," even "dog" are terms that do not define the bear in itself, but instead describe the relations that Lou has with the bear, terms that embody situational knowledges that Lou and the bear mutually enact. Her enthrallment transforms Lou, dramatizing that situated knowledges cannot be predetermined— because if there is no subject/object divide, then the very process of coming into knowledge will alter the knower. The openness of the "subject" to transformation by the "object" of knowledge discourages the presumption of mastery and domination.

As they enact feminist epistemologies and situated knowledges, *Bear* and the Xenogenesis Trilogy disrupt Enlightenment dualisms that have been complicit in the domination of nature, women, and racially marked others. Thus feminist epistemologies, operating at a crucial intersection between feminism and environmental philosophy, can work deconstructively to dislodge both "woman" and "nature" from their denigrated positions. Susan J. Hekman, however, sounds an important warning about the roots of some feminist epistemologies, that, she argues, "reif[y] the nature/culture dichotomy."

> All of the theorists who argue for a distinctive feminist standpoint appeal in some way to woman's special relationship to nature to ground the feminist epistemology that they advance. The contradiction in this position should be obvious: they are appealing to women's special relationship to nature to advance an epistemology that is intended to counter Enlightenment epistemology, an epistemology that rests on the association between women and nature.[58]

Whether feminist standpoint theorists appeal to "woman's special relationship with nature," depends, of course, on the theorist.[59] While I think Hekman has reason to be wary of theoretical formulations built on a supposed closeness between woman and nature, feminist epistemologies can construct alliances with nature that in no way depend on some sort of "natural" connections. The Xenogenesis Trilogy, for example, by inventing a third sex and another species to embody its epistemology, eludes the associations between nature, women, and racially marked others even as it promotes ways of knowing that do not deny the "being of the world." Similarly, in *Bear* the epistemological/romantic drama and the resulting situated knowledges are possible precisely because Lou does *not* presume any special affinity with or understanding of bears. If she were some sort of ursine Earth Mother to begin with there would be no story.[60] Because women have not been authorized as subjects or as knowers, there is a possibility that they will formulate different ways of being and knowing.[61] As Holler asserts, "it is no accident that having lived on the object side of the subject/object dichotomy, women would emphasize the subject inherent in the object."[62] By emphasizing the subject in the object, feminist epistemologies radically reconceptualize the very category of nature.

In *Bear*, for example, nature is no longer an entity-to-be-dominated—

no longer *female,* in other words. And indeed, the bear is male. But to say that is to say too much—or too little—for the fact that it is a woman who heads off to the wilderness on an epistemological quest reverberates gender trouble. To gender the subject female and to portray nature as male reverses the gender dynamics of wilderness tales and epistemological paradigms, "jamming the theoretical machinery itself."[63] Such reversals unmoor the ground of gender, as various creatures shuttle between male and female: Homer, the caretaker of the estate, expected that Lou would be a man; for most of the book Lou and the reader mistakenly believe that the last Colonel Cary was male; the "indubitably male" bear (35) is referred to as a "large hipped woman," a mother, and a housewife; and it is unclear whether the Great Bear constellation is accompanied by "*her* children" or "*his* thirty-seven thousand virgins" (70, 141, emphasis added). This gender play suggests the potential for feminist epistemologies to function deconstructively, as gender is destabilized by the heretofore oxymoronic position of "female knower." Thus, *Bear* and the Xenogenesis Trilogy demonstrate that feminist epistemologies and situated knowledges can dislodge gendered dualisms—even as they "play nature" transgressively and transformatively, embodying knowledges that refuse to distance, denigrate, or objectify the natural world.

Postmodern Natures

Though it may seem odd to discuss Leslie Marmon Silko's *Ceremony,* Gerald Vizenor's *Bearheart,* and Jane Rule's *Desert of the Heart* in the same section, racism and heterosexism have mapped "nature"—in revealingly contradictory ways—so as to make it an extremely difficult place for both Native Americans and lesbians to inhabit. Lesbians and gays have long been denounced as "unnatural," and thus, paradoxically, unfit for culture. Native Americans, on the other hand, have been systematically killed and culturally assaulted on the grounds that they are "too natural": "Because the Indian occupied large areas of land, he was considered a wild animal."[64] Because discourses of "nature" and the "natural" have been used to both validate and oppress, to celebrate and to denigrate, writing against this matrix demands complex tactics. Leslie Marmon Silko's *Ceremony* and Gerald Vizenor's *Bearheart* do not distance native cultures from the nature that has been used to denigrate them, but instead, represent nature from within their own traditions; such representations are consonant with "postmodern" natures that possess agency, transgress the divide between nature and culture, and dwell in an already politicized space. Jane Rule's *Desert of the Heart* also represents nature as a political place as it works to deconstruct the normative heterosexism of the "natural" in order to forge an alliance with a nature that is not hostile to lesbianism.

James Applewhite denounces postmodernism for treating nature as an "object of contempt."[65] However, a constellation of philosophy, ethics, environmental science, and feminist theory embraces postmodernism (one that departs from rather than extends modernism), epistemologically enriching and ethically enhancing environmental philosophy. Such postmodern natures echo Native American conceptions which, as Paula Gunn Allen explains, characterize the earth as "aware, palpable, intelligent, alive" and reject the notion that nature is an "inert resource" or "ever-dead other" located "somewhere over there while humanity is over here or that a great hierarchical ladder of being exists on which ground and trees occupy a very low rung, animals a slightly higher one, and man (never woman)—especially 'civilized' man—a very high one indeed."[66] Gilles Deleuze and Felix Guattari's provocative *A Thousand Plateaus* contests the "great hierarchical ladder" that Allen describes by playing out concepts such as rhizomes, strata, and assemblages that not only toss together the psychological, philosophical, and economic, but intrepidly ignore divisions between human life and nonhuman nature. The copious discussions of biological and geological phenomena in *A Thousand Plateaus*— not the usual fare for critical theorists—stand not as overcoded metaphors that illuminate aspects of humanity but as maps to another ontology and epistemology that refuse to demarcate distinctions between human and nonhuman. *A Thousand Plateaus* enacts an ecological view that stresses complex patterns of connection rather than binaries, "taproots with a more multiple, lateral, and circular system of ramification, rather than a dichotomous one."[67]

In order to evade the system of dichotomies that has produced nature as an inert, mindless mass, postmodern approaches to science stress the agency and even the consciousness of almost all forms of nature. Rupert Sheldrake, for example, proposes that the "laws of nature" be understood as *habits* that organisms have "inherited or acquired."[68] David Ray Griffin explains that "overcoming the subject/object dualism involves the attribution of other essential features of subjects, such as feeling, memory, and aim or decision, at least in embryonic form, all the way down" through bats, bees, bacteria, DNA—even to the atom itself.[69] Similarly, Carolyn

Merchant argues that nature is not an unchanging backdrop against which history plays out its drama, but an actor in its own right:

> Nonhuman nature, therefore, is not passive, but an active complex that participates in change over time and responds to human-induced change . . . The relation between human beings and the nonhuman world is thus reciprocal. Humans adapt to nature's environmental conditions; but when humans alter their surroundings, nature responds through ecological changes.[70]

Merchant's sound, even commonsensical argument makes it difficult to imagine nature as anything other than an actor. Merchant's philosophy is especially compelling because it recognizes that nature is a "human construct and a representation" while insisting that it is, at the same time, "a real, autonomous agent."[71] Characterizing nature as an agent, however, does not entail collapsing all differences between human and nonhuman nature. As Val Plumwood argues, we need theories (like Merchant's) that recognize the agency of the world but which "do not show disrespect for the otherness of nature by inscribing that agency with the cast of the conscious human mind."[72]

Donna Haraway's work radically recasts nature, releasing it from its subordinate role in the nature/culture dichotomy without ascribing a human consciousness to it. Haraway, in ever more innovative ways, disrupts the dichotomies between subject and object, knower and known, which have undergirded the domination of women, people of color, and nature. She stresses the positioned, partial perspective of the knower (as the previous section discusses), the agency of the known, and the "artifactualism" of nature. Nature is artifactual in the sense that even nature is something made, not something existing "out there" in some essential, eternal, and exploitable form. Even though the "artifactualism" of nature could be criticized as the ultimate in appropriation, in that it becomes just another product of culture, Haraway explains that nature is made, "but not entirely by humans; it is a co-construction among humans and nonhumans," which makes it a generative force, not a passive resource.[73] In order to portray nature's agency in ways that neither encapsulate it within models of human subjectivity nor perpetuate the nature/culture divide, Haraway encodes humans and nonhumans as "material-semiotic" actors. A "world full of cacophonous agencies," an "unquiet multitude of nonhumans,"[74] nature becomes "social," or, in William Bevis's terms, "urban." Bevis, explaining why "Welch's deer talk like philosophers in a Paris cafe," argues that Native Americans portray nonhuman nature as "humanlike beings," which are "apparently semiologists."[75] Along with Deleuze and Guattari, who contend that "not only do plants and animals, orchids and wasps, sing or express themselves, but so do rocks and even rivers, every stratified thing on earth,"[76] Haraway and Bevis characterize nature as a signifying force, not a blank slate awaiting the inscription of culture.

Indeed, nature can speak back to culture, not only shaping but helping to generate the stories we tell. Jim Cheney, for example, argues against totalizing discourse which "assimilates the world" to itself, and for a contextualizing discourse that "assimilates language to the situation": "For a genuinely contextualist ethic to include the land, the land must *speak* to us; we must stand in *relation* to it; it must *define* us, and we it."[77] Silko, in her letters to James Wright, supports Cheney's perspective: "[A]fter all, the stories grow out of the land as much as we see ourselves as having emerged from the land."[78] Arnold Krupat, on the other hand, has underlined the dangers of seeing Native American literatures as emerging from the land. He argues that attempts to include Native American literature in the canon were based, "mistakenly, to be sure, yet powerfully, nonetheless—on an appeal to the 'naturalness' of this literature, as though it was not the individuals and cultural practices but the very rocks and trees and rivers that had somehow produced the Native poem or story, and somehow spoke directly in them."[79] Certainly, when placed within a Western framework that divorces nature from culture, such a depiction of Native American literatures no doubt diminishes their artistry and denies their cultural genesis. Yet Krupat's comments immobilize Native American literatures within the very conception of nature that they have the potential to dismantle. For if Euro-American culture has petrified "Indians" by imaging them as indistinguishable from nature, the Native American stories that grow out of the land counter such moves by resisting them at their core—by demonstrating that nature is neither silent nor inert. Another compelling reason for Native American texts to foreground nature is that, as Gail Guthrie Valaskakis has argued, the Native American relationship with the land gives them a politically potent distinguishing "difference": it is "the basis for an Indian ideology that is their most effective political resource in negotiations with each other and the state."[80] Infused with this very "difference," Leslie Marmon Silko's *Ceremony* and Gerald Vizenor's *Bearheart* insist on the material and semiotic significance of nature. By dramatizing the agency, signifying power, and artifactualism of nature—a nature that is in no way severed from culture—*Ceremony* and *Bearheart* elude romanticized, tragic depictions that fossilize tribal cultures along with nonhuman nature.

Ceremony begins with a mystery—a mystery that unravels into webs of convergences. Tayo, fighting in World War II, somehow thinks a Japanese soldier is his uncle Josiah: "Tayo started screaming because it wasn't a Jap, it was Josiah, eyes shrinking back into the skull and all their shining black light glazed over by death." Rocky, his cousin, explains to him: "[I]t was impossible for the dead man to be Josiah, because Josiah was an old Laguna man, thousands of miles from the Philippine jungles and Japanese armies."[81]

The solution to this mysterious connection between the Laguna and the Japanese, the jungle and the desert is, at once, mythical and political.[82] One of the poetic segments of *Ceremony* tells how witches from many tribes had a contest, demonstrating their powers. The final witch merely tells a story—a story that will begin to happen as it is told. The witch tells of white-skinned people for whom "the world is a dead thing." "The[y] fear the world. / They destroy what they fear" (135). After they kill animals, poison the earth, and decimate many tribes, they find, in "these hills" their final weapon: "they will find the rocks, / rocks with veins of green and yellow and black. / They will lay the final pattern with these rocks / they will lay it across the world / and explode everything" (137). Nature, in this tale, is hardly a utopian, inviolate space. The tale describes the rocks—both in a mythic past and in an apocalyptic future—as "the final pattern" that "will lay . . . across the world / and explode everything." Although we receive this petrifying tale in the middle of the novel, Tayo does not understand its implications until near the end, when he understands how the mythic tale has manifest itself in the geopolitical landscape that surrounds him.

> And the top-secret laboratories where the bomb had been created were deep in the Jemez Mountains, on land the Government took from Cochiti Pueblo: Los Alamos, only a hundred miles northeast of him now, still surrounded by high electric fences and the ponderosa pine and tawny sandrock of the Jemez mountain canyon where the shrine of the twin mountain lions had always been. There was no end to it; it knew no boundaries; and he had arrived at the point of convergence where the fate of all living things, and even the earth, had been laid. From the jungles of his dreaming he recognized why the Japanese voices had merged with Laguna voices, with Josiah's voice and Rocky's voice; the lines of cultures and worlds were drawn in flat dark lines on fine light sand, converging in the middle of witchery's final ceremonial sand painting. (245–56)

This unnerving epiphany powerfully represents the "convergence where the fate of all living things, and even the earth, had been laid." Merging voices and converging lines of sand synchronize human expressivity with material, geographic markings. The complexity and intensity of this place insists on the contextualized ethic that Cheney describes: "[T]he land must *speak* to us; we must stand in *relation* to it; it must *define* us, and we it." Even to say the land must define us, however, distinguishes between the land and the people, which leads us astray from the way in which "the lines of cultures and worlds" are both drawn in sand.[83] As Edith Swan explains, " 'people' and 'place' " are "coterminous" as "[s]trands forming the interconnective tissue of relationships pull on the logical arrangement of the universe, and on Laguna symbolic geography."[84] As an artifactual place, the land has been created, in part, by Native American cultures, since the "tawny sandrock of the Jemez mountain canyon" is "where the shrine of the twin mountain lions had always been." This place, however, is mapped not only by the symbolic geography of the Lagunas, but by the U.S. military-industrial complex, making it a nature that cannot be thought of as an escape from culture, especially since the beginnings of the most destructive force of civilization reside here. Thus the land is not a space apart, nor a mere resource for culture, but a signifying topos, molded by cultural and historical forces but also shaping the patterns of voices, the lines of sand. Though Silko has criticized postmodernism for its self-referential language, which shimmers because "no history or politics intrudes to muddy" it, I would characterize this depiction of the land as postmodern precisely because it is "muddied" by history and politics.[85] "Nature" here—if it can even be termed that—is, in Haraway's terms, "effected in the interactions among material-semiotic actors, human and not."[86]

Various human and nonhuman actors play a role in the central drama of the novel—Tayo's quest to reclaim his stolen cattle. This drama quite effectively acts out a struggle between opposing conceptions of nature. Demonstrating that stories conjure reality, the Herefords, bred by white scientists according to their notions of what an "ideal cow" should be, embody Western notions of nature as mindless and inert—a "dead thing." When "a windmill broke down or a pool went dry," the "white-face Herefords" would not look for water themselves but would stand there waiting—some would even die, "still waiting" (79). Unlike these scientifically bred cattle that were too long separated from the land, as Josiah tells us, the Mexican cattle are resourceful, willful, and determined, breaking through fences as they head south. Thus, when Tayo reclaims his cattle, he is also reclaiming a Pueblo conception of nature, a conception that does not evacuate nature of mind or agency.[87] Indeed, the novel dramatizes the agency of nature when the mountain lion and the land itself become Tayo's allies, helping him to steal back the cattle. As he is hunting for his cattle, Tayo sprinkles "pinches of yellow pollen into the four footprints" of the mountain lion and thinks "Mountain lion, the hunter. Mountain lion, the hunter's helper" (196). Later, cowboys capture Tayo for "trespassing," but they free him when they find mountain lion tracks and are eager to hunt the cat. The freshly falling snow then covers the mountain lion's tracks, saving it from the cowboys' guns (205). Remarkably, even the shape of the land itself, a certain arroyo that traps cattle, helps Tayo in his ceremony of reclamation (210). The mountain lion, the snow, and the arroyo act as Tayo's allies. Tayo's ceremony, then, performs a Pueblo conception of nature against a "white face" one. As a "praxis-like activity,"[88] the ceremony wages a struggle that is both semiotic and material, for the Mexican cattle that Tayo reclaims not only embody a Pueblo, as opposed to a "white face," conception of nature, but also serve as a metonym of stolen Indian lands: "The spotted cattle wouldn't be lost any more, scattered though his dreams, driven by his hesitation to admit they had been stolen, that the land—all of it—had been stolen from them" (192). In an artifactual land, always already striated by struggles, ceremonies need political muscle.

The oppositional strength of the Mexican cattle becomes especially important in the context of how the novel genders nature.[89] In "The Feminine Landscape of *Ceremony*," Allen explains that the symbolism in *Ceremony* leads back to the "universal feminine principle of creation," Thought Woman. Although Allen explains that Thought Woman's acts of intellectual creation distinguish her from a mindless, Western Earth Mother, Allen's interpretation of the novel casts Ts'eh (an embodiment of Thought Woman) as somewhat stereotypically feminine, arguing that it is Ts'eh's "loving that heals Tayo, that and his willingness to take up her tasks of nurturing the plant and beast people she loves."[90] Yet Ts'eh does not inhabit a feminine realm divorced from political struggle. It is while Tayo makes love with her that he dreams of reclaiming the cattle. More significantly, she is the one who, with the help of the arroyo, actually captures the cattle for Tayo. Furthermore, as Edith Swan has demonstrated, Ts'eh is herself associated with the cattle through her "antelope aspects" and through her last name, Montaño, which is a colloquial term for "the summer range for grazing livestock along the higher plateaus of Mount Taylor.["][91] Dwelling within a Pueblo nature, the novel resists readings by which a feminine nature is taken to mean something mystical and removed from political significance, as it weaves Ts'eh to the strong-willed Mexican cattle and the contested land, creating a ceremony to remap both the conceptual and geographical terrain of nature.

Unlike Silko, Vizenor has close ties with postmodernism. In the introduction to *Narrative Chance: Postmodern Discourse on Native American Indian Literatures,* Vizenor argues that postmodernism can free tribal fictions from their reduction into "objective" cultural representations, "consumable cultural artifacts," and paralyzing narratives of tragedy.[92] Simultaneously a trickster tale and postmodern novel, *Bearheart* exemplifies Vizenor's view of the trickster as quintessentially tribal and postmodern. The rollicking and raunchy comedy waves away any whiff of a tragic narrative, while the novel's unruly episodic form eludes narrative control as it tosses from spectacle to startling spectacle.

The dystopian *Bearheart* portrays a United States in which environmental devastation leads to the collapse of civilization. As "tribes" of "white savages" and genetic mutants roam the country searching for food, the novel follows the journey of Proude Cedarfair, who "understood the language of cedar and learned to trust the voices of the crows. He became the rhythm of cedar trees and birds."[93] Standing in stark contrast to the dominant white culture's denigration of nature, Proude Cedarfair is able to decipher and merge with nonhuman creatures. The novel's postmodern, trickster-like representation of nature, however, wards off tragic or patronizing links between Native Americans and nature. Proude Cedarfair's transformations into birds and other creatures, for example, hardly fossilize him, but instead, allow him to move in a multiplicity of directions and beings, helping him to dodge government agents. The "cosmically erotic," "mythically connected"[94] sexual relations between Lilith Mae and her gang of boxer dogs transgress boundaries between humans and nature, as does the girl who gives birth to puppies. Nature's agency also muddies the boundaries between humans and nature. Crows teach a girl how to care for herself. Other "clown crows" "swooped down and dropped white excrement" on the soldiers that terrorize the circus pilgrims. This excremental attack even ends in a parodic inquisition regarding the agency of nature: " 'Did you tell those crows to shit?' 'No.' 'Then who did?' 'No one.' 'For the last time . . . Tell us who caused this?' 'The crows . . . Crows are not told what to do . . .' 'The crows have their own power.' "[95]

Metamorphosis, bestiality, and the antics of crows comically commingle human and nonhuman creatures, reveling in their energy, activity, and perpetual motion. "Terminal creeds," on the other hand, lock nature and Indians into a static, tragic condition. In a novel simmering with satire, some of the fiercest condemnation is aimed at a character named Belladonna, who preaches to the hunters and breeders how the Native American view of nature is superior to the white view.

> "Well, as I was explaining, tribal people are closer to the earth, the meaning and energies of the woodlands and mountains and plains . . . We are not competitive because we share our lives and dreams and use little from the earth . . ."
>
> ". . . My blood moves in the circles of mother earth and through dreams without time. My tribal blood is timeless and it gives me strength to live and deal with evil . . . "
>
> "Right on sister, right on," said the hunter with the trigger finger on his ear." (191–92)

The hunter's slangy response deflates Belladonna's worn-out rhetoric. While there certainly is truth to Belladonna's sermon, the truths have become rigid, the language clichéd. As one hunter responds, "Who gathers around them the frail hopes and febrile dreams and tarnished mother earth words?" (194).

The hunters and breeders who have objected to Belladonna's preaching begin to cheer her on, because

> . . . when questions are unanswered and there is no humor the messages become terminal creeds, and the good hunters and breeders here seek nothing that is terminal . . . So the questioners become celebrants when there is nothing more to learn. Terminal creeds are terminal diseases and when death is inevitable celebration is the best expression.
>
> Here come the sugar cookies. (193)

Poisoned by the cookies, Belladonna receives her just desserts. The fact that the "questioners become celebrants when there is nothing more to learn" criticizes affirmations that foreclose questioning. Belladonna's terminal creeds may allude to ecofeminism, especially since Belladonna was raped by white men, and the parallel "rape" of women and the earth has become a stock ecofeminist motif. Thus Vizenor satirizes ecofeminist celebrations of nature that are emotive, mystifying, and more importantly, that shut off questioning, debate, and comedy. He warns that terminal creeds, caught up in a tragic narrative, lead to terminal ends. One reason Belladonna's Earth Mother terminal creeds are so poisonous is that they can be too easily appropriated by capitalist America. As if acting out a Hawaiian travel ad, Belladonna slips a beaded necklace over the head of a bald banker, graciously giving away a metonym of Indian culture. But even more to the point, such "tarnished mother earth words," are terminal because they are *dead* serious; they deny nature its own wily, unpredictable, trickster agency.

While Belladonna's valorizations of nature are satirized as victimizing terminal creeds, it seems that the male, Proude Cedarfair, is allowed to achieve an unparodied relation with nature: He "understood the language of cedar and learned to trust the voices of the crows. He became the rhythm of cedar trees and birds. Silence and the languages of animals gave him power" (13). One could read the language here as clichéd, like Belladonna's, but it seems to have more beauty and dignity than hers. Furthermore, at the end of the novel, Proude Cedarfair and Inawa Biwide ascend, as bears, into the fourth world while Rosina and Sister Eternal Flame watch from the sidelines: "[T]he two women heard the bears roaring again ha ha haaaa. In seconds, faster than birds could soar, the bears roared from the four directions ha ha ha haaaa" (241). Belladonna is cast in a satiric tragedy, while Proude Cedarfair parades through a grand comic adventure. Is *Bearheart*'s masculinist politics of nature motivated by a belief that the overdetermined nexus of woman-native-nature is doomed to exploitation and reification, or by a male desire to reappropriate and exclude women from a source of power?

Whereas the more mythic *Ceremony* reaffirms the connections between nature and the feminine, *Bearheart* parodies those connections. Despite this important divergence, *Ceremony* and *Bearheart* show some striking similarities. Both apocalyptically warn of environmental catastrophe, both emphasize the power and centrality of nature without essentializing it, romanticizing it, or otherwise relegating it to a position somewhere else. Silko's *Ceremony* and Vizenor's *Bearheart* represent nature as an active, yet always already acted on, force. These novels embody Native American conceptions of nature that parallel postmodernist formulations.

While for most feminist theory and politics "nature" is a problematic terrain because of the historically entrenched discourses that bind woman to nature, for lesbian feminism the territory is more complex. As women, lesbians can be encoded or can identify themselves as "close" to nature, but, as queers, they have been denigrated as "unnatural." It is hardly sufficient to say that discourses of the "natural" have been invoked to uphold heteronormativity as an ideal, since the "natural" no doubt circulates *as* an ideal to a large extent *because* it is so thoroughly infused with heteronormativity. Moreover, as a bludgeon of heteronormativity, "the natural" is hardly intended as a loose expression but rather as a direct citing of the laws of "nature itself." And what nature intended, of course, is "reprosexuality": "the interweaving of heterosexuality, biological reproduction, cultural reproduction, and personal identity."[96] Rather than critiquing the re-prosexuality inscribed upon nature, some ecofeminism has, as Catriona Sandilands points out, promoted profoundly heterosexual metaphors "in which reproduction, in its narrowest sense, is often located as the 'apex' of woman's connection to nature."[97] This leaves little room for queer, green places, and, in fact, much queer theory, literature, and politics takes place in the big city and, understandably, repudiates all notions of "the nat-ural."[98] Bonnie Zimmerman argues that despite the historical trajectory of much gay literature, which has "endorse[d] the move from the country to the city," "the ecological and feminist movements of the 1960s and 70s" in-fluenced the development of a counter-novel: "The country was glorified, and lesbian novels became imbued with a profound pastoralism." Novels such as Sally Gearheart's *Wanderground,* for example, "affirm the natural-ness of lesbianism by claiming . . . that women have a special tie with nature."[99]

Jane Rule's *Desert of the Heart* makes no such direct claims for a female bond with nature. It attempts, rather, to "queer nature," which, in Sandi-land's terms "is a process by which all relations to nature become de-naturalized, by which we question the ways in which we are located in na-ture, by which we question the uses to which 'nature' has been put."[100] The very first paragraph of the novel queers nature by tugging upon the many strands tying it to marriage.

> Conventions, like clichés, have a way of surviving their own usefulness. They are then excused or defended as the idioms of living. For every-one, foreign by birth or by nature, convention is a mark of fluency. That is why, for any woman, marriage is the idiom of life. And she does not give it up out of scorn or indifference but only when she is forced to ad-mit that she has never been able to pronounce it properly and has com-mitted continually its grossest grammatical errors. For such a woman marriage remains a foreign tongue, an alien landscape, and, since she cannot become naturalized, she finally chooses voluntary exile.[101]

Just as "idiom," "the manner of expression which is natural or peculiar" to a language, juxtaposes the natural with the strange, these musings suggest the unnaturalness inherent within the natural. Marriage, as a "landscape," is no more natural than a "foreign tongue," especially since it remains ever "alien." Paradoxically, to become "naturalized" to marriage means going against one's nature, becoming socialized into a particular idiom that oth-ers accept as natural. This passage complicates the natural to such a de-gree that it can no longer serve as the bedrock of heterosexuality. The novel undertakes an even more complicated project. As Evelyn, the protagonist, exiles herself from the "alien landscape" of marriage by traveling to the alien landscape of the desert and her first lesbian relationship, the novel, in a sense, (de)naturalizes the desert, transforming nature into a space for lesbian desire.[102]

This is quite an undertaking, since, as much of the novel suggests, lesbian desire flouts all that is deemed natural. Ann Childs, the young woman Evelyn falls in love with, for example, revels in her freedom from nature. Ann, who works in a casino making change, explains why she has chosen such a physically exhausting job:

> Why did she do it? At the center of this desert industry, symbol of it, she wanted to take her place, for there was no nature. The apes could not have survived. Only man could have invented a living independent of earth, related to no physical need, yet satisfying them all. Out of his own nonanimal nature, he had found a weakness, a faith by which he could survive. Ann was novice to her world's only passionate belief. She moved from station to station, to serve and to witness. (94)

Despite Ann's nunlike devotion to an industry that has seemingly transcended the need for nature, her vocation demands that she endure the most "natural" suffering of women—pregnancy.

> She strapped her [change] apron very high, carrying it like a fetus in its seventh month, careful to lift and turn the weight as if it were her own flesh, for she had to walk some distance with it, and maneuver on and off escalators, her back burning, the veins in her legs aching with the drag of sixty pounds of dead weight: the ironic emancipation of woman, martyred to nothing but her own belligerence surely. (94)

This passage plays out Judith Butler's observation that "gender practices within gay and lesbian cultures often thematize 'the natural' in parodic contexts that bring into relief the performative construction of an original and true sex."[103] Despite Ann's belief in the liberating effects of a culture "independent from the earth," the casino—her cathedral of unfettered freedom—demands that she strap on a sixty-pound fetus-like weight. This parody of pregnancy, staged in a garishly unnatural environment, demonstrates that neither biology nor nature is the cause of women's oppression, since, as Wittig notes, "what we take for the cause or origin of oppression is in fact only the mark imposed by the oppressor."[104] Furthermore, this scene undercuts Ann's antinature stance by demonstrating that the nature she is fleeing from, like the change apron she straps on, is certainly a cultural construction.

Even as the novel parodies "the natural," it opens a space for a queer nature by disarticulating nature from a reproductive telos. As Ann and Evelyn discuss the desert, damnation, and fertility, Ann shifts the ground of the argument by reversing the valences of the terms. Their debate plays off the trajectories of lesbian novels, the "dying fall, a narrative of damnation, of the lesbian's suffering as a lonely outcast" and the "enabling escape, a narrative of the reversal of such descending trajectories."[105] Evelyn echoes the narratives of damnation or escape, while Ann, by boldly preferring damnation to salvation, refuses to be trapped by these conventions.

"The desert frightens me, I think. It looks too much like the seventh circle of hell. I'm afraid of damnation."

"Why?"

"Why?" Evelyn repeated, peering at Ann from behind her hand. She lay back again and closed her eyes. "I don't know. I've always supposed everyone is."

"Well, they're not. I, for instance, am a hell of a lot more frightened of being saved."

Evelyn chuckled.

"I'm serious," Ann protested. "Virtue smells to me of rotting vegetation. Here you burn or freeze. Either way it's clean."

"Sterile," Evelyn said and felt the word a laceration of her own flesh.

"I wonder. It's fertility that's a dirty word for me."

"Is it?"

"Yes, I'm terrified of giving in, of justifying my own existence by means of simple reproduction. So many people do or try to. And there are the children, so unfulfilling after all. And they grow up to do nothing but reproduce children who will reproduce, everyone's so busy reproducing that there's no time to produce anything. But it's such a temptation. It seems so natural—another dirty word for me. What's the point?" (107)

On a psychological level, debating the desert allows the women to discuss lesbianism without confronting it directly. More significantly, however, this passage forges a space for a queer nature, both by making the ideological trio of salvation, reproduction, and the natural the "dirty words," and by counterposing them to the desert, a nature that is—magnificently—not fecund.

Even though "natural" is a dirty word for Ann, the novel does not simply espouse an antinature stance. Nature, in fact, has been an important setting for lesbian love scenes, which take place "in the arms of Mother

Nature," according to Zimmerman, in order to insist on "the naturalness of lesbianism." More specifically, the "liquidity of oral sex" and the "connection between water and rebirth" lead to the ubiquity of water imagery in lesbian fiction.[106] Setting a pivotal erotic scene near water, Rule insists that this nature is not a "fertile" place. Evelyn, wary of this alien landscape, "wanted Ann to turn the car around and drive back to Reno, which, alien and hostile as it might be, was at least human. There was no way Evelyn could comprehend this unnatural, dead body of water, still, killing, blue" (104). Evelyn may be projecting her own culturally acquired fears of lesbianism onto the landscape in which her love for Ann has been staged. Yet at the same time, this description of the lake decisively rids it of any connection with reproduction—it is not only "dead," but "still, killing, [and] blue."

The narrative traces Evelyn's parallel responses to the desert and to Ann, from fear to a loving acceptance of both. At the lake, Evelyn "watched Ann wade out for the bottle of wine, that young, beautiful body she had so carefully admired an hour ago to take her mind off the terrors of the landscape. Its sudden erotic power bewildered and offended her" (109). Although Evelyn seeks solace from the "terrors of the landscape" in Ann's body, the erotic power of her body then upsets Evelyn, associating her fear of lesbianism with the fear of the landscape. Ann, too, seems to draw parallels between Evelyn's feelings toward the desert and her feelings toward their relationship: "Ann watched Evelyn look out over the near sage into the far space of the evening, the desert already in the shadow of the great mountains, and she hoped she could read in Evelyn's face some new awareness of the freedom and the peace of this still, unpeopled earth" (153). This passage links the desert with their relationship since "freedom" is crucial to Ann's sexuality. Finally, through Ann, Evelyn comes to accept the desert: "Being with Ann, Evelyn found it hard to remember what it was in the desert that had so terrified and appalled her" (166). Nature does not serve as a mere "objective correlative" for the women's relationship. The fact that nature is experienced via the body of Ann, the face of Evelyn, and Evelyn's "being with Ann" suggests instead that their desire actually drives the embrace of the desert as a "natural" but queer place.

By the end of the novel, Evelyn finally tells Ann, "Nothing else I've ever known has been as right and as natural as loving you" (214). Within the discourse of the novel, the word "natural" has become disarticulated from its heterosexist assumptions, so that Evelyn can use it to describe her love for Ann and Rule can claim nature as a lesbian space. The novel does not depict a lesbian pastoral that celebrates women as closer to nature; rather, it makes "gender trouble" by the "mobilization" and "subversive confusion" of the category of the "natural."[107] Gillian Spraggs condemns Evelyn's reclamation of the natural as a gesture of bad faith, arguing that "to refer lesbian desire and sexuality to the realm of 'nature' cannot help in defining a context for lesbian relationship within society."[108] But it can. Because "nature" and the "natural" have functioned as the ground for heterosexism, it is crucial for lesbians to combat these notions and to redefine nature as a queer, green place. Evelyn's lesbian desire and the "sterile" desert landscape become "natural" only through discursive subversion, deconstruction, and rearticulation, demonstrating that, paradoxically, "naturalization," is a mode of cultural work.

Although Kruger's photo declares, "We won't play nature to your culture," playing nature is an indispensable mode of feminist cultural critique, a mode of resistance to the "natures" that have been waged against women. Playing nature allows feminists to shift the discursive terrain of nature and the natural, opening up spaces for feminist articulations. Despite the fact that "woman" and "nature" are still an extremely volatile combination—especially when the "woman" is racially marked—*Song of Solomon*, the Xenogenesis Trilogy, *Bear, Ceremony*, and *Desert of the Heart* demonstrate the possibilities for radically recasting nature as a more hospitable ground for human and nonhuman life.

Chapter Seven: Cyborgs, Whale Tails, and the Domestication of Environmentalism

Gaia is a tough bitch—a system that has worked for over three billion years without people.

Lynn Margulis

The contemporary fictions of the last chapter "play nature" as a mode of cultural critique, recasting nature across the expanse of space that narrative allows. Even as they write nature as a feminist space, such texts as *Song of Solomon, Bear, Desert of the Heart,* and the Xenogenesis Trilogy avoid portraying nature as female. Indeed, several of these texts represent nature as a site that destabilizes rigid notions of gender and sexuality. The question remains, however, whether environmentalism, feminism, and feminist environmentalism should promote images of female natures or should work toward radically ungendered portrayals. Tracking the ubiquitous and surprisingly protean female natures that circulate through ecofeminism and popular culture helps us to answer this question.[1] Contemporary tropes of nature echo the natures of the preceding chapters— sometimes ironically, sometimes parodically, but always in illuminating ways. By way of a conclusion, then, in this chapter I examine contemporary figures of nature both as they function within the present political landscape and as they descend from the natures of the preceding chapters.

While the overwhelmingly detrimental legacy of connections between "woman" and "nature" would seem to necessitate a complete rejection of any female tropes, the issue is actually more complicated, especially when we consider such forceful feminist figures as Emma Goldman's Mother Earth or Mary Austin's desert mistresses. The very ubiquity of less appealing female natures may necessitate feminist portraits that gender nature—but with a vengeance. In *Rethinking Ecofeminist Politics* Janet Biehl repudiates ecofeminism, in part because of its reliance on metaphors, arguing that metaphors should not found political movements because "one of the functions of a political movement, let alone a radical one, is to explain the world, not to obscure it."[2] I would argue, though, that ethics, politics—indeed, most ways of thinking—are shaped by metaphors. Simply rejecting all metaphors hardly seems an option. As Donna Haraway puts it, "Theoretical work in social movements is often done through figuration—through imagining powerful cultural figures."[3] In a cultural context in which feminized tropes of nature seem unlikely to vanish, we need to understand the political entanglements and the potential force of specific metaphors.[4]

The most persistent figure linking woman and nature, of course, is the inescapable Mother Nature. Despite the fact that environmentalists continue to promote Mother Nature, this figure supports a domestic consumerism that threatens to sever environmentalism from the public sphere. The Mother Nature of an Earth Day television special, for example, neutralizes environmentalist passions by enclosing them within the domestic. The monstrous nature of the film *Habitat* moves in the reverse direction, devouring the domestic from within, suggesting the continued importance of nature as an undomesticated, feminist ground. Like *Habitat*, Susan Griffin's *Woman and Nature* portrays nature as a resistant feminist subject, even if that subject is, at times, rather monolithic. While it is important to formulate such heretical natures against that tedious hausfrau Mother Earth, promoting nongendered tropes is equally, if not more, crucial. Nongendered conceptions of nature are valuable not only for postmodern feminism, but for environmentalism, since they do not reduce nature to a caricatured mirror of human culture. The whale-tail portraits of an environmental group's promotional materials and Donna Haraway's figurations offer provocative models of natures that are not gendered but are nonetheless politically potent.

It's Not Nice to Domesticate Mother Nature

"Love Your Mother," chides a bumper sticker bearing the image of the planet. Catherine Roach, in an extensive analysis of this image, argues that

> it is problematic because of our tendency to relate to our mothers as
> ambivalent love-objects, expected to care for all our needs, and that for

this reason, instead of achieving the desired result of encouraging us toward environmental soundness, this slogan has almost the opposite effect of helping to maintain exploitative patterns toward the earth and mother.[5]

Similarly, Carolyn Merchant warns against reinstating "nature as the mother of humankind."[6] Patrick D. Murphy, in "Sex-Typing the Planet," argues that "sex-typing a gender-free entity" reinscribes a cultural dualism and an "anthropomorphism that *alienates* Earth by trying to render it in our image." Despite the convincing critiques put forth by Merchant in 1980 and Murphy in 1988, female figurations of nature have continued to proliferate, as Murphy himself laments in his 1994 essay, "My Mother's Name is Evelyn, not Gaia."[7] Environmental groups and environmentally oriented small businesses keep Mother Earth in circulation, affixing her to many a mug, T-shirt, poster, and advertisement. While in some ways it is gratifying to see *any* sign of environmentalist consciousness, I would like to reiterate the important warnings posted by Merchant, Murphy, and Roach, and add that portraying the earth as a mother also contributes to a domesticating discourse that is harmful to both women and the environment.

Hardly a direct descendent of Emma Goldman's expansive, resolute, and insurgent Mother Earth, the Mother Nature of a recent Earth Day TV special, played by a floral-crowned Bette Midler, is a whiny, dismissable character. Poor Mother Earth is sick, victimized by humanity.[8] This perfectly selfless mother doesn't really mind that she herself is dying but worries about the people who need her. She is placed in the town hospital and doctored by male physicians. Yet what saves Mother Earth is not medical science, but, lo and behold: capitalist consumers and good housekeepers. The old association between women and the earth is deployed here in a contradictory way. Mother Earth is a near-dead victim, to be saved by commercial capitalism (buying the right products); this echoes Merchant's account of how during the Scientific Revolution "[l]iving animate nature died, while dead inanimate money was endowed with life."[9] The way that the show manages to articulate environmentalism with capitalism supports Hall's explanation of why the right has been more successful than the left in connecting with popular trends: "Their strategy has been to align the positive aspirations of people with the market and the restoration of the capitalist ethic, and to present this as a natural alliance."[10] The Earth Day special not only supports a capitalist ethic, but also a patriarchal one because it portrays the planet as a victimized female and suggests that everyday environmental problem solving is "women's work." Even though the program displays both men and women suggesting environmental solutions, the message of the program—"what you can do at home to save the earth"—places the blame and responsibility on women, who (still) do the majority of the shopping and housecleaning. The program includes several TV families who demonstrate that earth saving is just another domestic chore. For example, the Bundys' bad housekeeper is admonished: "Imagine that your house was the earth. If you just dusted your house once in a while, imagine what the earth could be like." And, as the Cosbys teach us, if we just wouldn't open the lids on stove-top pots and pans, we would save energy, and thus save the earth. Domestic dust and renegade steam cloud our view of more threatening substances such as nuclear waste, chemical runoff, oil spills, and pesticides. Furthermore, these pat, simplistic solutions to systemic problems cast environmentalism as women's work, which not only reinforces women's domestic bondage but also lets corporate and military polluters off the hook.

Ironically, the program opens with Robin Williams as a smarmy Everyman boasting of Man's many great exploits, technologies, and environmental dominations. William's many phallic allusions to missiles and power worship show an awareness of feminist critiques of phallotechnology. The program quickly transforms systemic shortcomings into mere personal failings, however, as Everyman and the industrial polluter who confesses his misdeeds are represented as bad boys who have disappointed their Mother Nature. The industrial polluter explains that the government controls and the system are fine and don't need to be changed—he just has to learn how to behave. Mother Earth is invoked not only in order to cast women and nature as passive victims, but—perhaps even worse—to depict polluters as unruly children, thus making the problem personal and familial instead of political and systemic. It shifts the focus from capitalism to the home and places the blame not on military or corporate polluters, but ultimately on homemakers, who had better keep those pots fully covered.

Just as capitalism can pocket Mother Earth, a conservative environmentalism can embrace the care and nurturing discourse of ecofeminism. Such discourse is problematic in a number of ways. Ariel Salleh, for example, argues that "[u]nlike capitalist patriarchy, which is geared to short-term profits, women's lives straddling the *nature-woman-labor nexus* are embedded in a context of conservation and care."[11] Although Salleh sees women's "conservation and care" as antithetical to capitalist patriarchy, such a formulation not only elides the fact that women in industrialized nations often "care for" their families by acting as consumers (which makes them central to, not outside of capitalism), but it neglects the way in which discourses of nurturing can actually bolster capitalism. In *The Conservator*, the magazine of the Nature Conservancy, the article "Stewardship: Empowering the Land" echoes Salleh's ecofeminism: "Linda Wark may have articulated the leadership role of stewards best when she said, 'stewardship is not only the care and nurturing of natural areas, it's the care and nurturing of volunteers.'"[12] The feminized language supports *The Conservator*'s conservative politics: by alluding to the motherly realms of care and nurturing, it places ecological volunteer work into the separate sphere of the domestic, fencing it off from the public sphere of business, economics, and politics—issues that this organization, partly funded by big business, dares not disturb. Deane Curtin warns that an "ethic of care provides a very important beginning for an ecofeminist ethic, but it runs the risk of having its own aims turned against it unless it is regarded as part of a distinctively feminist political agenda that consciously attempts to expand the circle of caring for."[13] Limiting the realm of caring to the private world leaves government and corporate polluters untouched. If, as Timothy W. Luke contends, "[t]he Nature conservancy 'succeeds' in its own way because it accepts so much of what so many other ecological groups ardently picket, sue, and protest to stop—the market economy and corporate capitalism,"[14] then domestic discourses do not counter, but instead enable, the unchecked "freedom" of the market economy.

Of course, the what-I-can-do-at-home-to-save-the-earth movement has increased recycling and consumer awareness of environmental problems. People *can* have some small effect as consumers— "reducing" and "reusing," as well as purchasing less environmentally destructive products. Buying organic food, for example, is one of the few actions that directly benefits one's own health, the health of the environment, and the health of agricultural workers. Yet the rarity and the prohibitive prices of much organic food make such political actions an unattainable luxury item for many. Purchasing must be accompanied by political lobbying for policies that take into account the environmental benefits of organically grown foods in order to make them more affordable. Notwithstanding the tangible, albeit limited, benefits of bringing environmentalism to bear on the practices of consumers, the danger here is that environmental consumerism channels political energies into a depoliticized, indeed, pro-capitalist, privatized mode—and the potential for ecologically conscious consumerism to save the planet is limited, at best.[15] Lauren Berlant argues

that "the intimate public sphere of the U.S. present tense renders citizenship as a condition of social membership produced by personal acts and
values, especially acts originating in or directed toward the family
sphere."[16] Domestic citizenship has devastating effects on environmentalism's ability to articulate and mobilize political resistance, especially when
it insulates citizens from "external" environmental dangers and comforts
them with idealized images of the home. Representing the earth as a
mother supports notions of domestic citizenship only too well. Casting
the planet as a feminized victim and blaming bad housekeepers keeps environmentalism within the family sphere, leaving capitalist America free
to mind its own business.

This domestication of environmental politics proves a strange epi-
logue to the progressive women conservationists discussed in Chapter 3.
Whereas concern for the home provoked the women conservationists'
concern for natural resources, contemporary environmental consumerism takes the opposite path, turning concern for the earth back
into the home. And, whereas the women conservationists employed
their domestic talents to gain them an active role in the public sphere,
environmental consumerism reins environmental politics back into domestic enclosure, offering consumerism itself as the only link to a public
sphere. Furthermore, the domestic discourse of green consumerism
eliminates the potential for nature to serve as an undomesticated, feminist space, as the household itself mediates between (and divides)
women and nature.

Habitat: The Demolition of the Domestic

When "monsters signify,"[17] they have the potential to signify in
provocative and progressive ways. Despite the fact that the horrific often
recontains challenges to the status quo by scaring people into submission
and solidifying the boundaries of the "normal," the horrific can also function as a site of resistance and subversion.[18] The 1997 film *Habitat,* for example, can be read as a fantastic culmination of feminist forays into nature. Whereas Catherine Sedgwick, Sarah Orne Jewett, and Mary Austin
all pose nature as a liberating space outside of domestic enclosure, *Habitat* destroys the domestic from within. Aggressively inhabiting and transforming domestic space, nature consumes the very walls of domestic
enclosure. The monstrous nature of this film, in fact, seems to confirm
Carolyn Merchant's contention that "the feminist movement cannot suc-

ceed" unless "the home is liberated from its status as a 'women's sphere' to that of 'human habitat.' "[19]

Habitat is set in a dystopian future, where the ozone has been depleted and the species that have survived, including humans, have had to "adapt to a life sheltered from the sun."[20] Hank (Tcheky Karyo), the archetypal mad scientist, explains that since nature has been destroyed faster than it can repair itself, he needs to "give Mother Nature a kick in the butt" via "accelerated evolution," involving computers, a flood of water, and a jolt of electricity. When he "brings nature indoors," the rapidly evolving creatures rapidly take over the house, transforming it (at first) into a lush, tropical Eden. Hank himself evolves into a kind of disembodied, disaggregated "swarm," while his wife Clarissa (Alice Krige) ecstatically inhabits the Edenic house, floating along with her cloud of Pre-Raphaelite hair. Whereas the popular emphasis on what-you-can-do-at-home-to-save-the-earth transforms housekeeping into earthkeeping, making women responsible for cleaning up yet another domain, *Habitat* eliminates the need for housework, as Clarissa neither cleans nor cooks, but blissfully wanders, gathering an occasional meal for herself and her son. While her son yearns for a "normal" life, complaining that he is "so sick of eating what [she] scrape[s] off the walls," Clarissa insists that she "loves" living this way.

Tellingly, the habitat of Clarissa's bliss is also the domain of misogynist disgust. The males who intrude on this "animal's den," as Clarissa calls it, are punished for their transgressions—just as Clarissa warns—by ending up "on the wrong end of the food chain." The coach has the most violent reaction to the habitat, calling it "an exterminator's nightmare," and a "breeding ground for bugs." He even debates the nature of nature with Clarissa, who, incidentally, has a Ph.D. in microbiology. When the coach argues that "this isn't nature, Mrs. Symes—this is germs, bugs, bacteria," Clarissa informs him that such creatures thrive on our bodies. The coach—the maker of tough, disciplined, supposedly impermeable male bodies—responds to her insistence that our very bodies are, in fact, part of nature with misogynist disgust, calling Clarissa a "filthy, evil, flea-ridden whore" and a "witch." He concludes that "this is no animal den. No brothel. This is the womb of the queen bitch. This is you. A hundred times over." If it is Clarissa a hundred times over, it is with a vengeance: after shooting Clarissa, the coach is sucked down what looks like a giant anal sphincter; the centripetal visual image suggests the coach's compressing disgust of nature, the body, and woman.

From whence did such a disciplining device come? During the course of the film, as various men intrude on Clarissa's habitat, the formerly pastoral Eden evolves into a revoltingly biomorphic place. If it seems that misogyny itself catalyzes this transformation from the pastoral to the threateningly corporeal, it would not be the first time that the fall from Eden to wilderness turned upon the body of a woman. Although *Habitat,* like Fielding Burke's *Call Home the Heart,* pivots around this split between pastoral and corporeal natures, Clarissa does not deny her own bodily nature by projecting it onto someone else. Instead, happily dwelling at the very heart of the abject, she delights in the power of monstrous natures to revolt. In fact, the very vituperativeness of the coach's reaction to Clarissa suggests that her relationship to nature gives her some sort of power. Like the creatures Octavia Butler creates, who also live within walls of rippling flesh, Clarissa affirms her corporeality and her connections to animals and nature. As the culmination of women's texts that write nature as an undomesticated place for feminism, *Habitat* destroys the domestic from within, disrupting the boundaries between inside and outside, offering nature not as a distant refuge from culture but as an ally that is always as close as our own skin. The film can be read as a critique of environmental consumerism's claustrophobic insistence on the domestic: nature will not be placated by good housekeeping, nor will it respect the house as a separate domain. Furthermore, as the rhetoric of "family values" tries to coerce women back into domestic enclosure, the nature of *Habitat,* as it devours the domestic, acts as feminism's ally.

Gaia the Bitch, Mother Nature the Butch, and Feminists That Roar

Clarissa, cheerfully embracing centuries of misogynist connections between woman and nature, raises questions about the possibility for feminist renditions of female natures. How have contemporary environmental feminists portrayed nature, and to what extent do these portrayals enable a mobile, critical, and subversive subjectivity?

Mount St. Helens erupts on the cover of the 1981 issue of *Heresies,* on feminism and ecology. The volcano explodes from the bottom of the page; the smoke and dust fume past the top of the page, uncontained. The editors explain that they chose Mount St. Helens as the "connecting image," "both nurturing and destructive": "We called this issue of *Heresies* 'Earthkeeping/Earthshaking' because we plan to do both."[21] The words "Earthkeeping/Earthshaking" are repeated, wrapping around the cover, implying that earthkeeping necessitates earthshaking, which necessitates earthkeeping, and so on. Even though the slash represents a site of conflict for feminism, as cultural feminist nurturing clashes against radical feminist revolt, it also transforms this conflict into a pivotal space, allowing the feminist subject to negotiate the demands of the political moment—earthkeeping or earthshaking, as needed. Although the title certainly plays off women's traditional role as housekeepers, it also insists on feminist insurrection. Hardly a victimized or domestic(ated) mother, this nature erupts with uncontainable power, making quite a mess.

Feminist rearticulations of female natures are equally messy, as they carry with them such overwhelming cultural baggage. But perhaps this is the nature of most political interventions. As Paula A. Treichler notes, counterdiscourse is intimately related to the dominant discourse it struggles against: "Counter-discourse does not arise as a pure autonomous radical language embodying the purity of a new politics. Rather it arises from within the dominant discourse and learns to inhabit it from the inside out."[22] Perhaps the very ubiquity and tenacity of female natures, then, necessitates the discursive construction of natures that are female with a vengeance. If some articulations, like a female nature, are "powerfully forged" and "deeply resistant to change,"[23] then shifting the political valence of such formations (rather than simply dismissing them) is a crucial political strategy. Many feminists have recast the image of nature as female in quite provocative ways. Biologist Lynn Margulis, for example, critiques those who "want Gaia to be an Earth goddess for a cuddly, furry human environment" and retorts that, instead, "Gaia is a tough bitch—a system that has worked for over three billion years without people."[24] Against the heterosexism of Mother Earth, Catriona Sandilands proclaims the lavender-green slogan "Mother Nature is a butch!"[25] And Linda Vance insists that "nature is no June Cleaver," "no man's mother, or wife, or virgin," but instead a "wild and rowdy woman, a bad and unruly broad with no concern for her children, and no use to anyone but herself."[26] Like Mary Austin's portrayal of desert mistresses, the depiction of nature as a bitch, a butch, and a wild woman works against the historically entrenched discourses that feminize nature in order to dominate "her." Countering the long-suffering Mother Nature, they cast nature as a feminist subject who is by no means maternal. These unruly, heretical natures not only resist the domestication of Mother Earth, but they forge an alliance between feminism and environmentalism.

One of the most innovative and sustained attempts to forge an alliance between feminism and environmentalism is Susan Griffin's 1978 *Woman and Nature: The Roaring Inside Her.* Patrick D. Murphy's insightful analysis of *Woman and Nature,* which explores the text's postmodern structure, dialogic double voicing, and effective use of indirect discourse to "strip away the emotive, affective, and stylistic subterfuges" of the " 'great' Western male thinkers," demonstrates how *Woman and Nature* performs its epistemological critique.[27] This feminist tour de force presents a compelling history of the parallels between the exploitation, denigration, and mastery of woman and nature. Some of the parallels that Griffin cobbles together delight with their surprising aptness. Take, for example, the institution of marriage and the invention of plastic: "*We bear his name* to live with him after God's ordinance in the holy state of matrimony? *His knowledge is our knowledge, what he asks of us we give.* Matter impressed. *We are the background, the body, we receive.* Matter impressed with heat. The enlarging of the molecule. The polymerization of material. The desirable flexibility. The formation of plastic."[28] While some sentences clearly refer to either marriage or plastics, the two overlap, since "matter impressed" or "the desirable flexibility" refers to either the perfect plastic or the perfect wife.

The overlapping of woman and nature is visually depicted in "How the Forest Should Look," which cites forestry and office management manuals. This section, moving back and forth across the page, not only disrupts the imposition of order on trees and secretaries but also represents the messy space in which the feminist (and environmentalist) subject can maneuver.

> For harvesting trees, it is desirable that a stand be all of the same variety and age. Nothing should grow on the forest floor, not seedling trees, not grass not shrubbery. (In one case,

nineteen girls all
working on the same operation
were using ten
different methods.) Clearcutting
the virgin stand and replanting
the desired
species is
recommended. (58)

Composing across the field of the page, Griffin affirms a "new space" "*in which there is no center.* Space filled with her disintegration. Where all certainties change" (170). A very postmodern space indeed, where the decentered form not only resists the imposition of order, but opens up paths of escape. The jarring juxtapositions derail a linear narrative path and encourage, as Teresa de Lauretis puts it, the "movement" between "hegemonic discourses and the space-off, the elsewhere, of those discourses."[29]

Griffin's feminist subject, however, must also be an environmentalist, as the text makes it nearly impossible to divide "woman" from "nature." In "Our Ancient Rages," Griffin intertwines the life of Mary Wollestonecraft with the life of plankton to argue that passion is not the enemy of reason, since the life of plankton "depends on the turbulence of the seas" (182). The epigraph by Hutchinson, "the biosphere does not end where the light gives out," also suggests a biocentric critique of the limits of Enlightenment models, making the argument even more complex. Here is just one segment: "(But if the plankton sinks deeper, as it would in calm waters, she read) *But we say that to her passion, she brought lucidity* (it sinks out of the light, and it is only the turbulence of the sea, she read) *and to her vision, she gave the substance of her life* (which throws the plankton back to the light)" (183). Much of *Woman and Nature* is written in this demanding form, which neither collapses woman and nature into one entity nor divides them into two parallel but separate entities. This section can only be understood by simultaneously following the distinctiveness of the stories of Wollestonecraft and plankton *and* by reading one as the story of the other. This form demands that the reader engage the text not as a detached observer (xv), but as a positioned subject for whom nature is contiguous and knowledge is self-constituting. Moreover, the textual overlaps between "woman" and "nature" and the intertwined arguments encourage the formation of a feminist subjectivity that must also be environmentalist.

The utopian moments of *Woman and Nature,* however, collapse this complex discursive cartography, as they reach for unity by channeling both "woman" and "nature" into narrow and known entities, a "we" that many feminists bump up against. The lyrical affirmation that "We Are Mothers," for example, cannot overcome the overdetermination of the category (72). And when the text proclaims "We are the cows" it assumes that humans can know the innermost being of cows: "With our large brown eyes and our soft fur there was once something called beauty we were part of. It is this we remember when we bellow" (72). Speaking for the cows, in this unqualified and unabashed way shows, in Plumwood's words, a "disrespect for the otherness of nature" (136). Though Griffin, as she explains in her epigraph, seeks to write for "those robbed of language, who are called voiceless or mute, even the earthworms, even the shellfish and sponges," speaking for nature can be yet another form of silencing, as nature is blanketed in the human voice. Even a feminist voice is nonetheless human: representing cows as ruminating over the beauty of the mother-child bond no doubt says more about cultural feminism than it does about cows.

Moreover, when *Woman and Nature* sings of unity with nature, it unwittingly broadens the great divide between nature and culture. "Naming" begins: "Behind naming, beneath words, is something else. An existence named and unnameable" (190). Here Griffin marks the limits of discourse and human knowledge, but later in the passage these bounds are transcended: "But in a moment that which is behind naming makes itself known. Hand and breast know each one to the other . . . Air knows grass knows water knows mud knows beetle knows frost knows sunlight . . . before speaking, beneath words" (191). In this utopian moment, Griffin puts forth a sort of material knowledge that precedes and exists apart from language and culture. Like Irigaray in "When Our Lips Speak Together," she seeks to express something that cannot be expressed within patriarchal discourse. Yet the crucial difference is that whereas Irigaray continually marks the impossibility of her project with ironic linguistic failures and self-reflexiveness, Griffin plants hers in mystical realm that furthers the nature/culture divide. Like the heroine in Margaret Atwood's *Surfacing,* Griffin emerges into nature as a pure world apart from language and culture. This dualistic structure does not allow for the movement within, against, and beyond discourse that engenders feminist subjects. It neither opens up a pivotal space for "Earthkeeping/Earthshaking" nor allows for the playfully potent articulations of nature as bitch, butch, or wild woman. The full title, *Woman and Nature: The Roaring Inside Her,* indicates only one "her," a monolithic union of "woman" and "nature." Though the roar of nature reverberates throughout Griffin's text, it is sometimes muffled by the monolithic voice of woman.

Cyborgs, Whale Tails, and the Likeness of Lichen

As long as Mother Nature circulates through the culture, insurgent feminist natures such as Emma Goldman's anarchist Mother Earth, Mary Austin's desert mistresses, Susan Griffin's passionate plankton, Mother Nature the Butch, and Gaia the Bitch perform crucial cultural work, playfully but forcefully countering the baneful legacy of this trope. Such figures are, for the most part, deconstructive, in that they disrupt the calcified associations between woman and nature, surprising or confronting us with their strange aptness. They also forge new identities for women by recasting the prevalent trope of a female nature. While it is important to take up and transform the discourses that hold sway, to rearticulate rather than run from whatever has cultural potency, we must also develop and promote alternative visions. Finessing the slash between "earthkeeping" and "earthshaking," between gender minimizing and gender maximizing feminisms, feminists can play nature with a vengeance *and* forward tropes of nature that are, expressly, not gendered. For as necessary as they may be within particular historical moments, gendered tropes of nature remain problematic on two counts: they continue the tiresome, overburdened, and predominately pernicious link between woman and nature,[30] and they confine nature within overdetermined human categories. While feminist theory and environmental philosophy must dismantle the opposition between nature and culture, nature must not simply collapse into culture, but instead retain some sort of difference. Val Plumwood makes this argument quite persuasively in *Feminism and the Mastery of Nature,* explaining the need for recognizing "both the otherness of nature and its continuity with the human self."[31] Determining when to emphasize continuity and when to emphasize otherness, however, is a complicated matter that Plumwood does not address. Portraying nature as female, to take the topic at hand as a case in point, can stress the continuity of nature with a female self;[32] on the other hand, such gendered portrayals all but obliterate nature's otherness. The ossified category of "woman" dresses the Bear in pink pyjamas, making it seem immediately knowable in all-too-human terms.[33] The challenge, then, is to develop nongendered tropes of nature that emphasize continuity between humans and nature while still respecting nature's difference, that have some sort of cultural potency while gesturing toward what cannot be encompassed by, controlled by, or even entirely known by human culture. Donna Haraway's cyborg and coyote as well as the whale-tail portraits of the Whale Adoption Project offer provocative models.

As the last chapter outlined, Donna Haraway's work radically reconceptualizes nature. The fact that Haraway's account of the cyborg has been so incredibly influential perhaps best supports her claim that in the late twentieth century "the cyborg is our ontology; it gives us our politics."[34] While it may seem a bit problematic to include the cyborg within this discussion of nongendered tropes of nature, since Haraway has stated that the cyborg is a "polychromatic girl," Haraway has also stated that "the cyborg is a figure for whom gender is incredibly problematic; its sexualities are indeterminate."[35] The fact that the cyborg seems alien to gender categories is, I would argue, what enables the cyborg to embody a feminist connection with nature that does not reinvoke the woman-nature equation. The cyborg, both human and machine, not only seems utterly unfeminine, but disrupts the very categories of sex and gender. One of Haraway's "peculiar boundary creatures," the cyborg strikes to the root of the constellation of dualisms that have bound woman to nature, confusing "self/other, mind/body, culture/nature, male/female, civilized/primitive, reality/appearance, whole/part, agent/resource, maker/made, active/passive, right/wrong, truth/illusion, total/partial, God/man."[36] The cyborg inextricably connects humans to animals, to the body, to machines, which means that "[n]ature and culture are reworked; the one can no longer be the resource for appropriation or incorporation by the other." At the same time that the cyborg connects humans to nature, it knows that "the certainty of what counts as nature . . . is undermined, probably fatally."[37]

The coyote, a trickster figure, also undermines any kind of certainty about the nature of nature. Rejecting the image of the world as resource, as "mother/matter/mutter," Haraway promotes the notion of the world as a "witty agent": "The Coyote or Trickster, embodied in American Southwest Indian accounts, suggests our situation when we give up mastery but keep searching for fidelity, knowing all the while we may be hoodwinked."[38] The coyote embodies the notion of "nature" as a "material-semiotic actor," a "coding trickster with whom we must learn to converse."[39] Coyotes, like other nonhumans, have their own way of acting and signifying, which is not mediated by language, but which must be heard nonetheless: "for our unlike partners, well, the action is 'different,' perhaps 'negative' from our linguistic point of view, but crucial to the generativity of the collective. It is the empty space, the undecidability, the wiliness of other actors, the 'negativity.' "[40] Stressing the difference of nonhuman actions and semiotic systems allows Haraway to portray nature as a signifying, wily, agent—without collapsing it into human models of subjectivity.

Animal rights and environmental activists often stress connections between humans and animals in order to gain support for their projects. Whereas the postmodern cyborg rejects the unified Western self, some environmental and animal rights movements bridge the human/animal distinction by attempting to construct animals as individuals. For example, the Whale Adoption Project, addressing its letter "Dear Fellow Creature," urges us to adopt whales, "not just any whales, but whales that have been identified, named, and tracked."[41] The letter stresses the individuality of each whale, "each with distinctive markings and personality," and reminds us that when we adopt whales we won't be adopting "some nameless whales, but *special* whales, whales you pick out." Research showing that one of the most "astonishing discoveries is that individual whales, like humans, have distinctive personalities" supports this appeal. The letter includes a Whale Adoption list featuring the names, tail portraits, and personality sketches of each of the whales. On the one hand, constructing the whales or other animals as individuals fosters empathy and a sense of connection. Furthermore, elevating whales to the status of individuals frees them from their position as Other and denies humans their presumptuous position as the only species comprised of unique individuals. On the other hand, the very status of individual subject has depended on the contrasting ground of the Other. When whales become individuals, do they disrupt this pattern of domination, or do humans cast less lovable life forms as the natural background against which higher subjectivity emerges? If whales become valued because, like us, their "individuality" distinguishes them from a plethora of plankton, then what discursive maneuvers enable environmentalists to establish the plankton's claim to life? Furthermore, although the portraits of whale tails blur the boundary between human and nature, their movement is in a well-traveled direction—toward an already established model of human subjectivity. Very little movement occurs in the opposite direction—humans have "declined the invitation" to see themselves in light of evolutionary and ecological models, because, as Christopher Manes states, "Not everyone likes being likened to lichen."[42] Notwithstanding these difficulties, even though the whales are represented as "individuals" they are not reduced to mirrors of human subjectivity. Underscoring the whales' differences from humans, the Whale Adoption Project takes portraits of tails—not heads. These portraits stress kinship and affinity across the human/animal divide even while respectfully insisting on species difference. The portraits not only frame the whales as individual subjects but demand that humans learn new ways of reading subjectivity, encouraging us to decipher distinctive tail markings rather than decoding grimaces or grins. Like Haraway's cyborg and coyote, the whale tails portray continuity between humans and nature, while insisting that nature cannot be encompassed by, controlled by, or even entirely known by human culture.

Writing Nature as Feminist Space

Even though Haraway underscores the fact that the cyborg transgresses the boundaries between human and nature as well as between human and machine, it is telling that the cyborg has become much more popular as a creature of technology, rather than as a creature of nature. Patricia S. Mann, for example, in "Cyborgean Motherhood and Abortion," proposes the "cyborgean belief that children are social offspring and can be morally conceived only by acts of interpersonal agency."[43] This "cyborgean" formulation leaves little room for the body's agency, promoting instead, a Cartesian separation of mind and body that is a mark of feminism's continued flight from nature. Haraway's cyborg, on the other hand, is a feminist subject who does not distance herself from nature, who affirms "the pleasure of connection of human and other living creatures."[44]

Even as feminist theory has worked to maintain a safe, reasonable distance from the nature that has threatened to engulf woman, many feminists have traveled toward nature as a crucial site for cultural work. Inhabiting the very discourses that would bind them, feminists have transfigured the valence, meaning, and mapping of nature. Early twentieth-century feminists, including Emma Goldman, Agnes Smedley, and Tillie Olsen, trespassed across the boundaries that constitute nature as outside of culture, engaging in a "contest of mapping" that sought to align nature's political potency with leftist struggles. During roughly the same period, Nella Larsen, Edith Summers Kelley, and Fielding Burke dwell within the natures that rob women of reproductive control, dramatizing how these natures are constructed by religious ideologies, racism, and sexism. Notwithstanding the fact that nature, in these narratives, becomes the enemy by transforming women into the very nucleus of the domestic, in many other texts nature offers a feminist space of possibility because it is outside of, or antithetical to, domestic values and enclosures.

Understanding how and why North American women have written nature as an undomesticated ground is crucial for comprehending the landscape of late nineteenth-century and twentieth-century feminism. For even though the texts discussed here combat historically specific discourses of the domestic (those of the progressive movement, the Moynihan report, and environmental consumerism), they also establish a significant pattern of feminist "theory." They turn away from historically entrenched formulas that install nature as the ground of essentialism, and instead conceptualize nature as a place where, in Austin's words, "the law and the landmarks fail together." Nature, rather surprisingly perhaps, has served as a space for (nascent) poststructuralist feminisms, as the landmarks fail, gender unravels, and meanings come undone. Even when feminist texts "play nature," they do so deconstructively, shifting the discursive terrain rather than solidifying it. Whereas much feminist theory has accepted a transcendent conceptual system that severs nature from culture, many feminist writers have instead engaged in "situated theorizing" that transforms the very landscape it inhabits. Austin, along with Sarah Orne Jewett, Mary Inman, Rebecca Pitts, Edith Summers Kelley, Nella Larsen, Marian Engel, Leslie Marmon Silko, Jane Rule, and Octavia Butler, writes nature as a place that disrupts the calcified categories of gender, race, and sexuality. Feminism can learn a great deal by taking these writers seriously, for the most effective way to approach feminism's vexed relationship with nature is to radically rewrite the concept itself.

Notes

Introduction

1. Adrienne Rich, "Planetarium," in *The Fact of a Door Frame* (New York: Norton, 1984), 114.

2. Carolyn Merchant, *The Death of Nature: Women, Ecology, and the Scientific Revolution* (New York: Harper and Row, 1980), 9.

3. Ibid., 189, 295.

4. Denise Riley, *"Am I That Name?" Feminism and the Category of "Women" in History* (Minneapolis: University of Minnesota Press, 1988), 43.

5. Simone de Beauvoir, *The Second Sex*, trans. and ed. H. M. Parshley (New York: Random House, 1952), 281.

6. Dorothy Dinnerstein, *The Mermaid and the Minotaur: Sexual Arrangements and Human Malaise* (New York: Harper and Row, 1976), 102.

7. Sherry B. Ortner, "Is Female to Male as Nature Is to Culture?" in *Woman, Culture, and Society*, ed. Michelle Zimbalist Rosaldo and Louise Lamphere (Stanford: Stanford University Press, 1974), 73. Most feminists would now question the search for any one original cause of women's subordination (especially a cross-cultural one). Moreover, many of Ortner's claims do not hold up to cross-cultural scrutiny. Paula Gunn Allen, for one, challenges the assumption that all cultures oppress women when she asserts that some Native American cultures were not misogynist until contact with Europeans; see *The Sacred Hoop: Recovering the Feminine in American Indian Traditions* (Boston: Beacon, 1987). The devaluation of nature and the association of woman with nature are far from universal. Marilyn Strathern argues that the Hagen people of Papua New Guinea, for example, do not associate female and male with "nature" and "culture" or with the "wild" and the "tame" in any systematic way. Moreover, the gendered binary systems of nature/culture that Lévi-Strauss and other structuralists described are far from universal. Strathern explains that there is no "demarcated 'nature' or 'culture' in Hagen thought." "No Nature, No Culture: The Hagen Case," in *Nature, Culture, and Gender*, ed. Carol P. MacCormack and Marilyn Strathern (Cambridge: Cambridge University Press, 1980), 176.

8. Ortner, "Is Female to Male," 74.

9. Ibid., 87.

10. Ibid.

11. Beauvoir, *Second Sex,* 73–74.

12. Susan Bordo, *The Flight to Objectivity: Essays on Cartesianism and Culture* (Albany: State University of New York Press, 1987), 5.

13. For an analysis of seventeenth-century feminist writings arguing that "not nature, but culture, is the cause of the apparent deficiencies of women," see Riley, *"Am I That Name?"* 30.

14. Juliet Mitchell, "Women: The Longest Revolution" (1966), in *Women, Class, and the Feminist Imagination: A Socialist-Feminist Reader,* ed. Karen V. Hansen and Ilene J. Philipson (Philadelphia: Temple University Press, 1990), 70.

15. Gayle Rubin, "The Traffic in Women: Notes on the 'Political Economy' of Sex," reprinted in *Women, Class, and the Feminist Imagination: A Socialist-Feminist Reader,* ed. Karen V. Hansen and Ilene J. Philipson (Philadelphia: Temple University Press, 1990), 75.

16. Monique Wittig, *The Straight Mind and Other Essays* (Boston: Beacon Press, 1992), 15.

17. Ibid., 9.

18. Ibid., 13, 20.

19. Luce Irigaray, *This Sex Which Is Not One,* trans. Catherine Porter (Ithaca: Cornell University Press, 1985), 77.

20. Ibid.

21. Luce Irigaray, *Speculum of the Other Woman,* trans. Gillian C. Gill (Ithaca: Cornell University Press, 1985), 133.

22. Luce Irigaray, *Sexes and Genealogies,* trans. Gillian C. Gill (New York: Columbia University Press, 1993), 185–86.

23. Ibid., 187.

24. Ibid., 201.

25. Plumwood, in her important study *Feminism and the Mastery of Nature* (New York: Routledge, 1993), refuses this false dichotomy between denying or affirming an association between women and nature. Instead, she argues for a feminism of "critical affirmation" and a recognition of both continuity and nonhierarchical difference between humans and nonhuman nature.

26. Ariel Salleh, for example, makes the baldly reductive claim that "what is undeniably given is the fact that women and men do have existentially different relationships to 'nature' because they have different kinds of body organs." "Nature, Woman, Labor, Capital: Living the Deepest Contradiction," *Capitalism, Nature, Socialism* 6, no. 1 (March 1995): 33. Salleh's biological determinism not only underestimates the degree to which gender and sex are socially constructed but ignores feminism's vexed, complex, and historically shifting relation to the discourses of nature.

27. Noël Sturgeon, *Ecofeminist Natures: Race, Gender, Feminist Theory, and Political Action* (New York: Routledge, 1997), 11.

28. Nancy C. M. Hartsock, *Money, Sex, and Power: Toward a Feminist Historical Materialism* (Boston: Northeastern University Press, 1985), 246.

29. Judith Butler, "Contingent Foundations: Feminism and the Question of 'Postmodernism,' " in *Feminists Theorize the Political,* ed. Judith Butler and Joan W. Scott (New York: Routledge, 1992), 13.

30. My term, "situated theorizing," echoes Donna Haraway's term, "situated

knowledges," and is intended to suggest that writings that are not explicitly theoretical undertake a kind of theorizing that does not presume to float above, but rather is immersed within, a particular discursive landscape. See Donna Haraway, "Situated Knowledges: The Science Question in Feminism and the Privilege of Partial Perspective," in *Simians, Cyborgs, and Women: The Reinvention of Nature* (New York: Routledge, 1991).

31. Rosi Braidotti, *Patterns of Dissonance: A Study of Women in Contemporary Philosophy,* trans. Elizabeth Guild (New York: Routledge, 1991), 128–29.

32. Ibid., 129.

33. Diana Fuss, *Essentially Speaking: Feminism, Nature, and Difference* (New York: Routledge, 1989), 1.

34. Ibid., 1, 21.

35. Take, for example, Jacques Derrida's reading of Rousseau, which demonstrates how the sense of nature as presence is an illusion: "[W]e have read, *in the text,* that the absolute present, Nature, that which words like 'real mother' name, have always already escaped, have never existed; that what opens meaning and language is writing as the disappearance of natural presence." *Of Grammatology,* trans. Gayatri Chakravorty Spivak (Baltimore: Johns Hopkins University Press, 1974), 159. Derrida adroitly demonstrates that no pure and unmediated relation to nature is possible, as nature is always within textuality. But at the same time, by characterizing nature as a counterfeit presence, and moreover by holding nature out as the opposite of "writing," he strengthens the opposition between nature and culture and pushes nature further away from the center of textual or poststructuralist interest. Rousseau's ideal of nature as an unmediated illusory presence is justly exposed but not really deconstructed or transformed, as this very image of nature serves Derrida too well as a contrast to his theories. Even though there is "no outside-the-text," nature dwells outside the horizons of textuality, as textuality itself is predicated on the absence of a natural presence.

36. Mark Seltzer, *Bodies and Machines* (New York: Routledge, 1992), 155.

37. For a very different reading of what I call the discursive "vanishing frontier," see Alice A. Jardine's *Gynesis,* in which she argues that postmodern French philosophy has undertaken an "intensive exploration of those terms not attributable to *Man:* the spaces of the en-soi, Other, without history—the feminine . . . To give a new language to these other spaces is a project filled with both promise and fear, however, for these spaces have hitherto remained unknown, improper, unclean, non-sensical, oriental, profane." *Gynesis: Configurations of Woman and Modernity* (Ithaca: Cornell University Press, 1985), 72–73.

38. Seltzer, *Bodies and Machines,* 155.

39. Jody Berland and Jennifer Daryl Slack, "Introduction: On Environmental Matters," *Cultural Studies* 8, no. 1 (1994): 2.

40. Carolyn Merchant, *Ecological Revolutions: Nature, Gender, and Science in New England* (Chapel Hill: University of North Carolina Press, 1989), 7.

41. Gilles Deleuze and Felix Guattari, *A Thousand Plateaus: Capitalism and Schizophrenia,* trans. Brian Massumi (Minneapolis: University of Minnesota Press, 1987).

42. See Chapters 6 and 7.

43. Plumwood, *Feminism,* 124.

44. Ibid., 9.

45. Frederick Turner, *Beyond Geography: The Western Spirit against the Wilderness* (New York: Viking, 1980).

46. Frederick Jackson Turner, "The Significance of the Frontier in American History," in *The Early Writings of Frederick Jackson Turner,* ed. Everett E. Edwards (Madison: University of Wisconsin Press, 1938), 186.

47. Henry Nash Smith, *Virgin Land: The American West as Symbol and Myth* (Cambridge: Harvard University Press, 1950), 256, 253.

48. Plumwood, *Feminism,* 111.

49. Leo Marx, *The Machine in the Garden: Technology and the Pastoral Ideal in America* (New York: Oxford University Press, 1964), 29.

50. Annette Kolodny, *The Lay of the Land: Metaphor as Experience and History in American Life and Letters* (Chapel Hill: University of North Carolina Press, 1975), 158.

51. Ibid., 24, 87.

52. Vera Norwood, *Made from This Earth: American Women and Nature* (Chapel Hill: University of North Carolina Press, 1993). Kolodny's *The Land before Her: Fantasy and Experience of the American Frontiers, 1630–1860* (Chapel Hill: University of North Carolina Press, 1984) covers earlier historical periods in which women tended to embrace rather than critique the domestic. Although I do discuss Sedgwick's *Hope Leslie,* which is contemporaneous with some of the writers Kolodny studies, I stress that *Hope Leslie* stands as an anomaly within its period. Kolodny's extensively researched arguments remain compelling. Rachel Stein also poses similar questions. In *Shifting the Ground* she asks how American women writers have "perceived a pattern of negative identification with nature," and how they have "*turned over*" these problematic patterns, questioning assumptions that their contemporaries had viewed as natural fact." Analyzing the work of Emily Dickinson, Zora Neale Hurston, Alice Walker, and Leslie Marmon Silko, Stein concludes that it maps "more fertile social/natural geographies within which women, particularly women of color, may redefine themselves." *Shifting the Ground: American Women Writers' Revisions of Nature, Gender, and Race* (Charlottesville: University Press of Virginia, 1997), 4, 152.

53. Kolodny, *Land before Her,* 7.

54. Ibid., 5–6.

55. Norwood, *Made from This Earth,* 277.

56. Ibid., 237.

57. Ibid., 240.

58. In "Mama's Baby, Papa's Maybe," Hortense Spillers alerts us to the radically different relations black and white women have had to the domestic. "Mama's Baby, Papa's Maybe: An American Grammar Book," *Diacritics* (Summer 1987): 65–81. Claudia Tate, for example, argues that African American women, having been barred from the "institutions of womanhood, marriage, motherhood, and family" during slavery and having been forced to labor in someone else's domestic space, have "used their stories—'female texts'—of ideal domesticity to promote . . . 'the steady growth, development and advancement of the colored American in the very teeth of all kinds of obstacles.'" *Domestic Allegories of Political Desire* (New York: Oxford University Press, 1992), 25, 5.

59. See Gillian Rose, *Feminism and Geography: The Limits of Geographical Knowledge* (Minneapolis: University of Minnesota Press, 1993), for an insightful analysis of the "paradoxical space" of feminism.

60. Teresa de Lauretis, *Technologies of Gender: Essays on Theory, Film, and Fiction* (Bloomington: Indiana University Press, 1987), 26.

61. Lawrence Buell, *The Environmental Imagination: Thoreau, Nature Writing, and the Formation of American Culture* (Cambridge: Harvard University Press, 1995), 44.

62. A telling contemporary analog: the Association for the Study of Literature and Environment (ASLE) discussion list is divided between those interested in how environmental concerns intersect with race, gender, and class and those who think such issues are already overrepresented elsewhere and should have little or no place in a discussion list about "nature."

63. Karl Kroeber, *Ecological Literary Criticism: Romantic Imagining and the Biology of Mind* (New York: Columbia University Press, 1994), 140.

64. Ibid.

65. Ibid., 141.

66. Slavoj Žižek, *The Sublime Object of Ideology* (New York: Verso, 1989), 99.

67. Perhaps one of the most humorous examples of projecting moralism onto nature is Ernest Thompson Seton's 1907 "The Natural History of the Ten Commandments," *The Century Illustrated Monthly Magazine* 75 (November 1907): 24–33. Seton sets out to prove that the Ten Commandments are not mere "arbitrary laws given to man," but "fundamental laws of all creation" (24). Applying the Ten Commandments to animals, Seton judges some animals to be less moral than others. He laments, for example, that some animals are not monogamous, only the "higher and most successful animals" (26).

68. Ronald Takaki, *Iron Cages: Race and Culture in Nineteenth-Century America* (New York: Oxford University Press, 1990).

69. Ernesto Laclau and Chantal Mouffe, *Hegemony and Socialist Strategy: Towards a Radical Democratic Politics* (London: Verso, 1985).

70. De Lauretis, *Technologies of Gender*, 25.

71. Poetry, by contrast, gains some of its political effectiveness from its power to put forth subject positions, as Cary Nelson argues: "In part because of its long historical links with song and with the speaking voice, and in part because we are especially aware of its formal properties, poetry offers us subject positions we can take up consciously and with a paradoxically self-conscious sense of personal identification." *Repression and Recovery: Modern American Poetry and the Politics of Cultural Memory, 1910–1945* (Madison: University of Wisconsin Press, 1989), 124

One. Feminism at the Border

1. Slavoj Žižek, *The Sublime Object of Ideology* (New York: Verso, 1989), 126.

2. In contrast, Christopher Castiglia reads *Hope Leslie* within the domestic tradition, arguing that Sedgwick uses a " 'domestic' perspective to render Cooper's wilderness more humane" and brings "the wilderness—and American history—into the home." "In Praise of Extra-Vagant Women: *Hope Leslie* and the Captivity Romance," *Legacy* 6, no. 2 (fall 1989): 4.

3. Nina Baym, *Woman's Fiction: A Guide to Novels by and about Women in America, 1820–1870* (Ithaca: Cornell University Press, 1978), 27.

4. Mary Kelley, *Private Woman, Public Stage: Literary Domesticity in Nineteenth-Century America* (New York: Oxford University Press, 1984), 241.

5. Ibid., 199–200.

6. Carol J. Singley, "Catherine Maria Sedgwick's *Hope Leslie:* Radical Frontier Romance," in *The (Other) American Traditions: Nineteenth-Century Women Writers,* ed. Joyce W. Warren (New Brunswick: Rutgers University Press, 1993), 46.

7. Gillian Brown, *Domestic Individualism: Imagining Self in Nineteenth-Century Literature* (Berkeley: University of California Press, 1990), 7.

8. Tzvetan Todorov, *The Conquest of America,* trans. Richard Howard (New York: Harper and Row, 1984), 48.

9. Roderick Nash, *Wilderness and the American Mind* (New Haven: Yale University Press, 1967), 28.

10. Harriet Prescott Spofford, "Circumstance," in *Provisions: A Reader from Nineteenth-Century American Women,* ed. Judith Fetterly (Bloomington: Indiana University Press, 1985), 273.

11. Carl Gutiérrez-Jones, *Rethinking the Borderlands: Between Chicano Culture and Legal Discourse* (Berkeley: University of California Press, 1995), 66.

12. Helen Hunt Jackson, *Ramona* (Boston: Roberts Brothers, 1892), 281.

13. Ibid.

14. Lydia Maria Child, "She Waits in the Spirit Land," in *Hobomok and Other Writings on Indians,* ed. Carolyn L. Karcher (New Brunswick: Rutgers University Press, 1986).

15. Louise K. Barnett includes *Hope Leslie* in the genre of "frontier romance," American novels written between 1790 and 1860 that include Indian characters. She exposes the racism of this genre as a whole and reads *Hope Leslie* as a racist text. Although I agree that ultimately *Hope Leslie* is structured in a racist manner, I think the novel puts forth some remarkably anti-racist arguments, scenes, and images. Barnett's lumping of Sedgwick's novel in with all the others, I would assert, simplifies and sometimes distorts it. For example, Barnett uses one character's racist comment as evidence of the novel's racist ideology. The novel, however, criticizes this character's racism, as the heroine and hero refute the remark. The racial politics of *Hope Leslie* are complex, but its anti-racist intentions are hardly subtle: most of the "bad" white characters are the most racist and the white hero and heroine are the least racist of the Puritans. *The Ignoble Savage: American Literary Racism, 1790–1890* (Westport: Greenwood, 1975). See especially p. 91.

16. Catherine Maria Sedgwick, *Hope Leslie* (New Brunswick: Rutgers University Press, 1987), 6. Hereafter cited within the text.

17. Lydia Maria Child's 1830 "Chocorua's Curse" seems a direct critique of this avian image of female freedom. Child's story tells of Caroline Campbell, who, marked by "the exercise of quiet domestic love," did not have any use for "modern doctrines of equality and independence": "The bird will drop into its nest though the treasures of earth and sky are open." Even more striking, however, is that the bird's nest—the domestic realm—is destroyed by an Indian. When Chocorua murders Caroline and her children, the story seems to warn white women of the dangers of allying with Indians and abandoning their nests. "Chocorua's Curse," in *Hobomok and Other Writings on Indians,* ed. Carolyn L. Karcher (New Brunswick: Rutgers University Press, 1986), 164.

18. Paula Gunn Allen, *The Sacred Hoop: Recovering the Feminine in American Indian Traditions* (Boston: Beacon, 1987), 217.

19. Gail H. Landsman, "The 'Other' as Political Symbol: Images of Indians in the Woman Suffrage Movement," *Ethnohistory* 39, no. 3 (summer 1992): 274.

20. J. Hector St. John de Crévecoeur, *Letters from an American Farmer*, in *The Heath Anthology of American Literature*, ed. Paul Lauter, et al. (Lexington: D. C. Heath, 1990), 894. Not only did the land supposedly establish democracy, freedom, and individual rights, but according to Myra Jehlen, Americans imagined the influence of the land as something even more pervasive, molding the development of culture itself: "Americans saw themselves as building their civilization out of nature itself, as neither the analog nor the translation of Natural Law but its direct expression." *American Incarnation: The Individual, the Nation, and the Continent* (Cambridge: Harvard University Press, 1986), 3.

21. Singley, "Catherine Maria Sedgwick's *Hope Leslie*," 48.

22. Julia Kristeva, *Powers of Horror: An Essay on Abjection* (New York: Columbia University Press, 1982), 4.

23. Ibid., 10.

24. Landsman, "The 'Other' as Political Symbol," 247.

25. Dana D. Nelson, for example, argues that the novel succeeds in establishing a "space of authority for Sedgwick as a woman author through its challenges to male cultural authority," but "the text succumbs to the same processes of historical representation that it formerly condemned . . . in which Indian genocide is something that happens outside the agency of whites." *The Word in Black and White: Reading "Race" in American Literature, 1638–1867* (New York: Oxford University Press, 1992), 77. Whereas I argue that Hope Leslie, the character and the text, pushes Magawisca back into the wilderness, Lucy Maddox views Magawisca's departure as a submission to her father's patriarchal authority and a rejection of the opportunity to join Hope and Everell in "constituting a new, vital American family that is not defined by race." Maddox provocatively argues that Sedgwick, along with Lydia Maria Child, ends up "confirming the Puritan idea that the Indians are predestined to become extinct, since the only way they can be saved is to imitate the white women, and stop being Indians." *Removals: Nineteenth-Century American Literature and the Politics of Indian Affairs* (New York: Oxford University Press, 1991), 107, 110. Christopher Castiglia, however, asserts that a "sisterhood evolves" among the Indian and white women in the novel that substitutes "mutuality and support for subservience and hierarchy." "In Praise of Extra-Vagant Women," 10. Similarly, Carol J. Singley asserts that the "true bond—the real romance—in this novel is between Hope and Magawisca." "Catherine Maria Sedgwick's *Hope Leslie*," 47.

26. Trinh T. Minh-ha, *When the Moon Waxes Red: Representation, Gender, and Cultural Politics* (New York: Routledge, 1991), 12.

27. Nearly two centuries later Trinh, describing her contribution to a special journal issue on "Third World Women," sardonically comments on her role: "Eager not to disappoint, i [*sic*] try my best to offer my benefactors and benefactresses what they most anxiously yearn for: the possibility of a difference, yet a difference or an otherness that will not go so far as to question the foundation of their beings and makings." *Woman, Native, Other: Writing Postcoloniality and Feminism* (Bloomington: Indiana University Press, 1989), 88. *Hope Leslie* searches for a "possibility of a difference" in Native American culture, yet reasserts racist foundations of white "civilization."

28. Homi K. Bhabha, *The Location of Culture* (New York: Routledge, 1994), 70.

29. Žižek, *Sublime Object*, 126.

30. Ibid., 195.

31. Jane Flax argues, quite trenchantly, in *Thinking Fragments* that Lacan "recreates the myth of a solipsistic disembodied self" and that "his texts are best read as a phenomenology of what it is like to be confined within the narcissist's universe." Lacanian models may be useful for diagnosing Western dis-eased subjectivity predicated upon opposition to an other, but less helpful for formulating less destructive models. *Thinking Fragments: Psychoanalysis, Feminism, and Postmodernism in the Contemporary West* (Berkeley: University of California Press, 1990), 107, 93.

32. Ursula Le Guin, "The Ones Who Walk Away from Omelas," in *The Wind's Twelve Quarters* (New York: Harper, 1975).

Two. Darwinian Landscapes

1. Nina Baym, *Woman's Fiction: A Guide to Novels by and about Women in America, 1820–1870* (Ithaca: Cornell University Press, 1978), 26, 48.

2. Mary Kelley, *Private Woman, Public Stage: Literary Domesticity in Nineteenth-Century America* (New York: Oxford University Press, 1984), 42, 258.

3. Jane Tompkins, *Sensational Designs: The Cultural Work of American Fiction, 1790–1860* (Oxford: Oxford University Press, 1985), 168.

4. Amy Kaplan, "Manifest Domesticity," *American Literature* 70, no. 3 (September 1998): 583.

5. Ibid., 588, 582.

6. Charles Darwin, *The Origin of Species and The Descent of Man* (New York: Random House, n.d.), 373, 389.

7. Ibid., 411.

8. Ibid., 446.

9. Ibid., 448, 449, 460.

10. Gertrude Himmelfarb, *Darwin and the Darwinian Revolution* (New York: Doubleday, 1959), 352–53. Stephen J. Gould asserts that "our unwillingness to accept continuity between ourselves and nature" has been the "greatest impediment" to making peace with "Darwin and the implications of evolutionary theory." *Ever Since Darwin: Reflections in Natural History* (New York: Norton, 1977), 50. One of the earliest reviews of the *Descent*, by St. George Jackson Mivart in 1871, bears this out. Mivart vehemently insists that human mental faculties differ "in kind" from those of animals, thus reasserting the "gulf which lies between [man] and that of the highest brute." "Darwin's Descent of Man" (1871), reprinted in *Darwin and His Critics*, ed. David L. Hull (Chicago: University of Chicago Press, 1973), 383.

11. Darwin, *Descent*, 911.

12. Gillian Beer, *Darwin's Plots: Evolutionary Narrative in Darwin, George Eliot and Nineteenth-Century Fiction* (London: Routledge, 1983), 105.

13. Sarah Orne Jewett, *Country By-ways* (Boston: Houghton Mifflin, 1881), 101. Hereafter cited within the text.

14. Since this passage is so relevant here, it is worth quoting at length:

They share other instincts and emotions with us besides surprise, or suspicion, or fear. They are curiously thoughtful; they act no more from unconscious instinct than we do; at least, they are called upon to decide many questions of action or direction, and there are many emergencies of life when we are far more helpless and foolish than they. It is easy to say that other orders of living creatures exist on a much lower plane than ourselves; we know very little about it, after all. They are often gifted in some way that we are not; they may even carry some virtue of ours to a greater height than we do. (6)

While the language here is more lofty and less biomorphic than that of Darwin, the last sentence is certainly in line with Darwin in that it denies a ladder of species by emphasizing that different creatures are "successful" in various ways according to the niche they occupy.

15. Despite the anachronism, I use "lesbian" here for lack of a better term. As Paula Blanchard explains, "Jewett's deepest affections were always centered on women." Blanchard concludes, however, that these relationships were "romantic friendships" and not sexual. *Sarah Orne Jewett: Her World and Her Work* (Reading: Addison-Wesley, 1994), 54. Not only does the attempt to discern what is properly "sexual" seem problematic, however, but such categorizations cloak a more important point, that "[s]exuality, for Jewett, was not a fixed category." Marjorie Pryse, "Sex, Class, and 'Category Crisis': Reading Jewett's Transitivity," *American Literature* 70, no. 3 (September 1998): 526.

16. Carroll Smith-Rosenberg, *Disorderly Conduct: Visions of Gender in Victorian America* (New York: Oxford University Press, 1985), 252.

17. Sarah Orne Jewett, *Deephaven* (Boston: Houghton Mifflin, 1893), 226. Hereafter cited within the text.

18. Barbara A. Johns, " 'Mateless and Appealing': Growing into Spinsterhood in Sarah Orne Jewett," in *Critical Essays on Sarah Orne Jewett*, ed. Gwen L. Nagel (Boston: G. K. Hall, 1984), 150.

19. Judith Fetterley, "Reading *Deephaven* as a Lesbian Text," in *Sexual Practice/ Textual Theory: Lesbian Cultural Criticism*, ed. Susan J. Wolfe and Julia Penelope (Cambridge: Blackwell, 1993), 172.

20. Ann Romines, *The Home Plot: Women, Writing, and Domestic Ritual* (Amherst: University of Massachusetts Press, 1992), 41. Sarah Way Sherman, *Sarah Orne Jewett, an American Persephone* (Hanover: University Press of New England, 1989), 113.

21. Sherman, *Sarah Orne Jewett*, 113.

22. Margot Norris, *Beasts of the Modern Imagination: Darwin, Nietzsche, Kafka, Ernst, and Lawrence* (Baltimore: Johns Hopkins University Press, 1985), 42.

23. Ibid., 40.

24. Beer, *Darwin's Plots*, 125.

25. Romines, *Home Plot*, 46.

26. Mary Wilkins Freeman, "Christmas Jenny," in *A Mary Wilkins Freeman Reader*, ed. Mary B. Reichardt (Lincoln: University of Nebraska Press, 1997), 52. Originally published in 1888. Hereafter cited within the text.

27. Leah Blatt Glasser, *In a Closet Hidden: The Life and Work of Mary E. Wilkins Freeman* (Amherst: University of Massachusetts Press, 1996), 80.

28. Barbara A. Johns, " 'Love-Cracked': Spinsters as Subversives in 'Anna Malann,' 'Christmas Jenny,' and 'An Object of Love,' " *Colby Library Quarterly* 23, no. 1 (March 1997); Glasser, *In a Closet Hidden,* 83; Sarah W. Sherman, "The Great Goddess in New England: Mary Wilkins Freeman's 'Christmas Jenny,' " *Studies in Short Fiction* 17, no. 2 (spring 1980): 161–62.

29. See Elizabeth Meese, "Signs of Undecidability: Reconsidering the Stories of Mary Wilkins Freeman," in *Critical Essays on Mary Wilkins Freeman,* ed. Shirley Marchalonis (Boston: G. K. Hall, 1991).

30. Janice Daniel, "Redefining Place: *Femes Covert* in the Stories of Mary Wilkins Freeman," *Studies in Short Fiction* 33 (1996): 74.

31. Judith Butler, *Gender Trouble: Feminism and the Subversion of Identity* (New York: Routledge, 1990), 82.

32. *The Country of the Pointed Firs* was first published serially in *The Atlantic Monthly* in 1896; it was published as a book in the same year. Several other stories set in Dunnet Landing were added to later editions of *The Country of the Pointed Firs:* "The Queen's Twin" and "A Dunnet Shepherdess," which were first published in 1899, and the unfinished "William's Wedding." Since my argument does not focus on the genre or plot of *The Country of the Pointed Firs,* I will include discussions of the later stories, but distinguish them as such by noting their titles. All quotations will be from the following edition, hereafter cited within the text. Sarah Orne Jewett, *"The Country of the Pointed Firs" and Other Stories* (Garden City: Doubleday, 1956).

33. Elizabeth Ammons, "Material Culture, Empire, and Jewett's *Country of the Pointed Firs,*" in *New Essays on "The Country of the Pointed Firs,"* ed. June Howard (Cambridge: Cambridge University Press, 1994), 85.

34. Romines, *Home Plot,* 48.

35. Ibid., 90.

36. Vera Norwood, *Made from This Earth: American Women and Nature* (Chapel Hill: University of North Carolina Press, 1993), 195.

37. Michael Davitt Bell, "Gender and American Realism in *The Country of the Pointed Firs,*" in *New Essays on "The Country of the Pointed Firs,"* ed. June Howard (Cambridge: Cambridge University Press, 1994), 76.

38. Romines, *Home Plot,* 65.

39. Karen Halttunen, "From Parlor to Living Room: Domestic Space, Interior Decoration, and the Culture of Personality," in *Consuming Visions: Accumulation and Display of Goods in America, 1880–1920,* ed. Simon J. Bronnere (New York: Norton, 1989), 161.

40. Norwood, *Made from This Earth,* 196.

41. Susan Gillman, "Regionalism and Nationalism in Jewett's *Country of the Pointed Firs,*" in *New Essays on "The Country of the Pointed Firs,"* ed. June Howard (Cambridge: Cambridge University Press, 1994), 111; Ammons, "Material Culture," 96.

42. Elizabeth Ammons, "Going in Circles: The Female Geography of Jewett's *Country of the Pointed Firs,*" *Studies in the Literary Imagination* 16, no. 2 (fall 1983): 89.

43. Elizabeth Ammons, "Jewett's Witches," in *Critical Essays on Sarah Orne Jewett,* ed. Gwen L. Nagel (Boston: G. K. Hall, 1984), 178.

44. Josephine Donovan, "Sarah Orne Jewett and the World of the Mothers," in *New England Local Color Literature: A Women's Tradition* (New York: Frederick Ungar, 1983), 113.

45. Sherman, *Sarah Orne Jewett*, 92.

46. Lynne Huffer, *Maternal Pasts, Feminist Futures: Nostalgia, Ethics, and the Question of Difference* (Stanford: Stanford University Press, 1998), 19.

47. Bell, "Gender and American Realism," 69; Margaret Roman, *Sarah Orne Jewett: Reconstructing Gender* (Tuscaloosa: University of Alabama Press, 1992), 211.

48. Judith Fetterley, " 'Not in the Least American': Nineteenth-Century Literary Realism," *College English* 56, no. 8 (December 1994): 889.

49. Roman, *Sarah Orne Jewett*, 208.

50. Pryse, "Sex, Class, and 'Category Crisis,' " 525, 529.

51. Darwin, *Descent*, 911.

52. Ibid., 867.

53. Antoinette Brown Blackwell, *The Sexes throughout Nature* (New York: G. P. Putnam's Sons, 1875), 20.

54. Ibid., 43.

55. Ibid., 44.

56. Ibid., 115.

57. Quoted in Lester Ward, "Our Better Halves," *Forum* 6 (November 1888): 267.

58. W. K. Brooks, "The Condition of Women from a Zöological Point of View," *Popular Science Monthly* (June 1879): 145.

59. Quoted in Ward, "Our Better Halves," 268.

60. Ward, "Our Better Halves," 268.

61. Sarah Orne Jewett, *A Country Doctor* (Boston: Houghton Mifflin, 1884), 54.

62. Ibid., 60, 61, 71, 79. Hereafter cited within the text.

63. Sherman, *Sarah Orne Jewett*, 175.

64. Josephine Donovan, *After the Fall: The Demeter-Persephone Myth in Wharton, Cather, and Glasgow* (University Park: Pennsylvania State University Press, 1989), 32.

65. Josephine Donovan, "Breaking the Sentence: Local-Color Literature and Subjugated Knowledges," in *The (Other) American Traditions: Nineteenth-Century Women Writers*, ed. Joyce W. Warren (New Brunswick: Rutgers University Press, 1993), 232.

66. R. v. Krafft-Ebing, *Psychopathia Sexualis* (Chicago: Login Brothers, 1928), 579.

67. Donovan, *After the Fall*, 40.

68. Ward, "Our Better Halves," 275.

69. Ibid.

70. Ibid., 272.

71. Ibid.

72. Eliza Burt Gamble, *The Evolution of Woman: An Inquiry into the Dogma of Her Inferiority to Man* (New York: G. P. Putnam and Sons, 1894), v, 8.

73. Grant Allen, "Woman's Place in Nature," *Forum* 7 (May 1889): 263.

74. Ibid.

75. Meese, "Signs of Undecidability," 158.

76. Martha J. Cutter, "Beyond Stereotypes: Mary Wilkins Freeman's Radical Critique of Nineteenth-Century Cults of Femininity," *Women's Studies* 21 (1992): 383. Mary R. Reichardt argues that heroines in Freeman's stories "who resist social and religious codes often end up deeply reenmeshed in the very confines that have prompted their revolt in the first place." *Mary Wilkins Freeman: A Study of the Short Fiction* (New York: Twayne, 1997), 31. Romines notes the "way [Freeman's] plots enact the complex interplay between the impulse to escape for a more expansive, less prescriptive 'terri-

tory,' as in so many of the works of the male canon, and the need for a continuing relationship with women's domestic culture." *Home Plot*, 126. Eileen Razzari Elrod writes that Freeman "remained unresolved concerning gender issues, insisting on exposing and defying stereotypes, and then, alternately, reinforcing them." "Rebellion, Restraint, and New England Religion: The Ambivalent Feminism of Mary Wilkins Freeman," in *Studies in Puritan American Spirituality: Literary Calvinism and Nineteenth-Century American Women Authors*, ed. Michael Schuldiner (Lewiston: Edwin Mellen, 1997), 232.

77. Josephine Donovan, "Silence of Capitulation: Prepatriarchal 'Mothers' Gardens' in Jewett and Freeman," *Studies in Short Fiction* 23, no. 1 (winter 1986): 43.

78. Mary E. Wilkins Freeman, *Six Trees* (New York: Harper and Brothers, 1903), 33. Cited hereafter within the text.

79. Robert M. Luscher, "Seeing the Forest for the Trees: The 'Intimate Connection' of Mary Wilkins Freeman's *Six Trees*," *ATQ: American Transcendental Quarterly* 3, no. 4 (December 1989): 373.

80. Beer, *Darwin's Plots*, 9.

81. Shirley Marchalonis, "Another Mary Wilkins Freeman: *Understudies* and *Six Trees*," *ATQ: American Transcendental Quarterly* 9, no. 2 (June 1995): 96.

Three. The Undomesticated Nature of Feminism

1. Nancy Cott, *The Grounding of Modern Feminism* (New Haven: Yale University Press, 1987), 174.

2. Dolores Hayden, *The Grand Domestic Revolution: A History of Feminist Designs for American Homes, Neighborhoods, and Cities* (Cambridge: MIT Press, 1981), 274.

3. Jeannette Eaton, "The Woman's Magazine," *Masses* 7, no. 1 (October/November 1915): 19; see also Silas Bent, "Woman's Place Is in the Home: So, at Least, Ten Million Readers Are Urged to Believe," *Century* 116 (June 1928): 204–13.

4. Molly Ladd-Taylor, *Mother-Work: Women, Child Welfare, and the State, 1890–1930* (Urbana: University of Illinois Press, 1994), 43.

5. Theodore Roosevelt, *The Foes of Our Own Household* (New York: George H. Doran, 1917), 239, 237.

6. Theda Skocpol, *Protecting Soldiers and Mothers: The Political Origins of Social Policy in the United States* (Cambridge: Harvard University Press, 1992); Gwendolyn Mink, *The Wages of Motherhood: Inequality in the Welfare State, 1917–1942* (Ithaca: Cornell University Press, 1995).

7. Carroll Smith-Rosenberg, *Disorderly Conduct: Visions of Gender in Victorian America* (New York: Oxford University Press, 1985).

8. Charlotte Perkins Gilman, *Women and Economics* (New York: Harper and Row, 1966), 269; see also Gilman's often overlooked *The Home: Its Work and Influence* (Urbana: University of Illinois Press, 1972). My truncated contrast between Gilman and Austin by no means does justice to Gilman's complex critical and visionary writings on the home.

9. Smith-Rosenberg, *Disorderly Conduct*, 289.

10. Annette Kolodny, *The Land Before Her: Fantasy and Experience of the American Frontiers, 1630–1860* (Chapel Hill: University of North Carolina Press, 1984), 5–6.

11. Vera Norwood, "Crazy-Quilt Lives: Frontier Sources for Southwestern Women's Literature," in *The Desert Is No Lady: Southwestern Landscapes in Women's Writing and Art*, ed. Vera Norwood and Janice Monk (New Haven: Yale University Press, 1987), 75.

12. Vernon Young, "Mary Austin and the Earth Performance," *Southwest Review* 35, no. 3 (summer 1950), 154. Patrick D. Murphy's incisive analysis of Austin's recent reception reveals that misogyny continues to shape the response to Austin's work. Murphy argues that Edward Abbey's introduction to Austin's *The Land of Little Rain* "trashes Austin's style, which is 'too fussy, even prissy,' " and judges the value of the book by determining "the degree to which [Austin] aligns herself with normative male thinking and writing on a traditionally male subject." *Literature, Nature, and Other: Ecofeminist Critiques* (Albany: State University of New York Press, 1995), 36.

13. Marjorie Pryse, introduction to *Stories from the Country of Lost Borders*, by Mary Austin (New Brunswick: Rutgers University Press, 1987), xxi.

14. Margaret Russell Knudsen, "The Conservation of the Nation's Natural Resources," *Proceedings of the First National Conservation Congress* (1909), 207.

15. Elmo R. Richardson, for example, attributes the conservation movement to a "handful of men in the West and the East." *The Politics of Conservation: Crusades and Controversies: 1897–1913* (Berkeley: University of California Press, 1962), 158–59. During their own time, however, the women conservationists were credited with founding the conservation movement.

16. Carolyn Merchant, "Women of the Progressive Conservation Movement: 1900–1916," *Environmental Review* 8, no. 1 (spring 1984): 65.

17. Lydia Adams-Williams, "A Million Women for Conservation," *Conservation, Official Organ of the American Forestry Association* 15 (1909): 346–47.

18. Karen J. Blair, *The Clubwoman as Feminist: True Womanhood Redefined, 1868–1914* (New York: Holmes and Meier, 1980), 119.

19. Lydia Adams-Williams, "Conservation—Woman's Work," *Forestry and Irrigation* 14, no. 6 (June 1908): 350–51.

20. Mrs. Overton G. Ellis, *Proceedings of the First National Conservation Congress* (1909), 150.

21. See Samuel P. Hays, *Conservation and the Gospel of Efficiency: The Progressive Conservation Movement, 1890–1920* (Cambridge: Harvard University Press, 1959), for a history of the progressive conservation movement's utilitarian "gospel of efficiency." The very fact that "conservation" became the dominant term reveals the prevailing force of a utilitarian philosophy of nature—a philosophy that those promoting "protection" or "preservation" of nature would reject. "Conservation" rests on the assumption that nature is, above all, a resource for human use. Dr. W. J. McGee in his 1909 "The Cult of Conservation" best expresses the utilitarian spirit when he describes the "new patriotism" sweeping the country: "Its object is the conservation of national resources; its end the perpetration of People and States and the exaltation of Humanity." "The Cult of Conservation," *Conservation: Woods and Waters, Soils and Ores* 14, no. 9 (September 1908): 469. The utilitarian arguments for conservation reach an absurd dimension in Irving Fisher, who argues in 1909 that human health and vitality should be promoted because stronger, healthier, and longer lived people are better able to use "natural resources": "[T]he conservation of health will tend in several ways to the conservation of wealth. First of all, the more vigorous and long-lived the race, the better

utilization can it make of its natural resources. The labor power of such a race is greater, more intense, more intelligent, and more inventive." "National Vitality, Its Wastes and Conservation," in *Report of the National Conservation Commission, with Accompanying Papers* (Washington, D.C.: Government Printing Office, 1909), 747. Fisher seems worried that if there are not enough energetic humans eager to convert nature into "wealth," the vast "natural resources" of this country would be—horror of horrors—"wasted." Though utilitarianism, by definition, subordinates nature to a resource for human use, here even humans themselves are subordinated to the "larger" goal of efficiently consuming nature.

22. Ellen Foster, *Proceedings of the First National Conservation Congress* (1909), 91.

23. Despite women's educational and political accomplishments, when forestry and conservation "came of age as technical professions" around 1912, according to Carolyn Merchant, women were shut out—no longer appearing in the journal of the American Forestry Association or participating in the national conservation congresses in which they had played a major role. "Women of the Progressive Conservation Movement: 1900–1916," 77.

24. Foster, *Proceedings*, 92.

25. W. J. McGee, "The Relations among the Resources," *Proceedings of the First National Conservation Congress* (1909), 96; Ellis, *Proceedings*, 148.

26. Senator Clap, *Proceedings of the Second National Conservation Congress* (1910), 108.

27. Marion A. Crocker, *Proceedings of the Fourth National Conservation Congress* (1912), 258.

28. Stephen Fox provides one explanation as to why conservation was so appealing to WASPs, who felt "besieged by the new groups": "By recalling America as it was, or as it was imagined, and by calling forth the sturdy pioneer values now seemingly passing on to the aliens, conservation offered psychic release from the new tensions. Conservation seemed clean, efficient, invoking a vision of rushing streams and fragrant forests and cultural homogeneity, all in sharp contrast to the redolent immigrant districts of most cities." Take for example Hornaday's 1913 reprimand of Italians for killing birds in Little Italy. His specific complaint gives way to a more diffuse hysteria: "Wherever they settle, their tendency is to root out the native American and take his place and his income. . . . The Italians are spreading, spreading, spreading." As Fox quips, "This in a book about wildlife!" *John Muir and His Legacy: The American Conservation Movement* (Boston: Little, Brown, 1981), 347.

29. Mrs. Matthew T. Scott, "Address," in *Proceedings of the Second National Conservation Congress* (1910), 276.

30. Ibid., 275.

31. The biographical information that follows relies on Mary Austin, *Earth Horizon* (Boston: Houghton Mifflin, 1932); Benay Blend, "Mary Austin and the Western Conservation Movement: 1900–1927," *Journal of the Southwest* 30, no. 1 (spring 1988); Augusta Fink, *I-Mary: A Biography of Mary Austin* (Tucson: University of Arizona Press, 1983); Esther Lanigan Stineman, *Mary Austin: Song of a Maverick* (New Haven: Yale University Press, 1989).

32. Austin, *Earth Horizon*, 129.

33. Ibid., 266. In Austin's article "Why Americanize the Indian," she protests the American ideal of "destroying Indians *as Indians*," raging against the many absurdi-

ties: "I have never yet discovered an Indian who understood why he should be morally obligated to cut his hair and wear trousers in honor of a gentle Jesus who is always pictured to him in long hair and in a garment much more like an Indian blanket than a modern suit of clothes." Despite her incisive criticism of the Indian Bureau's policies, she gratingly calls the Indians "our Indians," not to mention "simple primitives," and "small, backward people in [our] midst." "Why Americanize the Indian?" *Forum* 82, no. 3 (September 1929): 169. For discussions of Austin's views of American Indians, see Lois Palken Rudnick, "Re-Naming the Land," in *The Desert Is No Lady: Southwestern Landscapes in Women's Writing and Art,* ed. Vera Norwood and Janice Monk (New Haven: Yale University, 1987); Elémire Zolla, *The Writer and the Shaman* (New York: Harcourt, Brace, Jovanovich, 1973); and Richard Drinnon, *Facing West: The Metaphysics of Indian-Hating and Empire-Building* (Minneapolis: University of Minnesota Press, 1980). Elizabeth Ammons concludes that Austin "was racist. At the same time, however, I think, her interest in Indians was for the most part a genuine attempt to participate in the values of a culture she believed more life-supporting than the one into which she was born." *Conflicting Stories: American Women Writers at the Turn into the Twentieth Century* (New York: Oxford University Press, 1991), 102.

34. Austin's autobiography, *Earth Horizon,* titled after an Indian song in which "man wanders in search of the Sacred Middle," suggests that her own feminist quest was influenced by an understanding of nature that she gained from Native American cultures. Furthermore, Austin envisions American feminism as progressing toward an Indian ethos when she suggests that American feminism should displace domesticity by invoking nature as the "Sacred Middle." *Earth Horizon,* 280.

35. Ibid., 198.

36. Blend, "Mary Austin," 19.

37. Ibid., 14.

38. Rudnick, "Re-Naming the Land," 26.

39. Another critic who reads Austin within a domestic framework is Shelley Armitage, who introduces her book with the "135 jars of jams and jellies [that] were found in storage" when Austin died, noting that this "domestic expression of the essential country woman in Austin was often overlooked by those who knew her." *Wind's Trail: The Early Life of Mary Austin* (Santa Fe: Museum of New Mexico Press, 1990), 3.

40. Mary Austin, *Stories from the Country of Lost Borders* (New Brunswick: Rutgers University Press, 1987), 165. Reprint of *The Land of Little Rain* (1903) and *Lost Borders* (1909). Hereafter cited within the text.

41. Emily Dickinson, *The Complete Poems of Emily Dickinson,* ed. Thomas H. Johnson (Boston: Little, Brown, 1957).

42. Annette Kolodny, *The Lay of the Land: Metaphor as Experience and History in American Life and Letters* (Chapel Hill: University of North Carolina Press, 1975), 88.

43. Melody Graulich, " 'O Beautiful for Spacious Guys' : An Essay on the 'Legitimate Inclinations of the Sexes,' " in *The Frontier Experience and the American Dream: Essays on American Literature,* ed. David Mogen, Mark Busby, and Paul Bryant (College Station: Texas A & M University Press, 1987), 191.

44. Contrary to other feminists of her generation, such as Emma Goldman, Mabel Dodge Luhan, or Margaret Sanger, Austin thought sex was somewhat overrated and women's sexual freedom important, but not overwhelmingly so—she even apologizes

for the scarcity of sex in her autobiography. Unlike Luhan, for whom mysticism and primitivism merged with a feminist reclamation of sexuality and the cult of the orgasm, Austin saw sex as more troubling, more compromising. She saw women such as Luhan consumed with the need to inspire the genius of men, while she wanted to be a *Woman* of Genius. For Luhan's views on nature, sex, and Pueblo culture see her autobiographical works, *Winter in Taos* (New York: Harcourt, Brace, 1935) and *Edge of the Taos Desert: An Escape to Reality* (Albuquerque: University of New Mexico Press, 1987), as well as Lois Palken Rudnick's fascinating biography, *Mabel Dodge Luhan: New Woman, New Worlds* (Albuquerque: University of New Mexico Press, 1984).

45. Mary Austin, *The Ford* (Boston: Houghton Mifflin, 1917), 384.

46. Rudnick, "Re-Naming the Land," 11.

47. David Wyatt, *The Fall into Eden: Landscape and Imagination in California* (New York: Cambridge University Press, 1986), 76.

48. Mary Austin, *Starry Adventure* (Cambridge: Riverside, 1931), 379.

49. Austin, *The Ford,* 373.

50. Ibid., 234.

51. Mary Austin, *The American Rhythm* (New York: Harcourt, Brace, 1923), 55. The vague, mystical assertions in *The American Rhythm* and the lack of "evidence" and developed arguments left Austin's book wide open for criticism. Arthur Davidson Ficke wrote Austin: "I am absolutely stumped by your calm assumption of the existence of a general 'American rhythm'—a thing the existence of which you nowhere demonstrate." T. M. Pearce, ed., *Literary America, 1903–1934: The Mary Austin Letters* (Westport: Greenwood, 1979), 241. Witter Bynner's skepticism betrays white supremacism. He objects to the very possibility that Indians could have influenced white culture: "I should say that there is more influence from Queen Elizabeth down through Gershwin on Hopi Indian songs than on so-called American rhythm from any Amerindian whatever." Pearce, *Literary America*, 232. Within *The American Rhythm* itself Austin anticipated and dismissed such ethnocentric criticism of her theory. For a sympathetic reading of Austin's *The American Rhythm,* see James Ruppert, "Discovering America: Mary Austin and Imagism," in *Studies in American Indian Literature: Critical Essays and Course Designs,* ed. Paula Gunn Allen (New York: Modern Language Association, 1983): 243–58, and "Mary Austin's Landscape Line in Native American Literature," *Southwest Review* 68, no. 4 (autumn 1983): 376–90.

52. Mary Austin, *The Young Woman Citizen* (New York: Woman's Press, 1918), 93.

53. Mary Austin, "Regional Culture in the Southwest," *Southwest Review* 14 (July 1929): 474–75.

54. See Chapter 7 for an analysis of Griffin's work.

55. Melody Graulich, afterword to Mary Austin's *Cactus Thorn* (Reno: University of Nevada Press, 1988), 188. Hereafter cited within the text.

56. Fink, *I-Mary,* 233.

57. The feminism of this transformation may be undercut, however, by the story's implication in the racist literary tradition of proving the worth of Indian characters by portraying their extraordinary self-sacrifice to whites. Catherine Maria Sedgwick in *Hope Leslie,* for example, at pains to prove to her audience that an Indian woman could be a heroine, has Magawisca get her arm lopped off in order to save her white lover from death. *Hope Leslie* (New Brunswick: Rutgers University Press, 1987). Rayna Green argues that America's "Pocahontas Perplex" has defined the "good Indian," es-

pecially the Indian woman, according to whether she helps white men. "The Pocahontas Perplex: The Image of Indian Women in American Culture," in *Unequal Sisters: A Multicultural Reader in U.S. Women's History*, ed. Ellen Carol DuBois and Vicki L. Ruiz (New York: Routledge, 1990).

58. H.D., *Trilogy* (New York: New Directions Books, 1973), 3, 59.

59. Mary Austin, "Regionalism in American Fiction," *English Journal* 21 (February 1932): 106, 105. Marjorie Pryse has argued that in response to the ideology of separate spheres that "partitions women off," women created "their own regions" in order to use " 'location' in geographical regions as itself their strategy to explore hierarchies of cultural subordination." Her argument emphasizes the political significance of regionalism by downplaying the importance of place: "For even though the literal topography of place matters for some of these writers, especially Celia Thaxter and Mary Austin, the texts are not 'about' place in a literal sense. Rather, 'geographical region' stands in the same relation to 'regionalism' as 'female' stands to 'feminism': 'region' and 'female' are naturalizing terms but they do not serve as the 'essences' of regionalism or feminism." " 'Distilling Essences': Regionalism and 'Women's Culture,' " *American Literary Realism, 1870–1910* 25, no. 2 (winter 1993): 8, 9. Austin did envision the Southwest in a way that explored hierarchies of gender, as Pryse argues. But many of Austin's texts *are* about place in a "literal" sense; her own theories about regionalist fiction explicitly require that the land play a significant and active role. Though Austin's articulations of nature are, of course, enmeshed within and grate against the discursive formulations of her time, she struggled to represent the sovereignty, semiotics, and agency of the land itself.

60. Faith Jaycox, "Regeneration through Liberation: Mary Austin's 'The Walking Woman' and Western Narrative Formula," *Legacy* 6, no. 1 (spring 1989): 10.

61. Melody Graulich, introduction to "The Walking Woman," in *Western Trails: A Collection of Short Stories by Mary Austin*, ed. Melody Graulich (Reno: University of Nevada Press, 1987), 91.

62. Austin probably wanted to prevent her 1909 *Lost Borders* from encountering the same fate as her previous novel *Santa Lucia*, which was published in 1908 and withdrawn from bookstores the same year because, as a tale of a woman's adultery and suicide, it was " 'unfit for general reading.' " See Karen S. Langlois, "Mary Austin's *Woman of Genius:* The Text, the Novel and the Problem of Male Publishers and Critics and Female Authors," *Journal of American Culture* 15, no. 2 (summer 1992): 79–86. Austin's voluminous writings cannot be reduced to a monolith, however; her article "The Failure of Free Love," (*Harper's Weekly* 58 [March 21, 1914]: 25–28) contradicts the sexually liberated feminisms of both Dulcie and the Walking Woman.

63. Cott, *Grounding of Modern Feminism*, 42.

64. Though Austin draws on the prevalent notion of nature as an "outside" to culture, her depiction of the desert can hardly be reduced to such a view. The land of lost borders resists Anglo culture, but it sustains many Native and Mexican American cultures. Furthermore, the desert Austin presents is replete with nonhuman inhabitants living in complex relationships with each other and with humans—a different "culture" that serves as a critique and utopia. In 1931 Henry Smith observed that unlike most "nature writers," Austin does not think of " 'nature' as an escape," nor as "a retreat from men, cities, and society, but a real avenue of approach to them." "The Feel of the Purposeful Earth," *New Mexico Quarterly* 1, no. 1 (February 1931): 23.

65. Jane Tompkins, *West of Everything: The Inner Life of Westerns* (Oxford University Press, 1992), 39–40.

66. See Jaycox, "Regeneration," for a revealing analysis of how Austin uses literary conventions of the Western to write "The Walking Woman" as a "feminist western."

67. Austin, *Stories from the Country*, 156.

Four. Emma Goldman's *Mother Earth* and the Nature of the Left

1. Molly Ladd-Taylor, *Mother-Work: Women, Child Welfare, and the State, 1890–1930* (Urbana: University of Illinois Press, 1994), 104, 105.

2. Ellen Key, *The Renaissance of Motherhood* (New York: Source Book Press, 1970), 109. Originally published in 1914.

3. Along with *The Renaissance of Motherhood*, see Key's *Love and Marriage* (New York: Source Book Press, 1970), originally published in 1911, and *The Woman Movement* (Westport: Hyperion, 1976), originally published in 1912.

4. Emma Goldman and Max Baginski, "Mother Earth," *Mother Earth* 1, no. 1 (March 1906): 1.

5. Ibid., 2.

6. Emma Goldman, "Observation and Comments," *Mother Earth* 1, no. 10 (December 1906): 2.

7. Goldman and Baginski, "Mother Earth," 2–3.

8. Ibid., 4.

9. The use of the term "natural" to support arguments that it would seem to controvert suggests how powerful the appeal to the "natural" must have been. For example, an essay appearing in Margaret Sanger's *The Woman Rebel* promotes free love by embracing the ideal of the natural to justify its position, arguing that marriage is unnecessary for a "man and woman who under a natural condition avow their love for each other": "A reciprocal, spontaneous voluntary declaration of love and mutual feelings by a man and woman is the expression of Nature's desires. Were it not natural it would not be so and being natural it is right." "Marriage," *The Woman Rebel* 1, no. 2 (April 1914): 16. While it is not surprising that this piece appeals to the natural in order to justify free love, it is peculiar that an unqualified promotion of the natural as right would appear within *The Woman Rebel* since it would seem to contradict the arguments for women's reproductive control.

10. Emma Goldman, "Observation and Comments," *Mother Earth* 1, no. 2 (April 1906): 2.

11. Emma Goldman, "Anarchism: What It Really Stands For," in *Red Emma Speaks: An Emma Goldman Reader*, ed. Alix Kates Shulman (New York: Random House, 1972), 59.

12. Tillie Olsen, *Yonnondio: From the Thirties* (New York: Dell, 1974), 11–13.

13. Margaret Anderson, "An Inspiration," *Mother Earth* 10, no. 1 (March 1915): 435.

14. Margaret Anderson describing Goldman's 1916 imprisonment, quoted in Shulman, *Red Emma Speaks*, 105.

15. Similarly, Suzanne Clark asserts that "the maternal as exemplified by Goldman was not complicit with a patriarchal family structure but rather with woman as pow-

erful." *Sentimental Modernism: Women Writers and the Revolution of the Word* (Bloomington: Indiana University Press, 1991), 60.

16. Jennifer Daryl Slack, "The Theory and Method of Articulation in Cultural Studies," in *Stuart Hall: Critical Dialogues in Cultural Studies,* ed. David Morley and Kuan-Hsing Chen (New York: Routledge, 1996), 125.

17. Roderick Frazier Nash, *The Rights of Nature: A History of Environmental Ethics* (Madison: University of Wisconsin Press, 1989), 55–59.

18. Aldo Leopold, *A Sand County Almanac: And Sketches Here and There,* with an introduction by Robert Finch (New York: Oxford University Press, 1949), 224–25.

19. Donald C. Swain, *Federal Conservation Policy: 1921–1933* (Berkeley: University of California Press, 1963), 169.

20. In "Hobbling Back to Nature," *The Nation* lambasts the upper-class bias of the back-to-nature movements: "What makes the movement Back to Nature all the more difficult is the fact that our tenements are for the most part filled with people who have just come from Nature, and cannot be persuaded to go back, because 'they have been there.'" "Hobbling Back to Nature," *The Nation* 84, no. 2177 (March 21, 1907): 260.

21. Swain, *Federal Conservation Policy: 1921–1933,* 142.

22. William T. Hornaday, *Our Vanishing Wildlife: Its Extermination and Preservation* (New York: Charles Scribner's Sons, 1913), 105.

23. Ibid., 106.

24. Franklin D. Roosevelt, "The Civilian Conservation Corps," in *American Environmentalism: Readings in Conservation History,* ed. Roderick Frazier Nash (New York: McGraw-Hill, 1990), 140.

25. H. F. Osborne, quoted in Donna Haraway, *Primate Visions: Gender, Race, and Nature in the World of Modern Science* (New York: Routledge, 1989), 26.

26. Robert Fechner, quoted in Nash, *American Environmentalism,* 143, emphasis added.

27. Jean Baudrillard, *The Mirror of Production,* trans. Mark Poster (St. Louis: Telos Press, 1975), 57.

28. Theodore Roosevelt, quoted in Roderick Frazier Nash, *Wilderness and the American Mind* (New Haven: Yale University Press, 1967), 150.

29. Ibid., 150.

30. Haraway, *Primate Visions,* 55.

31. Nash, *Wilderness,* 143.

32. Ibid., 141–42.

33. Stewart H. Holbrook, "The Original Nature Man," *The American Mercury* 39, no. 156 (December 1936): 424.

34. Nash, *Wilderness,* 201.

35. Robert Marshall, "The Problem of the Wilderness," *Scientific Monthly* 30 (1930): 143, emphasis added.

36. Mark Seltzer, *Bodies and Machines* (New York: Routledge, 1992), 149.

37. I can't help but wonder, in passing, about the possible parallels between the wilderness cults of the early twentieth century and the macho strand of the current men's movement, exemplified by Robert Bly.

38. "We Americans and the Other Animals," *Century Magazine* 67 (February 1904): 626.

39. Judith Butler, "Contingent Foundations: Feminism and the Question of 'Postmodernism,' " in *Feminists Theorize the Political*, ed. Judith Butler and Joan W. Scott (New York: Routledge, 1992), 6.

40. Mary Inman, "Manufacturing Femininity," in *Writing Red: An Anthology of American Women Writers, 1930–1940*, ed. Charlotte Nekola and Paula Rabinowitz (New York: Feminist Press, 1987), 304, emphasis added.

41. Ibid.

42. The only exception to her thesis is motherhood, the "strictly 'biological' problem of womanhood" for which she advocates the following "provisions by society": "adequate contraceptive aid, four months leave from work, with pay, for the mother; and nurseries." Rebecca Pitts, "Women and Communism," in *Writing Red: An Anthology of American Women Writers, 1930–1940*, ed. Charlotte Nekola and Paula Rabinowitz (New York: Feminist Press, 1987), 324, 327.

43. Ibid., 325.

44. Ibid., 327–28.

45. Josephine W. Johnson, *Now in November* (New York: Feminist Press, 1991), 100; Nancy Hoffman, afterword to *Now in November*, 256.

46. Johnson, *Now in November*, 36, 35.

47. Ibid., 36, 100.

48. Hoffman, afterword, 270.

49. Agnes Smedley, *Daughter of Earth* (New York: Feminist Press, 1987), 106–7.

50. Ibid., 191.

51. Ibid., 245–46.

52. Ibid., 276.

53. Nancy Hoffman, in the afterword to *Daughter of Earth,* compares Smedley's views on childbirth to those of other radical women novelists of the 1930s and claims that "even among her sisters in this special circle, Smedley presents the most radical and daring 'reading' of childbearing: It must not happen." Afterword to *Daughter of Earth*, by Agnes Smedley (New York: Feminist Press, 1987), 410. Along with writing for the socialist paper *The Call*, Smedley wrote for Margaret Sanger's *Birth Control Review* from 1917 until 1920.

54. Butler, "Contingent Foundations," 20.

55. Olsen began writing *Yonnondio* in 1932 and continued intermittently until 1936. Nearly forty years later Olsen revised but did not finish the novel. It was published in 1974.

56. This scene also politicizes a mother's struggle to provide for her children by illustrating the near impossibility of following the government nutrition wheel. As Constance Coiner argues, Olsen and Le Sueur "implied that the 'personal is political' long before that phrase became a household slogan among younger feminists." From a feminist perspective, what was constituted by the Communist Party as "political" was quite narrow. "The Party at least tacitly endorsed the traditional sexual division of labor, and domestic issues, when they counted at all, were not priorities." "Literature of Resistance: The Intersection of Feminism and the Communist Left in Meridel LeSueur and Tillie Olsen," in *Left Politics and the Literary Profession*, ed. Lennard J. Davis and M. Bella Mirabella (New York: Columbia University Press, 1990), 165, 164.

57. Deborah Rosenfeldt, "From the Thirties: Tillie Olsen and the Radical Tradition," *Feminist Studies* 7, no. 3 (fall 1981): 398.

58. Tillie Olsen, *Yonnondio: From the Thirties* (New York: Dell, 1974), 98.

59. Ibid.

60. Ibid., 102.

61. Anna W. Shannon, biographical afterword to *Call Home the Heart*, by Fielding Burke (New York: Feminist Press, 1983).

62. The violent strikes by textile workers in Gastonia County, North Carolina in 1929 were covered by the national media and became, for the left, "a symbol of imminent class warfare in America." Joseph R. Urgo, "Proletarian Literature and Feminism: The Gastonia Novels and Feminist Protest," *Minnesota Review* 24 (spring 1985): 66. Along with *Call Home the Heart*, five other novels were written about the Gastonia strikes: Sherwood Anderson's *Beyond Desire*, Grace Lumpkin's *To Make My Bread*, Myra Page's *Gathering Storm*, William Rollins's *The Shadow Before*, and Mary Heaton Vorse's *Strike*.

63. Shannon, biographical afterword, 441, 443.

64. Sylvia J. Cook, critical afterword to *Call Home the Heart*, by Fielding Burke (New York: Feminist Press, 1983), 454–55.

65. Fielding Burke, *Call Home the Heart* (New York: Feminist Press, 1983), 229.

66. Ibid., 285.

67. Ibid., 313.

68. In *Yonnondio*, the chapter describing the family's healthy, exhilarating stint on a farm is flanked by chapters that narrate the horrors of mines and slaughterhouses, respectively. According to *Daughter of Earth*, farm life is preferable to other lower class environments, as Marie explains: "Our life there had indeed been poor, but as I see it now, it had been healthy and securely rooted in the soil." Smedley, *Daughter of Earth*, 34.

69. Burke, *Call Home the Heart*, 430.

70. Ernesto Laclau, *New Reflections on the Revolution of Our Time* (London: Verso, 1990), 34.

71. Cary Nelson, *Repression and Recovery: Modern American Poetry and the Politics of Cultural Memory, 1910–1945* (Madison: University of Wisconsin Press, 1989), 133.

72. Gillian Rose, *Feminism and Geography: The Limits of Geographical Knowledge* (Minneapolis: University of Minnesota Press, 1993), 155.

Five. Reproduction as a Natural Disaster

1. Carroll Smith-Rosenberg, *Disorderly Conduct: Visions of Gender in Victorian America* (New York: Oxford University Press, 1985), 245–46.

2. Stuart Hall, "The Problem of Ideology: Marxism without Guarantees," in *Stuart Hall: Critical Dialogues in Cultural Studies*, ed. David Morley and Kuan-Hsing Chen (New York: Routledge, 1996), 43.

3. Smith-Rosenberg, *Disorderly Conduct*, 118.

4. Paula Rabinowitz, *Labor and Desire: Women's Revolutionary Fiction in Depression America* (Chapel Hill: University of North Carolina Press, 1991), 136.

5. Linda Gordon, *Woman's Body, Woman's Right: A Social History of Birth Control in America* (New York: Grossman, 1976), 188.

6. "Unnatural?" *Birth Control Review* 4, no. 11 (November 1920): 1; W. J. Robinson, "Is Birth Control Unnatural?" *Birth Control Review* 2, no. 3 (April 1918): 14; Margaret Sanger, "How Nature Gets Even," *Birth Control Review* (September 1918): 13.

7. J. A. Rogers, "The Critic," *Messenger* 7, no. 4 (April 1925): 165–66.

8. Jesse M. Rodrique, "The Black Community and the Birth-Control Movement," in *Unequal Sisters: A Multicultural Reader in U.S. Women's History,* ed. Ellen Carol DuBois and Vicki L. Ruiz (New York: Routledge, 1990), 336.

9. Without diminishing the importance of women's struggles for sexual freedom, it is important to keep in mind that certain groups in the 1920s were only too happy to promote women's sexual fulfillment within heterosexual relations in order to vilify lesbianism and in order to "remove the cause for, and mean the end of, women's demands for rights and independence. As one doctor baldly put it, 'the driving force in many agitators and militant women who are always after their rights, is often an unsatisfied sex impulse, with a homosexual aim. Married women with a completely satisfied libido rarely take an active interest in militant movements.' " Nancy Cott, *The Grounding of Modern Feminism* (New Haven: Yale University Press, 1987), 159.

10. Gordon, *Woman's Body,* 207.

11. Margaret Sanger, *My Fight for Birth Control* (New York: Farrar and Rinehart, 1931), 49.

12. Ibid., 81.

13. Women radicals of the 1930s echoed earlier Marxist debates about the relation between reproduction and capitalism. "In 1913 Rosa Luxemburg in Germany and Anatole France in France proposed that workers undertake a 'birth-strike,' a cessation of childbearing in order to stop the flow of exploited manpower [*sic*] into the industrial and military machines. Karl Kautsky and other orthodox Marxists rebutted those heretical proposals with the classic Marxist retort to Malthusian ideas: that a reduction in the proletarian birthrate would harm socialism by dulling the revolutionary fervor of the working class and weakening its numerical strength." David M. Kennedy, *Birth Control in America: The Career of Margaret Sanger* (New Haven: Yale University Press, 1970), 21–22.

14. Gordon, *Woman's Body,* 288.

15. John D'Emilio and Estelle B. Freedman, *Intimate Matters: A History of Sexuality in America* (New York: Harper and Row, 1988), 247.

16. Ibid., 289.

17. Kennedy, *Birth Control,* 113.

18. Fielding Burke, *Call Home the Heart* (New York: Feminist Press, 1983), 7. Hereafter cited within the text.

19. Rabinowitz, *Labor and Desire,* 56.

20. Though Ishma learns the secret of birth control, the reader never does. As Rabinowitz explains, "The text censors itself. Four different times Ishma tries to learn how to control her fertility, but each time the narrator abruptly shifts point of view and the desired 'information' is never divulged to the reader." *Labor and Desire,* 93.

21. For more on the question of race see Suzanne Sowinska, "Writing across the Color Line: White Women and the 'Negro Question' in the Gastonia Novels," in *Radical Revisions: Rereading 1930s Culture,* ed. Bill Mullen and Sherry Lee Linkon (Urbana: University of Illinois Press, 1996), 120–43, and Anna Shannon Elfenbein, "A Forgotten Revolutionary Voice: 'Woman's Place' and Race in Olive Dargan's *Call Home the Heart,*" in *The Female Tradition in Southern Literature,* ed. Carol S. Manning (Urbana: University of Illinois Press, 1993), 193–208.

22. Charlotte Goodman, afterword to *Weeds*, by Edith Summers Kelley (New York: Feminist Press, 1982), 354–56.

23. Ibid., 357.

24. Updegraff, quoted in Goodman, afterword, 353.

25. Edith Summers Kelley, *Weeds* (New York: Feminist Press, 1982), 12. Hereafter cited within the text.

26. Even as the association of Judith's sexuality with the natural endorses these tabooed areas of sexuality, it forecloses the possibility of lesbianism. A strong fear of the "unnatural" "mannish lesbian" prevailed during the 1920s. If the psychoanalysts and physicians of the time had come into contact with a girl like Judith, a classic "tomboy," she would have been warned about her "dangerous predispositions for 'inversion'" and strongly encouraged to "marry quickly and have children." See Smith-Rosenberg, *Disorderly Conduct*, 116. Even though lesbianism is not offered as an option in this novel, the representation of marriage and, especially childbearing, as a naturalistic nightmare does challenge the standard medical prescription. For information on how the lesbian baiting of the 1920s affected feminist groups, see Cott, *Grounding of Modern Feminism*, 156–62.

27. Kelley, quoted in Goodman, afterword, 361.

28. Ibid.

29. Upton Sinclair's *The Jungle*, first published in 1906, contains a rather harrowing birth scene, but it is told almost entirely from a male perspective. The novel does not represent the drama of childbirth itself; it focuses instead on the husband's frantic labors to locate and find enough money to pay a doctor or midwife. *The Jungle* (New York: Signet, 1980).

30. Charlotte Goodman reads some of the earlier references to animals more ominously. "Judith's fate is prefigured early in the novel as Kelley describes the sad fate of the minnows, butterflies, mud turtles, and grasshoppers that the young child tries to domesticate in an assortment of containers; the 'curse of blight and disaster' that befalls them will befall her too when she becomes a prisoner of her tenant shanty as an adult." "Widening Perspectives, Narrowing Possibilities: The Trapped Woman in Edith Summers Kelley's *Weeds*," in *Regionalism and the Female Imagination*, ed. Emily Toth (University Park: Pennsylvania State University, 1985), 103.

31. Donald Pizer, *Realism and Naturalism in Nineteenth-Century American Literature* (Carbondale: Southern Illinois University Press, 1984), 11.

32. Unlike *Weeds*, which contrasts women to male farmers, who at least have means to control rampant fertility, Ellen Glasgow's *Barren Ground* focuses on a female farmer, and thus sets up an equivalence between the farmer's need to control nature and the feminist's need to control her body. Like the weeds in *Quicksand* and *Weeds*, the broomsedge in *Barren Ground* symbolizes rampant, natural fecundity. Yet unlike the other two novels, *Barren Ground* associates the fertility of broomsedge with barrenness, resignifying barrenness to mean a fecundity that is undesirable to both farmers and feminists, while disarticulating "nature" from uncontrolled reproduction. Ellen Glasgow, *Barren Ground* (New York: Harcourt Brace Jovanovich, 1925).

33. Robinson, "Is Birth Control Unnatural?" 1.

34. Mark Seltzer, *Bodies and Machines* (New York: Routledge, 1992), 29–31.

35. Ibid., 164.

36. Angela Davis, *Women, Race, and Class* (New York: Vintage, 1983).

37. Zora Neale Hurston, *Their Eyes Were Watching God* (Urbana: University of Illinois Press, 1978), 21, italics in original.

38. Hazel Carby, *Reconstructing Womanhood: The Emergence of the Afro-American Woman Novelist* (New York: Oxford University Press, 1987), 174.

39. W. E. B. DuBois, "Opinion," *Crisis* 24, no. 6 (October 1922): 248.

40. Rogers, "The Critic," 165.

41. Angelina Weld Grimké, *The Closing Door, Birth Control Review* (September 1919): 10–14 and (October 1919): 8–12. See also *Birth Control Review* 3, no. 9 (September 1919) and 16, no. 6 (June 1932) for several articles about African Americans and birth control. Along with *The Closing Door,* see Grimké's play *Rachel* and her story "Goldie" (all reprinted in *Selected Works of Angelina Weld Grimké,* ed. Carolivia Herron [New York: Oxford University Press, 1991]). Interestingly, "Goldie," a story about lynching that does not mention reproduction, was published in *Birth Control Review* (November–December 1920).

42. Rodrique, "The Black Community," 335.

43. Nella Larsen, *"Quicksand" and "Passing"* (New Brunswick: Rutgers University Press, 1986), 118. Hereafter cited within the text.

44. Jean Toomer, *Cane* (New York: Modern Library, 1994), 4, 5.

45. Ibid., 22.

46. Luce Irigaray, *This Sex Which Is Not One,* trans. Catherine Porter (Ithaca: Cornell University Press, 1985), 78.

47. Mrs. Birney, founder of the National Congress of Mothers, for example, supported her cause by stating that "nature has set her seal upon woman as the caretaker of the child." Quoted in Theda Skocpol, *Protecting Soldiers and Mothers: The Political Origins of Social Policy in the United States* (Cambridge: Harvard University Press, 1992), 335.

48. Elizabeth Grosz, *Volatile Bodies: Toward a Corporeal Feminism* (Bloomington: Indiana University Press, 1994), 23.

Six. Playing Nature

1. Thanks to Cary Nelson for complicating my reading of this work.

2. Judith Butler, "Contingent Foundations: Feminism and the Question of 'Postmodernism,' " in *Feminists Theorize the Political,* ed. Judith Butler and Joan W. Scott (New York: Routledge, 1992), 16.

3. Ibid.

4. Rita Felski, *Beyond Feminist Aesthetics: Feminist Literature and Social Change* (Cambridge: Harvard University Press, 1989), 148, emphasis added.

5. Amanda Anderson, "Cryptonormativism and Double Gestures: The Politics of Poststructuralism," *Cultural Critique* 21 (spring 1992): 73.

6. Ibid.

7. Cynthia Davis, "Self, Society, and Myth in Toni Morrison's Fiction," in *Toni Morrison: Modern Critical Views,* ed. Harold Bloom (New York: Chelsea House, 1990), 21–22.

8. Toni Morrison, *Song of Solomon* (New York: New American Library, 1977), 37, 340. Hereafter cited within the text.

9. bell hooks, "Marginality as a Site of Resistance," in *Out There: Marginalization and Contemporary Cultures,* ed. Russell Ferguson et al. (New York: New Museum of Contemporary Art, 1990), 34.

10. See Jacqueline de Weever, "Toni Morrison's Use of Fairy Tale, Folk Tale, and Myth in *Song of Solomon,*" *Southern Folklore Quarterly* 44 (1980): 143.

11. Patricia Hill Collins, *Black Feminist Thought: Knowledge, Consciousness, and the Politics of Empowerment* (Boston: Unwin Hyman,1990), 170–71.

12. Melvin Dixon, *Ride Out the Wilderness: Geography and Identity in Afro-American Literature* (Urbana: University of Illinois Press, 1987), 17.

13. Susan Willis, *Specifying: Black Women Writing the American Experience* (Madison: University of Wisconsin Press, 1987), 97.

14. Willis, *Specifying,* 98–99.

15. Collins, *Black Feminist Thought,* 229–30.

16. Barbara Christian, "Community and Nature: The Novels of Toni Morrison," *Journal of Ethnic Studies* 7, no. 4 (winter 1980): 68.

17. Michael Awkward, *Negotiating Difference: Race, Gender, and the Politics of Positionality* (Chicago: University of Chicago Press, 1995), 150.

18. Margaret Atwood, *Surfacing* (New York: Warner Books, 1972), 143. Hereafter cited within the text.

19. Atwood may be alluding to Sarah Orne Jewett's story "A White Heron," which also allies females with nature and reveals the cruelty in the "scientific" quest for knowledge. An ornithologist offers Sylvia ten dollars for the location of a white heron's nest, because he wishes to kill the heron, stuff it, and add it to his collection. Sylvia sides with the heron, giving up the extraordinary sum of money: "Sylvia cannot speak; she cannot tell the heron's secret and give its life away." Sarah Orne Jewett, *The Country of the Pointed Firs and Other Stories* (Garden City: Doubleday, 1956), 171. See Vera Norwood, *Made from This Earth: American Women and Nature* (Chapel Hill: University of North Carolina Press, 1993) for a comparison of Atwood and Jewett.

20. This was hardly Atwood's intention. In an interview she explains that the novel takes an "anti-coercion stand," not an " 'antiabortion' stand." "Using What You're Given, an Interview with Margaret Atwood," interview by Jo Brans, *Southwest Review* 68, no. 4 (autumn 1983): 302.

21. Judith McCombs, "Crossing Over: Atwood's Wilderness Journals and Surfacing," in *Essays on the Literature of Mountaineering,* ed. Armand E. Singer (Morgantown: West Virginia University Press, 1982), 116.

22. Patricia Jagentowicz Mills, "Feminism and Ecology: On the Domination of Nature," *Hypatia* 6, no. 1 (spring 1991): 170. Barbara Hill Rigney argues that the woman/nature myth in *Surfacing* condemns not only abortion but also contraceptive technology as a violation of nature. *Margaret Atwood* (Totowa, N.J.: Barnes and Noble, 1987), 42.

23. Carolyn Merchant, *The Death of Nature: Women, Ecology and the Scientific Revolution* (New York: Harper and Row, 1980); Jane Flax, "Political Philosophy and the Patriarchal Unconscious: A Psychoanalytic Perspective on Epistemology and Metaphysics," in *Discovering Reality,* ed. Sandra Harding and Merrill B. Hintikka (D. Reidel,

1983), 260; Nancy C. M. Hartsock, *Money, Sex, and Power: Toward a Feminist Historical Materialism* (Boston: Northeastern University Press, 1985); Donna Haraway, *Simians, Cyborgs, and Women: The Reinvention of Nature* (New York: Routledge, 1991).

24. Sandra Harding's "Feminist Epistemology in and after the Enlightenment" (in *Whose Science? Whose Knowledge?*) provides an extensive account of and rebuttal to the critiques of feminist epistemologies. The concept of "feminist epistemology" is itself problematic in that it can imply that gender is the primary axis of oppression. As Harding argues, however, since there "are no gender relations per se but only gender relations as constructed by and between classes, races, and cultures," the theorizing of standpoint theories "must be accompanied at every point by richer conceptualizations and analyses of the interlocking relationships between sexism, racism, heterosexism, and class oppression." Sandra Harding, *Whose Science? Whose Knowledge? Thinking from Women's Lives* (Ithaca: Cornell University Press, 1991), 178–79. Nancy C. M. Hartsock's term "epistemologies of marked subjectivities" embraces these interlocking relations, but is rather unwieldy. "Postmodernism and Political Change: Issues for Feminist Theory," *Cultural Critique* 14 (winter 1989–1990): 15–33. A note on terminology: it should be clear that by "feminist epistemology" I am referring to feminist standpoint theories and Haraway's theory of "situated knowledges," but not to feminist empiricisms.

25. See Stacy Alaimo, " 'Skin Dreaming': The Bodily Transgressions of Fielding Burke, Octavia Butler, and Linda Hogan," in *Ecofeminist Literary Criticism: Theory, Interpretation, Pedagogy,* ed. Patrick Murphy and Greta Gaard (Urbana: University of Illinois Press, 1998).

26. Collins, *Black Feminist Thought,* 208–17.

27. Eric White, "The Erotics of Becoming: Xenogenesis and *The Thing," Science-Fiction Studies* 20 (1993): 394–408.

28. Hartsock, *Money, Sex, and Power,* 246.

29. Octavia Butler, *Imago* (New York: Popular Library, 1989), 167–68.

30. Octavia Butler, *Dawn* (New York: Popular Library, 1987), 117.

31. Butler, *Imago,* 33.

32. Frances Bonner, "Difference and Desire, Slavery and Seduction: Octavia Butler's Xenogenesis," *Foundation: The Review of Science Fiction* 48 (spring 1990): 52; Michelle Erica Green, " 'There Goes the Neighborhood': Octavia Butler's Demand for Diversity in Utopias," in *Utopian and Science Fiction by Women: Worlds of Difference,* ed. Jane L. Donaweerth and Carol Kolmerten (Syracuse: Syracuse University Press, 1994), 188; Donna Haraway, *Primate Visions: Gender, Race, and Nature in the World of Modern Science* (New York: Routledge, 1989), 379–80.

33. As John B. Cobb Jr. explains, "[A] very simple idea impressed upon us by ecology is that things cannot be abstracted from relations to other things. They may be moved from a natural set of relations to an artificial one, such as in the laboratory, but when these relations are changed, the things themselves are changed." "Ecology, Science, Religion: Toward a Postmodern Worldview," in *The Reenchantment of Science: Postmodern Proposals,* ed. David Ray Griffin (Albany: State University of New York Press, 1988), 107.

34. Linda Holler, "Thinking with the Weight of the Earth: Feminist Contributions to an Epistemology of Concreteness," *Hypatia* 5, no. 1 (spring 1990): 5.

35. For reasons why maintaining some sort of conception of objectivity is impor-

tant for feminism, see Harding, *Whose Science?* 157–61. In "Situated Knowledges," Haraway poses the problem of "how to have *simultaneously* an account of radical historical contingency for all knowledge claims and knowing subjects, a critical practice for recognizing our own 'semiotic technologies' for making meanings, *and* a no-nonsense commitment to faithful accounts of a 'real' world." *Simians, Cyborgs, and Women,* 187.

36. Harding, *Whose Science?* 161.

37. Evelyn Fox Keller, *Reflections on Gender and Science* (New Haven: Yale University Press, 1985), 117.

38. June Goodfield, quoted in Keller, *Reflections,* 115.

39. Haraway, *Simians, Cyborgs, and Women,* 191.

40. Ibid., 190.

41. Marian Engel, *Bear* (Toronto: McClelland and Stewart, 1976), 29, 34. Hereafter cited within the text.

42. Coral Ann Howells, "Marian Engel's 'Bear': Pastoral, Porn, and Myth," *Ariel* 17, no. 4 (October 1986): 105–14.

43. Similarly, Howells argues that the novel exposes "the hidden dynamics of women's romantic fiction" as it rehabilitates pornography for women. "Marian Engel's 'Bear,' " 109.

44. Roberta Rubenstein, in her provocative reading of the novel, argues that Engel attempts "to represent and inscribe a female erotics at least partly outside of phallocentric discourse." "Animal Idylls: Female Desire, Fantasy, and the Reconstructed Other," *LIT* 4 (1993): 133.

45. Janice Radway, *Reading the Romance: Women, Patriarchy, and Popular Literature* (Chapel Hill: University of North Carolina Press, 1984), 147.

46. Haraway, *Simians, Cyborgs, and Women,* 191.

47. Ibid.

48. Harding, *Whose Science?* 150.

49. Haraway, *Simians, Cyborgs, and Women,* 198.

50. Howells, "Marian Engel's 'Bear,' " 109–10.

51. Elspeth Cameron, "Midsummer Madness: Marian Engel's Bear," *Journal of Canadian Fiction* 21 (1977–1978): 91; Howells, "Marian Engel's 'Bear,' " 106.

52. S. A. Cowan, "Return to 'Heart of Darkness': Echoes of Conrad in Marian Engel's 'Bear,' " *Ariel* 12, no. 4 (October 1981): 90.

53. Gerry Turcotte proposes a similar reading of this scene: "It could be argued that Lou's desire to be penetrated is 'wrong,' not because transgressive but rather because it mirrors or re-enacts the patriarchal sexual 'norm.' " "Sexual Gothic: Marian Engel's 'Bear' and Elizabeth Jolley's 'The Well,' " *Ariel* 26, no. 2 (April 1995): 77. Margaret Gail Osachoff offers perhaps the most original reading of this scene, arguing that because Lou anthropomorphizes the bear he wounds her "in defense of his own identity." "The Bearness of Bear," *University of Windsor Review* 15, no. 1–2 (1979–1980): 19. While this is a striking argument, I think that to say Lou anthropomorphizes the bear flattens the complex epistemological drama that the novel enacts.

54. Donna Haraway, *Modest_Witness@Second Millennium: Female Man_Meets_OncoMouse: Feminism and Technoscience* (New York: Routledge, 1997), 199.

55. Thanks to Brady Harrison for this insight.

56. Judith Butler, *Gender Trouble: Feminism and the Subversion of Identity* (New York: Routledge, 1990), 144.

57. Holler, "Thinking with the Weight of the Earth," 7.

58. Susan J. Hekman, *Gender and Knowledge: Elements of a Postmodern Feminism* (Boston: Northeastern University Press, 1990), 127–28.

59. Hekman's arguments are no doubt an apt critique of two of the theorists she discusses, Mary Daly and Dorothy Dinnerstein. Hartsock's theory, however, does not posit a natural affinity between woman and nature, but instead argues that the gendered division of labor shapes consciousness: "If material life structures consciousness, women's relationally defined existence, bodily experience of boundary challenges, and activity of transforming both physical objects and human beings must be expected to result in a world view to which dichotomies are foreign." *Money, Sex, and Power,* 242.

60. Many of *Bear*'s critics, however, have assumed that "nature and women, like nature and Canadians, have some special affinity," according to Margery Fee. "Articulating the Female Subject: The Example of Marian Engel's *Bear,*" *Atlantis* 14, no. 1 (spring 1988): 21

61. Quite pertinent here is the way in which Evelyn Fox Keller explains the difference of McClintock's approach to science. Rather than arguing that McClintock's methods and epistemologies derive from the fact that she is a woman, Keller argues that they emerge from the fact that she is *not* a man and thus need not replicate masculinist practices. "The Gender/Science System: Or, Is Sex to Gender as Nature Is to Science?" *Hypatia* 2, no. 3 (fall 1987): 38.

62. Holler, "Thinking with the Weight of the Earth," 19–20.

63. Luce Irigaray, *This Sex Which Is Not One,* trans. Catherine Porter (Ithaca: Cornell University Press, 1985), 78.

64. Vine Deloria, *Custer Died for Your Sins: An Indian Manifesto* (Norman: University of Oklahoma Press, 1988), 8.

65. James Applewhite, "Postmodernist Allegory and the Denial of Nature," *Kenyon Review* 11, no. 1 (winter 1989): 1–17.

66. Paula Gunn Allen, *The Sacred Hoop: Recovering the Feminine in American Indian Traditions* (Boston: Beacon, 1987), 119, 59.

67. Gilles Deleuze and Felix Guattari, *A Thousand Plateaus: Capitalism and Schizophrenia,* trans. Brian Massumi (Minneapolis: University of Minnesota Press, 1987), 5.

68. Rupert Sheldrake, "The Laws of Nature as Habits: A Postmodern Basis for Science," in *The Reenchantment of Science: Postmodern Proposals,* ed. David Ray Griffin (Albany: State University of New York Press, 1988), 80.

69. Griffin explains: "Daniel Koshland and his colleagues have provided evidence of rudimentary forms of 'memory' and 'decision' in bacteria. Going even further down, there is reason now to believe that DNA and RNA macromolecules are not simply passive entities which change as their parts are changed, but that they are active organisms which actively transpose their parts. Going even further, it has been suggested that the Pauli Principle provides reason to think of an atom as a self-regulating whole." David Ray Griffin, introduction to *The Reenchantment of Science,* 15.

70. Carolyn Merchant, *Ecological Revolutions: Nature, Gender, and Science in New England* (Chapel Hill: University of North Carolina Press, 1989), 8.

71. Carolyn Merchant, *Earthcare: Women and the Environment* (New York: Routledge, 1996), 221.

72. Val Plumwood, *Feminism and the Mastery of Nature* (New York: Routledge, 1993), 136.

73. Donna Haraway, "The Promise of Monsters: A Regenerated Politics for Inappropriate/d Others," in *Cultural Studies,* ed. Lawrence Grossberg, Cary Nelson, and Paula Treichler, with Linda Baughman and John M. Wise (New York: Routledge, 1991), 297.

74. Haraway, "Promise of Monsters," 297; Haraway, *Modest Witness,* 297.

75. William Bevis, "Native American Novels: Homing in," in *Recovering the Word: Essays on Native American Literature,* ed. Brian Swann and Arnold Krupat (Berkeley: University of California, 1987), 602.

76. Deleuze and Guattari, *A Thousand Plateaus,* 44.

77. Jim Cheney, "Postmodern Environmental Ethics: Ethics as Bioregional Narrative," *Environmental Ethics* 11 (summer 1989): 129.

78. Leslie Marmon Silko to James Wright, *The Delicacy and Strength of Lace,* ed. Anne Wright (Saint Paul: Graywolf Press, 1986), 24.

79. Arnold Krupat, *The Voice in the Margin: Native American Literature and the Canon* (Berkeley: University of California Press, 1989), 98.

80. Gail Guthrie Valaskakis, "Indian Country: Negotiating the Meaning of Land in Native America," in *Disciplinarity and Dissent in Cultural Studies,* ed. Cary Nelson and Dilip Parameshwar Gaonkar (New York: Routledge, 1996), 166.

81. Leslie Marmon Silko, *Ceremony* (New York: Penguin, 1977), 8. Hereafter cited within the text.

82. As Louis Owens explains: "Rather than interweaving 'planes,' definable as 'human,' 'myth/ritual,' and 'socio/cultural'—or working in several 'dimensions' we might label 'myth,' 'history,' 'realism,' and 'romance'—Silko spins an elaborate web that makes distinguishing between such concepts impossible." *Other Destinies: Understanding the American Indian Novel* (Norman: University of Oklahoma Press, 1992), 168.

83. One of the reasons it may be impossible to distinguish nature from culture in this novel is because, according to Elizabeth Meese's compelling reading, the novel "calls into question the security of bounded identity and place" by extending "people, places, things, and time beyond the boundaries, the outlines of their identities, so that the 'identifiable' substance, the substance of identity, comes in and out, is as diffuse as the wind." *(Ex)Tensions: Re: Figuring Feminist Criticism* (Urbana: University of Illinois Press, 1990), 41. Without stable, bounded entities it is impossible to map distinct, dichotomous realms of nature and culture.

84. Edith Swan, "Laguna Symbolic Geography and Silko's *Ceremony,*" *American Indian Quarterly* 12, no. 3 (summer 1988): 235. While Robert M. Nelson presents a careful and informative analysis of the landscape of the novel, his reading of the external landscape as a "relatively objective place" to which the more subjective patterns of culture and internal consciousness conform lays down rather rigid distinctions—distinctions that the "Laguna symbolic geography" that Swan delineates does not uphold. *Place and Vision: The Function of Landscape in Native American Fiction* (New York: Peter Lang, 1993).

85. Leslie Marmon Silko, "Here's an Odd Artifact for the Fairy-Tale Shelf," *Studies in American Indian Literature* 10, no. 4 (1986): 179.

86. Haraway, "Promise of Monsters," 298.

87. Similarly, Rachel Stein argues that *Ceremony,* as well as *Almanac of the Dead,* presents "the struggle of Indian-identified characters to regain their imperiled connection to the land through reconstruction and reassertion of the traditional stories." *Shifting the Ground: American Women Writers' Revisions of Nature, Gender, and Race* (Charlottesville: University Press of Virginia, 1997), 115.

88. Alan Wald, "The Culture of 'Internal Colonialism': A Marxist Perspective," *Multi-Ethnic Literatures of the United States* 8, no. 3 (fall 1981): 26.

89. For a remarkably detailed analysis of the "archetypal configuration of feminocentric values distilled from literary and cultural dimensions at Laguna Pueblo," see Edith Swan, "Feminine Perspectives at Laguna Pueblo: Silko's *Ceremony*," *Tulsa Studies in Women's Literature* 11.2 (fall 1992): 309–28.

90. Allen, *Sacred Hoop*, 120.

91. Swan, "Laguna Symbolic Geography," 242–44.

92. Gerald Vizenor, "A Postmodern Introduction," in *Narrative Chance: Postmodern Discourse on Native American Indian Literatures,* ed. Gerald Vizenor (Albuquerque: University of New Mexico Press, 1989), 5–6.

93. Gerald Vizenor, *Darkness in Saint Louis Bearheart* (St. Paul: Truck Press, 1978), 13.

94. Gerald Vizenor, interview by Laura Coltelli, in *Winged Words: American Indian Writers Speak,* ed. Laura Coltelli (Lincoln: University of Nebraska Press, 1990), 176.

95. Vizenor, *Darkness*, 227–28. Hereafter cited within the text.

96. Michael Warner, "Introduction: Fear of a Queer Planet," *Social Text* 9, no. 4 (1991): 9.

97. Catriona Sandilands, "Lavender's Green? Some Thoughts on Queer(y)ing Environmental Politics," *Undercurrents* 6, no. 1 (1994): 21.

98. Robert McRuer argues that it is crucial for the "queer world" not to be "contained in New York and San Francisco," but instead, to "transform the most apparently 'inappropriate' places." *The Queer Renaissance: Contemporary American Literature and the Reinvention of Lesbian and Gay Identities* (New York: New York University Press, 1997), 115.

99. Bonnie Zimmerman, *The Safe Sea of Women: Lesbian Fiction, 1969–1989* (Boston: Beacon Press, 1990), 137, 45.

100. Sandilands, "Lavender's Green?" 22.

101. Jane Rule, *Desert of the Heart* (Tallahassee: Naiad, 1964), 5. Hereafter cited within the text.

102. While I agree with Zimmerman that by "redefining nature, Rule appropriates it for lesbian use," I depart from her reading of this redefinition: "The desert appears sterile and empty, as homosexuality may to ignorant onlookers, but in fact the desert is a natural landscape bursting with life." The image of the desert landscape "bursting with life" still operates within the terms of a reprosexuality that the novel critiques. Zimmerman also argues, however, that Rule represents the desert as "antinatural": "Like the gambling casino, the desert symbolizes free will and choice—the characteristics that make us fully human. Lesbianism is in its way antinatural; that is, it disrupts the biological 'imperative' linking sex and reproduction. The casino in the desert, love blooming between two women: both are representations of the human will creating life in any landscape." *Safe Sea*, 43. The novel certainly celebrates the exhilarating freedom and self-determination of an "antinatural" lesbianism. Conflating the gambling casino with the desert is problematic, however, since it precludes the novel's complex transformations of the category of nature.

103. Butler, *Gender Trouble*, x.

104. Monique Wittig, *The Straight Mind and Other Essays* (Boston: Beacon Press, 1992), 11.

105. Catherine R. Stimpson, *Where the Meanings Are: Feminism and Cultural Spaces* (New York: Routledge, 1989), 98.

106. Zimmerman, *Safe Sea*, 44, 82.

107. Butler, *Gender Trouble*, 34.

108. Gillian Spraggs, "Hell and the Mirror: A Reading of *Desert of the Heart*," in *New Lesbian Criticism: Literary and Cultural Readings*, ed. Sally Munt (New York: Columbia University Press, 1992), 128.

Seven. Cyborgs, Whale Tails, and the Domestication of Environmentalism

1. An earlier and quite different version of this chapter first appeared as "Cyborg and Ecofeminist Interventions: Challenges for Environmental Feminism," *Feminist Studies* 20, no. 1 (spring 1994): 133–52.

2. Janet Biehl, *Rethinking Ecofeminist Politics* (Boston: South End Press, 1991), 84.

3. Donna Haraway, "Overhauling the Meaning Machines," interview by Marcy Darnovsky, *Socialist Review* 21, no. 2 (1991): 67.

4. For an extensive critique of Biehl see Ariel Salleh, "Second Thoughts on Rethinking Ecofeminist Politics: A Dialectical Critique," *ISLE: Interdisciplinary Studies in Literature and Environment* 1, no. 2 (fall 1993): 93–106.

5. Catherine Roach, "Loving Your Mother: On the Woman-Nature Relation," *Hypatia* 6, no. 1 (spring 1991): 56.

6. Carolyn Merchant, *The Death of Nature: Women, Ecology, and the Scientific Revolution* (New York: Harper and Row, 1980), xvii.

7. Patrick D. Murphy, "Sex-Typing the Planet: Gaia Imagery and the Problem of Subverting Patriarchy," *Environmental Ethics* 10 (1988): 165; Patrick D. Murphy, "My Mother's Name Is Evelyn, Not Gaia," *American Nature Writing Newsletter* 6, no. 1 (spring 1994): 12–13.

8. "Earth Day Television Special," ABC. Aired April 22, 1990.

9. Merchant, *Death of Nature*, 288.

10. Stuart Hall, *The Hard Road to Renewal: Thatcherism and the Crisis of the Left* (New York: Verso, 1988), 218.

11. Ariel Salleh, "Nature, Woman, Labor, Capital: Living the Deepest Contradiction," *Capitalism, Nature, Socialism* 6, no. 1 (March 1995): 38.

12. "Stewardship: Empowering the Land," *Conservator* (autumn 1990): 2.

13. Deane Curtin, "Toward an Ecological Ethic of Care," *Hypatia* 6, no. 1 (1991): 71.

14. Timothy W. Luke, "The Nature Conservancy or the Nature Cemetery: Buying and Selling 'Perpetual Care' as Environmental Resistance," *Capitalism, Nature, Socialism: A Journal of Socialist Ecology* 6, no. 2 (June 1995): 11.

15. An important exception here is *The Green Guide*, published by "Mothers & Others," which declares on its masthead that "Environmental Change Begins at Home." *The Green Guide*, an excellent source of information about environmental

and health issues, promotes not only ecoconsumerism, but also consumer activism, encouraging its readers to organize and make political demands.

16. Lauren Berlant, *The Queen of America Goes to Washington City: Essays on Sex and Citizenship* (Durham: Duke University Press, 1997), 5.

17. Donna Haraway, "The Actors Are Cyborg, Nature Is Coyote, and the Geography Is Elsewhere: Postscript to 'Cyborgs at Large,'" in *Technoculture,* ed. Constance Penley and Andrew Ross (Minneapolis: University of Minnesota Press, 1991), 22.

18. In "Endangered Humans," for example, I argue that despite the popular desire to preserve a subjectivity that transcends nature, *12 Monkeys* and the Carnosaur films depict human bodies that are inextricably wired into matter and human "wilds" for which nature can never be external. Stacy Alaimo, "Endangered Humans? Wired Bodies and the Human Wilds," *Camera Obscura* 40/41, no. 14 (January 1997).

19. Carolyn Merchant, *Earthcare: Women and the Environment* (New York: Routledge, 1976), 166.

20. *Habitat,* written and directed by René Daalder. Transfilm Kinsborough Pictures Ecotopica B.V., 1998.

21. *Heresies #13, Feminism and Ecology: Earthkeeping/Earthshaking* 4, no. 1 Issue 13 (1981).

22. Paula A. Treichler, "Feminism, Medicine, and the Meaning of Childbirth," in *Body/Politics: Women and the Discourses of Science,* ed. Mary Jacobus, Evelyn Fox Keller, and Sally Shuttleworth (New York: Routledge, 1990), 132.

23. Hall, *Hard Road,* 10.

24. Lynn Margulis, "Gaia Is a Tough Bitch," in *The Third Culture: Beyond the Scientific Revolution,* ed. John Brockman (New York: Touchstone, 1995): 140.

25. Catriona Sandilands, "Lavender's Green? Some Thoughts on Queer(y)ing Environmental Politics," *Undercurrents* 6, no. 1 (1994): 20.

26. Linda Vance, "Ecofeminism and the Politics of Reality," in *Ecofeminism: Women, Animals, Nature,* ed. Greta Gaard (Philadelphia: Temple University Press, 1993), 132.

27. Patrick D. Murphy, *Literature, Nature, and Other: Ecofeminist Critiques* (Albany: State University of New York Press, 1995), 41.

28. Susan Griffin, *Woman and Nature* (New York: Harper Colophon Books, 1978), 101. Hereafter cited within the text.

29. Teresa de Lauretis, *Technologies of Gender: Essays on Theory, Film, and Fiction* (Bloomington: Indiana University Press, 1987), 26.

30. As Stephanie Lahar puts it, they "tend to reify precisely the unexamined woman/nature associations ecofeminism has challenged since its beginnings." "Ecofeminist Theory and Grassroots Politics," *Hypatia* 6, no. 1 (1991): 38.

31. Val Plumwood, *Feminism and the Mastery of Nature* (New York: Routledge, 1993), 160.

32. Linda Vance, for example, admits that "[g]iving nature a female identity reinforces [her own] sense of solidarity with the nonhuman world." "Ecofeminism and the Politics of Reality," in *Ecofeminism: Women, Animals, Nature,* ed. Greta Gaard (Philadelphia: Temple University Press, 1993): 136.

33. See Chapter 6.

34. Donna Haraway, *Simians, Cyborgs, and Women: The Reinvention of Nature* (New York: Routledge, 1991), 150.

35. Donna Haraway, "Cyborgs at Large: Interview with Donna Haraway," interview by Constance Penley and Andrew Ross, in *Technoculture,* ed. Constance Penley and Andrew Ross (Minneapolis: University of Minnesota Press, 1991), 20, 19.

36. Donna Haraway, "The Actors Are Cyborg, Nature Is Coyote, and the Geography Is Elsewhere: Postscript to 'Cyborgs at Large,' " in *Technoculture,* ed. Constance Penley and Andrew Ross (Minneapolis: University of Minnesota Press, 1991), 21; Haraway, *Simians, Cyborgs, and Women,* 177.

37. Haraway, *Simians, Cyborgs, and Women,* 151, 153.

38. Ibid., 201, 199.

39. Ibid., 201.

40. Donna Haraway, "The Promise of Monsters: A Regenerated Politics for Inappropriate/d Others," in *Cultural Studies,* ed. Lawrence Grossberg, Cary Nelson, and Paula Treichler, with Linda Baughman and John M. Wise (New York: Routledge, 1991), 313.

41. Whale Adoption Project, letter to author, summer 1990.

42. Christopher Manes, "Nature and Silence," in *The Ecocriticism Reader: Landmarks in Literary Ecology,* ed. Cheryll Glotfelty and Harold Fromm (Athens: University of Georgia Press, 1996), 22.

43. Patricia S. Mann, "Cyborgean Motherhood and Abortion," in *Provoking Agents: Gender and Agency in Theory and Practice,* ed. Judith Kegan Gardiner (Urbana: University of Illinois Press, 1995), 145.

44. Haraway, *Simians, Cyborgs, and Women,* 152.

Index

Allen, Paula Gunn, 31–32, 157, 162
Ammons, Elizabeth, 47, 50–51
Anderson, Amanda, 137
Atwood, Margaret, *Surfacing*, 19, 129, 135–137, 140–144, 182
Austin, Mary, 16, 17, 21, 22, 37, 63–66, 70–84, 171, 176, 179, 186–187; *The American Rhythm*, 77, 204n. 51; *Cactus Thorn*, 78–80; *The Ford*, 76–77; and literary regionalism, 205n. 59; *Lost Borders*, 72–75, 80–84; *Starry Adventure*, 76
Awkward, Michael, 140

Barnett, Louise K., 194n. 15
Baudrillard, Jean, 96
Baym, Nina, 27, 38–39
Beauvoir, Simone de, 3–4, 8
Beer, Gillian, 41, 45, 61
Bell, Michael David, 51
Berlant, Lauren, 175
Bevis, William, 158
Bhabha, Homi, 35–36
Biehl, Janet, 172
Birth control, 87, 102, 108–129, 142–144
Blackwell, Antoinette Brown, *The Sexes throughout Nature*, 53
Blend, Benay, 71–72
Bodies, 87–90, 102; Darwinian, 40–41, 44–45, 61–62; as habitat, 177–178; of Oankali, 145–147; reproductive, 108–110, 116–118, 120–124, 127–129
Bonner, Frances, 146
Braidotti, Rosi, 10–11
Brown, Gillian, 28
Buell, Lawrence, 17–18
Burke, Fielding, *Call Home the Heart*, 18, 20, 88, 98, 102–106, 108–110, 114–117, 128, 178
Butler, Judith, 9, 98, 102, 136, 154, 167
Butler, Octavia, Xenogenesis Trilogy, 17, 37, 129, 144–147, 155–156, 178

Cameron, Elspeth, 153
Carby, Hazel, 124
Cheney, Jim, 159, 161
Child, Lydia Maria, *Hobomok*, 30; "She Waits in Spirit Land," 29
Class, 67–70, 87–107, 109–116, 125, 127, 137, 139
Coiner, Constance, 208n. 56

Collins, Patricia Hill, 139, 145
Colonialism, 35–36
Conservation, rhetoric of, 67–70, 96, 201–202n. 21, 202n. 28. *See also* Environmentalism
Consumerism. *See* Environmentalism: and environmental consumerism
Contest of mapping, 18, 87–88, 93–107
Cook, Sylvia J., 104
Cowan, S. A., 153
Curtin, Deane, 175
Cutter, Martha, 58

Daniel, Janice, 47
Darwin, Charles, 21, 40–42, 44–45, 50, 53, 61–62
Davis, Angela, 123
De Crévecoeur, J. Hector St. John, 32
De Lauretis, Teresa, 17, 181
Deleuze, Gilles, and Felix Guattari, 12, 157, 159
Derrida, Jacques, 191n. 35
Dinnerstein, Dorothy, 3
Dixon, Melvin, 138
Domestic space, 14–17, 27–28, 38–40, 43–50, 63–65, 69–70, 109, 114–116, 172–178, 192n. 58
Donovan, Josephine, 51, 54–56

Earth Day television special, 173–176
Ecofeminism, 8–9, 78, 109, 143, 171–172, 174–175, 179–184
Engel, Marian, 17, 37; *Bear*, 129, 135, 144–145, 148–156 .
Environmentalism, 66–71, 94–98, 171–185; and environmental consumerism, 172–176, 178. *See also* Conservation, rhetoric of; Ecofeminism; Progressive women conservationists
Evolution, 21, 40–41, 52–58, 60–62. *See also* Darwin, Charles

Felski, Rita, 136
Feminism. *See* Birth control; Domestic space; Ecofeminism; Feminist theory; Lesbianism; Motherhood; New Woman
Feminist theory, and ecofeminism, 8–9, 136; and evolution, 41, 53, 57; epistemology of, 9, 144–156, 214n. 24; and gender, 5, 98–99; and gender-minimizing feminisms, 16–17,